THE
HEARTBEAT
OF GOD

365 DAILY DEVOTIONS

chris baxter

ClearDay

THE HEARTBEAT OF GOD

Published by Clear Day Publishing, a division of Clear Day Media Group LLC, Waco, TX. cleardaypublishing.com.

Published in association with Lux Creative {theluxcreative.com}

Scripture quotations taken from the New American Standard Bible®, Copyright © 1960, 1962, 1963, 1968, 1971, 1972, 1973, 1975, 1977, 1995 by The Lockman Foundation Used by permission. (www.Lockman.org)

ISBN: 978-0-9863734-3-5

Library of Congress Control Number: 2015951857

Cover Design: Carolynn Seibert {carolynnseibert.com}

Printed in the United States of America.

Acknowledgements

Thank you, Mac, my husband and my Superman. I appreciate the way you always, always stand by me. And thank you, kids: Maggie, Bink, Davis, and Emmy. Your constant encouragement with my writing keeps me going forward.

Thank you, sweet friends, who helped "write" and proof this devotional. Your texts, emails, and phone conversations concerning the different names and numerous attributes of God are sprinkled throughout all the pages of this book. I wrote these prayers with each of you in mind.

Thank you, David and Melinda Seibert, for believing in me. Without your help, this book would still be less-than-half-written, hidden in my living room cabinet. I appreciate your knowledge, expertise, and most of all, your friendship.

And thank You, dear Lord, for quietly sitting with me as I slowly discovered the depth and width and height and breadth of Your heartbeat. And now, what You have "whispered in my ear, I am proclaiming upon the housetops" (from Matt. 10:27).

Dear Reader,

In my journey of faith with the Lord, I have found a treasure principle that keeps me close to Him. Whenever confusion, worry, fear, or doubt creeps into my heart, I have chosen to consciously replace these feelings with the phrase, *"O God, You are ..."*, filling in the blank with one of His beautiful names or wonderful attributes. This practice of prayer begins to change my mindset from focusing on the flesh to claiming a truth of the Spirit. As a result, I experience *life and peace* (Rom. 8:6). Calling on the Lord in this way has not only helped me in the moment, but it has also deepened my knowledge and understanding of God's heartbeat. God is LOVE! All through Scripture, His names and His character, from the Old Testament to the New Testament, exemplify His love for us, His love in us, and His love through us. I pray you will find this treasure for yourself in the following pages of this book.

Each devotional prayer is filled with Scripture verses and/or Scripture phrases taken from the New American Standard Bible. Some Bible quotations are exact; some however, are paraphrased without altering the meaning of the verse. I have inserted these verses and phrases in every prayer so you can pray His word in a flowing manner. If you choose to dig deeper into His word, the Bible verses that are used in each daily prayer are referenced, in order, at the bottom of the page.

While reading and meditating on the Scriptures and uplifting words within this 365-day devotional, I pray that you will be overwhelmed with the matchless heartbeat of God.

His love endures forever,

Chris Baxter

Inheritance

Blessed be the God and Father of our Lord Jesus Christ, who has blessed us with every spiritual blessing in the heavenly places in Christ.

EPHESIANS 1:3

O God, You are my Inheritance. *You became poor that through Your poverty, I might become rich.* Jesus, I thank You. You took my sin and caused me to be *holy and blameless in Your sight. ... You crowned me with lovingkindness and compassion. ... You have clothed me with garments of salvation, You have wrapped me with a robe of righteousness. I will rejoice greatly in the Lord, my soul will exult in my God. For I was afflicted, storm-tossed, and not comforted; but now, You have set my stones in antimony, and You have laid my foundations in sapphires. Moreover, You have made my battlements of rubies, and my gates of crystal, and my entire wall of precious stones.* How can my soul not rejoice in this love of my majestic King? O God, forgive me when I do not choose to see the unseen. Why do I live like a slave when You have set me free? Cause me to remember all You *have freely bestowed on me through Your Beloved Son: redemption ... forgiveness ... and grace.* Righteous Ruler, my heart is full of praise! Most of all, I thank You for Your most marvelous mystery: to think I have been *sealed with the Holy Spirit of promise, Your pledge to me* while I walk on this earth. Because Your Spirit forever lives in me, I will rejoice in my salvation, I will walk like an ambassador, and I will live for You, my glorious King.

**2 Corinthians 8:9; Ephesians 1:4; Psalm 103:4; Isaiah 61:10;
Isaiah 54:11-12; Ephesians 1:6-8, 13-14**

Freedom

Everyone who commits sin is the slave of sin ... So if the Son makes you free, you will be free indeed.

JOHN 8:34,36

O God, You are Freedom. Jesus, You came to earth as the perfect Son of God; You saw the condition of every man's heart; and You conquered sin so that we can live forever. *For the law of the Spirit of life in Christ Jesus has set me free from the law of sin and death.* I praise You that I am no longer bound to religious do's and don'ts, and I praise You that I am no longer captive to addictive human habits. You, O God, have cut these chains; You have severed these cords. Yes, *You have brought my soul out of prison.* I rejoice in You, my Savior! Continually remind my heart of flesh that it is *for freedom that You set me free; therefore, help me to stand firm so I do not become subject again to a yoke of slavery.* My enemy lures me, O God. *Sin is crouching at my door; and its desire is for me, but I must master it.* O God, help me to be subject to You alone; cause me to *resist the devil so that he will flee from me.* Only You, loving God, *have called me to freedom*—no one and nothing else can *give me abundant life* on this earth! I want to daily *abide in Your word, and be Your disciple. Because then I will know the truth, and the truth will set me free.*

Romans 8:2; Psalm 142:7; Galatians 5:1; Genesis 4:7; James 4:7; Galatians 5:13; John 10:10; 8:31-32

Everlasting God

And there (Abraham) called on the name of the LORD, the Everlasting God.
GENESIS 21:33

O God, You are the Everlasting God. *Lord, You sat as King at the flood; yes, You sit as King forever.* I praise You; for *You have been our dwelling place in all generations. Before the mountains were born, You gave birth to the earth and the world, even from everlasting to everlasting, You are God.* Thank You for being *the same, yesterday, today, and forever.* I can't help but humanly wonder, "Do You ever wrestle with weariness? Or does fatigue ever set in?" But then, I remember Your words of truth, *Do you not know? Have you not heard? The Everlasting God, the Lord, the Creator of the ends of the earth does not become weary or tired! I praise You, O God, for Your ongoing supply of strength, power, and might; and I thank You for giving these to Your people.* I ask You to come fill me again; renew me, O Lord. I will wait for You, and I know You will come. *For You are the One who rides upon the highest heavens, which are from ancient times; and You speak forth with Your voice, Your mighty voice. … And You Yourself, the God of Israel, gives strength and power to Your people. Blessed be God!* Indeed, You are from Everlasting to Everlasting.

Psalms 29:10; 90:1; Hebrews 13:8; Isaiah 40:28-29; Psalm 68:33,35

Friend

Thus the LORD used to speak to Moses face to face, just as a man speaks to his friend.

EXODUS 33:11

O God, You are my Friend! How can this statement be possible? The Maker of the universe and the Keeper of time is also the *One who wakes me in the morning for a visit?* The One who names the stars in heaven and establishes the seasons on earth is also the *One who cares about my ways and numbers each of my steps?* This truth is so mind-boggling I can hardly grasp it! But by faith, I will accept it. Yes, my soul is marvelously intertwined between Your awesome majesty and Your intimate mercy; in this place, I choose to stay. But to think, *I did not choose You, You chose me!* Dear Jesus, thank You for laughing with me, crying with me, speaking to me, and minute by minute walking this life with me. And then, my Confidant and Companion, to think, *You laid Your life down for me; ah, there is no greater love than this.* How can this humbled sinner thank You for *enduring my iniquity?* And how can this contrite heart thank You *for remaining silent like a lamb before its shearers?* All I have to give You is my life. And to think, that's all You want. Yes, because of this greater love, I will visit with You in the morning, and *I will hold Your hand in the daytime*, and *I will listen to Your counsel in the night.* How sweet to think, You are my awesome God and my intimate Friend.

Isaiah 50:4; Job 31:4; John 15:16; 15:13; Isaiah 53:6-7; 42:6; Psalm 16:7

God of Time

My times are in Your hand.

PSALM 31:15

O God, You are the God of Time. Nothing escapes Your progressive pendulum, and nothing inhibits Your predestined plan. *Yes, there is an appointed time for everything. And there is a time for every event under the sun.* O God, my heart rejoices over Your divinely selected day, even the chosen "silent night," to bring salvation to the world. Did a tender tear fall from heaven at this *acceptable time?* And yet, *Your great love sent the Messiah forward.* God of my salvation, thank You for coming; thank You for living; thank You for marching forward to Your predetermined death saying, *The hour has come.* Dear Father Time, I marvel at Your outstretched hands of grace and mercy. Your extreme compassion has traveled through history and overtaken my soul. Now, I too, want to march forward, following Your footsteps, *doing all that You have prepared beforehand for me to do while walking on this earth.* To think that You have celebrated me as Your unique design born to live *for such a time as this.* Therefore, I will celebrate YOU with my life! *Please teach me to number my days, O Lord*—may they be marked with Your name, not mine. Tell me again that *You live in me and that You are pleased with me.* Yes, take my appointed days and make them Yours, O God of Time.

Ecclesiastes 3:1; 2 Corinthians 6:2; Romans 5:8; John 17:1; Ephesians 2:10; Esther 4:14; Psalm 90:12; Philippians 2:13

Maker

*Know that the L*ORD *Himself is God; it is He who made us, and not we ourselves; we are His people and the sheep of His pasture.*

PSALM 100:3

O God, You are our Maker. And how extraordinarily complex You have formed mankind! *Our frame is made of only dust;* yet, *we are Your image bearers… You have made us to be earthen vessels;* yet, *we incredibly contain the surpassing greatness of Your power.* We are as *earthly tents;* yet, *we house Your holy presence.* We are as a *blade of grass, a fleeting flower… a vanishing vapor;* yet You have given us the capacity to hold a *love that is from everlasting to everlasting.* O God, how You must cherish mankind! *For the heavens are Yours; but the earth You have given to the sons of men.* While on this earth, *make me to know Your ways, O Lord; teach me Your paths.* Fill my frail frame with Your almighty strength; change my broken ways into Your binding beauty; breathe into my fleeting life Your majestic glory. I am humbled by *Your love that has been poured into me through Your Spirit.* Yes, *I will come and worship and bow down, and I will kneel before the Lord my Maker.*

Psalm 103:14; Genesis 1:26; 2 Corinthians 4:7; 5:4-5; Psalm 103:15; James 4:14; Psalms 103:17; 115:16; 25:4; Romans 5:5; Psalm 95:6

Radiant

*And there was a radiance around Him. As the appearance of the rainbow in the clouds
on a rainy day, so was the appearance of the surrounding radiance.*
EZEKIEL 1:27–28

O God, You are Radiant! You are full of vibrant color; You are full of awesome light.
Your face is like the sun, shining in its strength. I wonder at these ancient words of
truth: *Who is this who comes from Edom, with garments of glowing colors from Bozrah,
this One who is majestic in apparel, marching in greatness and strength?* And then
I humbly bow my knee with Your redemptive reply, *It is I who speak in righteousness,
mighty to save.* O awesome God, Holy One, You indeed are mighty to save! Yes, You sent
Jesus, *the radiance of Your glory and the exact representation of Your nature,* to rescue
me. Your beautiful brilliance has become my bountiful blessing! Dear Savior, as I seek
You, *allow Your face to shine upon me.* Yes, I will *look to You and be radiant, and my
face will never be ashamed.* Thank You, God my Savior. I love Your vibrant color; I love
Your awesome light.

Revelation 1:16; Isaiah 63:1; Hebrews 1:3; Psalms 80:3; 34:5

Teacher

The Teacher is here, and is calling for you.

JOHN 11:28

O God, You are the Teacher. Thank You for *making wise the simple.* And I praise You for this sweet promise to my heart of faith: *I will lead the blind by a way they do not know; in paths they do not know, I will guide them. I will make darkness into light for them and rugged places into plains. These are the things I will do, and I will not leave them undone.* Again, I say thank You! *For You give wisdom; and from Your mouth come knowledge and understanding. … You instruct me and teach me the way in which I should go, and You counsel me with Your eye upon me.* You promised in Your word that *You would pour out Your spirit on me; and that You would make Your words known to me.* Because of Your Son, O God, Your Spirit has come! And *He teaches me all things, and brings Your words to my remembrance.* O how I love Your words of instruction; O how I love Your words of truth. *They are a lamp to my feet, and a light to my path.* Keep me on Your path, O Lord. I want to walk with You, step by step. Yes, cause my heart to proclaim, *Teacher, I will follow You wherever You go.*

Psalm 19:7; Isaiah 42:16; Proverbs 2:6; Psalm 32:8; Proverbs 1:23; John 14:26; Psalm 119:105; Matthew 8:19

Savior

*I, even I, am the L*ORD*, and there is no savior besides Me.*
ISAIAH 43:11

O God, You are the Savior! Yes, You looked from heaven and *saw, and it was displeasing in Your sight that there was no justice. And You saw there was no man, and You were astonished that there was no one to intercede.* Then You said, *I, the Lord, will answer them Myself, as God of Israel I will not forsake them.* And *because You loved the world so much* You, O God, *gave Your only begotten Son, that whoever believes in Him should not perish, but have everlasting life.* I praise You, O my Father, for sending *Your Son to be the Savior of the world.* Because of Your lovingkindness, because of Your grace, because of Your plan, I have *been delivered from the domain of darkness and transferred into the kingdom of Your beloved Son.* O God, You are Jesus, and Jesus, You are God—*You are One. . . . the Righteous God and the Savior!* I thank You, God the Son, for paving the path for me to reach You, God the Father. I will forever sing praises that Your righteous hand reached down to *deliver me from my strong enemy,* yet not without having it pierced through first. *For You bared Your holy arm in the sight of all nations, that all the ends of the earth may see Your salvation.* Yes my God, You are the Savior of the world.

**Isaiah 59:15-16; 41:17; John 3:16; I John 4:14; Colossians 1:13;
John 10:30; Isaiah 45:21; Psalm 18:17; Isaiah 52:10**

Breath of Life

Then the LORD *God formed man of dust from the ground, and breathed into his nostrils the breath of life.*

GENESIS 2:7

O God, You are the Breath of Life. Only You, Mighty One, can give vitality to mortal man. Yes, You alone, are able to take *a field of dry bones, where hope is depleted, and then breathe life into them from the four winds; and only You can cause them to stand on their feet as an exceedingly great army!* Please, Giver of Life, come breathe on me in this way! I, too, want to stand with hope; and I, too, want to fight with power. Day by day, fill me with Your continual Spirit of truth; awaken my soul to Your word. Yes, I pray again, just as You, Conqueror of death, came to Your disciples *and breathed on them*, please come and breathe Your life-giving Spirit into me this day. Renew me, refresh me, revive me. And then, convict my heart to never allow Your sweet presence to lay dormant *in this temple of Yours; cause Your rushing wind from heaven* to blow continually through the windows of my soul. Remind me always, *You breathed Your last* so I would not have to. Yes, You alone can give mortal man immortality! I praise You for this ongoing, never-ending, all-encompassing Breath of Life.

Ezekiel 37:1,9-10; John 20:22; Acts 2:2; Mark 15:37

Father

For you have not received a spirit of slavery leading to fear again, but you have received a spirit of adoption as sons by which we cry out, "Abba! Father!"

ROMANS 8:15

O God, You are my Father. I can hardly humanly grasp that *You call me "child."* Keep reminding me that You are not some faraway, uninterested parent; but instead, You are my devoted, intentional Father. You do not miss one heartbeat, one blink, one breath of mine! Yes, You *know the number of hairs on my head.* O Father, really? Do You really *delight in me? Do You really call me by name? ... Am I really precious in Your sight?* Yes, *I am Yours, and You know me* and love me. When I say, "Don't leave me," You don't. And when I cry, "I am afraid," You respond. And when I complain, "It hurts," You heal. Thank You for enveloping me in this love of Yours, O God. And even when I feel Your parental hand of *discipline, I will recall, this too, is Your hand of love.* Father, continue to teach me. Father, continue to *abide with me.* Father, I never ever want to run away from home. Yes, I want to forever and ever stay with You, my Abba.

John 1:12; Matthew 10:30; Psalm 18:19; Isaiah 43:1,4; John 10:14; Hebrews 12:5-6; John 14:23

One Who Weeps

Jesus wept.

JOHN 11:35

O God, You are the One Who Weeps. Thank You for entering into my suffering and trials, and being *deeply moved in spirit.* Your heartfelt tears help heal my hurt. But I also wonder, do You cry tears of another kind? Are the raindrops that fall from heaven really teardrops that fall for Your people? Does Your heart ache for us to know You and to understand You? Dear Jesus, when You walked the earth, *You wept for the city that rejected You.* I hear You pleading then and now, *O Jerusalem, Jerusalem, the city that kills the prophets and stones those sent to her! How often I wanted to gather your children together, just as a hen gathers her brood under her wings, and you would not listen.* Yes, You *long to be gracious, and You wait on high to have compassion.* In the meantime, Your tears must fall for those who are *not willing.* I thank You, O God, that You did not stop with a brief fit of emotion. Instead, Your broken heart caused You to move with resolute compassion, keeping Your eyes steadfastly fixed upon the cross. You moved in spite of rejection-the *blows in the face,* the *thorns on Your brow,* the *nails in the hands,* the *sword in the side.* And these are the ones You wept for? And these are the ones You died for? O Savior, You wept and died for me! Thank You for Your passionate pursuit in spite of the sin of Your people. And now I wonder, when those You long for finally come to You, do You also weep tears of joy? Yes, raindrops from heaven must be mingled with both teardrops of longing and teardrops of laughter. Indeed, You are the God who is *deeply moved within.*

**John 11:33; Luke 19:41; 13:34; Isaiah 30:18; 30:15;
John 19:1-5,16-18,34; 11:38**

One Who Rejoices

He will rejoice over you with shouts of joy.

ZEPHANIAH 3:17

O God, You are the One Who Rejoices. You are the God of song and You are the God of dance. How pleased You must be to see Your people worship You in this way. In ancient times, You instructed Your people to throw *seven celebrations a year, filled with rest and rejoicing, praise and exultation.* And I know You were there when *Miriam led a victory dance at the edge of the Red Sea*; I know You were there when *King David danced with all his might.* Ah yes, You were also there when *the prodigal son came home. … You ran to him, You embraced him, You kissed him. … and You rejoiced over him with music and dancing.* And isn't it true that *all of heaven celebrates when one who is lost is now found?* Certainly, *there is a time to laugh . … and there is a time to dance;* and You, King of Love, are the source of my joy! Yes, *I will exult in You, O God,* as *You exult over me.* You have filled me to overflowing. Hear *the melody in my heart to You, O Lord.* Indeed, You make my heart beat, beat; You make my hands clap, clap; You make my feet tap, tap. Yes, Lord, come; let us rejoice, let us sing, let us dance.

Leviticus 23:1-44; Exodus 15:20; 2 Samuel 6:14; Luke 15:20-25,5-7; Ecclesiastes 3:4; Isaiah 61:10; Zephaniah 3:17; Ephesians 5:19

Unchanging

Jesus Christ is the same yesterday and today and forever.
HEBREWS 13:8

O God, You are Unchanging. *You sat as King at the flood; You sit as King forever.* You promise to give strength to Your people, and to bless them with peace. Please, I ask for Your strength and peace right now. It seems as if I need You even more today than I did yesterday. As the ebb and flow of different, diverse, or delightful circumstances come my way, help me to remember, You remain *Faithful and True.* Thank You, Father, and thank You, Friend. Guide me as I step into this season of change, and help me remember my unknown is completely known by You! *But one thing I do know: that You, O God, are for me!* Hold my hand as I *walk by faith, not by sight. ... Clothe me with Your strength and dignity, and cause me to smile at the future. ... Put a new song in my mouth* as I embrace the days ahead—a song of joy, a song of peace. Continue to remind me I am not alone. Yes, Faithful One, You are my constant, my steady, and my strength. I will humbly hold in my heart Your determined and unchanging vow, *For the mountains may be removed and the hills may shake, but My lovingkindness will not be removed from you, and My covenant of peace will not be shaken.* Thank You, Eternal Father, and thank You, Forever Friend.

Psalm 29:10-11; Revelation 19:11; Psalm 56:9; 2 Corinthians 5:7;
Proverbs 31:25; Psalm 40:3; Isaiah 54:10

Overcomer

In the world you have tribulation, but take courage; I have overcome the world.
JOHN 16:33

O God, You are the Overcomer. I ask You, please, overcome me! *Overcome my heart, overcome my soul, overcome my mind, overcome my strength.* My heart cries, "Increase my faith;" my soul pleads, "Immerse me in Your truth;" my mind begs, *"Throw out everything that is against You;"* my strength shouts, "Fill me with Your power." O God, *greater are You who lives in me than the one who is in the world.* Rise up in me; *let me hear Your victory song and Your shouts of joy over me.* Fight through me as I obey Your voice in this battle. Yes, help me to remember obedience brings unending PEACE to this war in my soul! Again, rise up in me, my Overcomer, and cause me to fervently *fight the good fight of faith*, all the while, claiming Your victory. *My heavenly armor is on, O God*; and only because of You, Almighty One, I have the ability to *overwhelmingly conquer all things*—all struggles, all trials, all tactics of my enemy. Again, fight through me while I trust in You. *Yes, for Your name's sake, do not delay, O Lord; listen and take action.* Please Overcome me.

Mark 12:30; 2 Corinthians 10:5; 1 John 4:4; Zephaniah 3:17;
1 Timothy 6:12; Ephesians 6:11; Romans 8:37; Daniel 9:19

Sustainer

It shall be that you will drink of the brook, and I have commanded the ravens to provide for you there.

1 Kings 17:4

O God, You are my Sustainer. I am waiting by the brook, O God; please come, renew my faith so that I may drink. Cause my eyes to look up and see the "bread of heaven" that You have sent. *Yes, Lord, restore me to the joy of Your salvation and sustain me with a willing spirit.* My heart is heavy, and my soul is sad. I need You. I come to You. You *promise to sustain all who fall, and raise up all who are bowed down.* Here I am, head down, knees bent. In this place, I will consider the *lilies of the field—they do not toil nor spin, yet they grow.* And then, *I will recall to mind: Your mercies are new every morning. I will not lose hope*—Your promises are mine for the taking. Yes, I will remember, *when I am weak, Your power is perfected in me.* And when I am downcast, *You cause Your face to shine upon me.* And *when I am waiting, You will surely come.* So, I will *drink of the brook*; and in this place of refuge and rest, You, O God, will sustain me. *Great is Your faithfulness.*

Psalms 51:12; 145:14; Matthew 6:28; Lamentations 3:21-23;
2 Corinthians 12:9; Psalms 80:3; 40:1; 1 Kings 17:6; Lamentations 3:23

Sanctifier

I am the LORD who sanctifies you.

LEVITICUS 22:32

O God, You are the Sanctifier. I am on the upward *climb of Your holy hill, O Lord.* Only You, my Savior, can help me *keep my hands clean and my heart pure;* and only You, Righteous One, can help me *keep my soul from falsehood and deceit.* I cannot walk this road alone. Continue to hold my hand; continue to direct my steps. I want my steps to match Yours—for I am Your image-bearer, *set apart for Your glory.* So, do Your work, O God. Continue to *sanctify me in Your truth. ... Please help me to discern my errors, and please acquit me of hidden faults. Also, keep back Your servant from presumptuous sins, let them not rule over me. I want to die to my flesh* so the world can see You in me; *You have called me to this purpose!* So come, dear Jesus, *increase as I decrease. ... Refine me like gold. ... Continue to transform me into Your image from glory to glory. ... Grow me up in all aspects of You.* I want to *sanctify You as Lord of my heart so that I may always be ready to share with everyone who asks about the hope that lives in me.* YOU are my hope as I walk forward and upward with joyful endurance. And I know You will see me through to the very last step; and there, I will rejoice as I finally meet You, the perfect One, face to face.

Psalms 24:3-4; 4:3; John 17:17; Psalm 19:12-13; Romans 8:13;
1 Thessalonians 4:7; John 3:30; Malachi 3:3;
2 Corinthians 3:18; Ephesians 4:15; 1 Peter 3:15

Righteous Judge

He will judge the world in righteousness and the peoples in His faithfulness.

PSALM 96:13

O God, You are the Righteous Judge. You know all things, You see all things—You discern the hidden motives of every heart. No one can stand before You; *no one is worthy, no, not one. … Even all our righteous deeds are like a filthy garment.* Yes, *we have all sinned and fall short of Your glory.* Who then can save me? And how can I even take one step toward Your throne? Tell me, *who will set me free from this body of death?* O Righteous Judge, You answer this question by the *sacrificial slaying of Your perfect Son.* Your love sent Him to be the *just for the unjust; and through His obedience, many will be made righteous.* I praise You, Holy God, for Your eyes see Jesus first, then me. Yes, You are a *God who delightfully exercises lovingkindness first, then justice and righteousness.* Because of Your mercy at the cross, *my life is hidden in Christ. … And now, there is no more condemnation! For the law of the Spirit of life in Christ Jesus has set me free from the law of sin and death.* Hallelujah! Because of Christ, I am worthy; because of Christ, I am holy; because of Christ, I am blameless; because of Christ, I am free! Your grace has saved me; and because of this truth, today, this minute, my soul will delightfully dance before Your throne.

Psalm 14:3; Isaiah 64:6: Romans 3:23; 7:24; Isaiah 53:5; Romans 5:18-19; Jeremiah 9:24; Colossians 3:3; Romans 8:1-2

Hiding Place

For in the day of trouble He will conceal me in His tabernacle; in the secret place of His tent He will hide me.

PSALM 27:5

O God, You are my Hiding Place. My soul is safe with You. *Though a host encamp against me, my heart will not fear, though a war arise against me, in spite of this I will be confident.* For You have *covered me with Your pinions, and under Your wings I take refuge; Your faithfulness is a shield and bulwark.* Yes, You are my Defender, and I am safe with You. Thank You, strong and loving God, for Your protection, and thank You for Your peace. Your sanctuary is my delight; for in this place, *You surround me with songs of deliverance.* I drink in Your love songs! Yes, *the nearness of God is my good. ... You restore me to the joy of Your salvation, You sustain me with a willing spirit.* So, I will continue to *abide in the shadow of the Almighty.* Hear me sing back to You, O God, *My refuge and my fortress, my God in whom I trust! Yes, under Your wings I will sing for joy.* Hear me harmonize with the heavenly hosts, *You are my hiding place.*

Psalms 27:3; 91:4; 32:7; 73:28; 51:12; 91:1-2; 63:7; 32:7

Intricate One

I will give thanks to You, for I am fearfully and wonderfully made.
PSALM 139:14

O God, You are the Intricate One. You knew me before I existed; when I was nothing, I was something to You. You knew me as a beautiful thought, and You know me now. *My frame was not hidden from You, when I was made in secret, and skillfully wrought in the depths of the earth. Your eyes have seen my unformed substance; and in Your book they were all written.* May I never believe the lie that I am a haphazard mistake— heavens no! Nor let me think that my weaknesses and shortcomings are Your failures and oversights—again, good heavens, no! Make me understand and believe that I am an intricately designed piece of art formed by the flawless Master Himself. Yes, I am a "Master-piece." You dotted my eyes a choice color; You printed the lines on my hand; and You set a unique rhythm to my heart. O God, how *wonderful are Your works, and my soul knows it very well!* Yes, dear Maker, let me rest in *Your detailed design.* Your artistry is inside me, and all around me. Because of this truth, my eyes, head, hands, and heart will delightfully praise You as the Intricate One.

Psalms 139:15-16,14

Famous One

Do you not know? Have you not heard?

ISAIAH 40:28

O God, You are the Famous One! *Praise the Lord from the heavens; praise Him in the heights! Praise Him, all His angels; praise Him, all His hosts! Praise Him, sun and moon; praise Him, all stars of light! … Let the rivers clap their hands; let the mountains sing together for joy.* Jesus, You are the *Name above all names;* You are the *King above all kings.* Yes, mighty rulers will *cast their crowns before Your throne saying, Worthy are You, our Lord and our God, to receive glory and honor and power.* O yes, let us *praise the Lord! Praise God in the sanctuary; praise Him in His mighty deeds; praise Him according to His greatness. Praise Him with trumpet sound; praise Him with harp and lyre. Praise Him with timbrel and dancing; praise Him with stringed instruments and pipe. Praise Him with loud cymbals; praise Him with resounding cymbals. Let everything that has breath praise the Lord.* You, O God, in heaven and on earth, are indeed, the Famous One!

**Psalms 148:1-3; 98:8; Philippians 2:9; 1 Timothy 6:15;
Revelation 4:10-11; Psalm 150:1-6**

My Burden Bearer

Blessed be the Lord, who daily bears our burden, the God who is our salvation.
PSALM 68:19

O God, You are my Burden Bearer. You eagerly say to my fainting heart, *Come to Me, ... My heavy-laden child, and I will give you rest. ... For My yoke is easy, and My load is light.* Help me respond to Your gentle and humble invitation, I pray. Prompt me to *lay aside every encumbrance and the sin that so easily entangles me.* Help me to put down my weight of worthless worry, my pounds of prideful pressure, and my accumulating faithless questions. Why do I carry this load, O Lord? For these are nothing but *chains around my neck. Loosen me of these things, I pray!* Again, help my heart to obey Your sweet command, *Cast all your anxiety upon Me, because I care for you.* Yes, Lord, cause me to remember that *You Yourself bore my griefs. ... and the chastening for my well-being fell on You.* O Savior, I humbly thank You for this extreme measure of care! Here, dear Lord, are my concerns about the past, my thoughts about the present, and my questions about the future. Change my focus from these earthly things, so that I can *re-fix my eyes on You. You are the author and finisher of my faith*—the One who carried my debts all the way to the cross. Thank You, my King of love, my Burden Bearer. Both hear and see me praise You with empty hands raised high to the heavens.

**Matthew 11:28-30; Hebrews 12:1; Isaiah 52:2; 1 Peter 5:7 ;
Isaiah 53:4-5; Hebrews 12:2**

Resurrection

And they found the stone rolled away from the tomb.

LUKE 24:2

O God, You are the Resurrection! *O death, where is your victory; O death, where is your sting? The sting of death is sin, and the power of sin is the law; but thanks be to God, who gives us victory through our Lord Jesus Christ.* Yes, You, O God, have raised Jesus from the dead and He is Lord of life. I hear my Savior's words of truth beckoning me, saying, *I am the resurrection and the life; he who believes in Me shall live even if he dies. . . . Do you believe this?* And then, I proclaim with my whole heart, *Yes, Lord; I have believed that You are the Christ, the Son of God, even He who comes into the world.* Thank You for coming, dear Jesus! And thank You for conquering sin and death on the cross. Because of this act of grace, my sin no longer keeps me from You. For *I have been crucified with Christ; and it is no longer I who live, but Christ lives in me; and the life which I now live in the flesh, I live by faith in the Son of God, who loved me, and delivered Himself up for me.* O God, help me to live by this faith that I proclaim! And help me to never underestimate *the surpassing greatness of Your power that now lives in me*—please, reign in me! May I and all those who call You Savior respond to Your eager plea every morning, *Awake sleeper, arise from the dead, and I will shine on you.* Yes, O God, awaken my soul to Your Resurrection.

**1 Corinthians 15:55-57; John 11:25-27; Galatians 2:20;
Ephesians 1:19; 5:14**

Potter

Then I went down to the potter's house, and there he was, making something on the wheel.

JEREMIAH 18:3

O God, You are the Potter. I hear You say to my heart, *Behold, like clay in the potter's hand, so are you in My hand.* I praise You, O God, for holding me. Once my heart was hard as stone and my neck was stiff with pride; but You came to me, and in Your mercy You *sprinkled clean water on me and cleansed me from all my filthiness and all my idols. Moreover, You put a new heart and a new spirit within me.* You made my hard heart soft; You made my stiff neck relax. Thank You, O God! Because of Your grace, I am now a workable piece of clay. Continue to make me willing to receive Your living water, Your living word. Keep me in the center of Your wheel; and there, keep Your collected hold on me with Your purposeful hands. Make me, mold me, move me into the vessel of Your choosing. Please help me not to fight against Your design, or ask in frustration, *What are You doing?* I know You know how to create *beauty from ashes. ... man from dust*; so, help me to trust You. Yes, *I am Your workmanship, created in Christ Jesus for Your good works.* I am humbled to be *Your earthen vessel, O God, filled with Your power and Your glory.* Indeed, I do love my Potter's hands.

Jeremiah 18:6; Ezekiel 36:25-26; Isaiah 45:9; 61:3; Genesis 2:7; Ephesians 2:10; 2 Corinthians 4:7

One Who Pursues

I will give them a heart to know Me, for I am the LORD.
JEREMIAH 24:7

O God, You are the One Who Pursues. My hand-in-hand relationship is a direct result of Your *love for me; yes, You first loved me. … You have allured me and spoken kindly to me. … You have healed me, and You have saved me.* Dear Father, thank You for *drawing me to Yourself through Your Son.* I hear and receive and live by Your sweet proclamation of love, *Nothing will separate you from My love—neither death, nor life, nor angels, nor principalities, nor things present, nor things to come, nor powers, nor height, nor depth, nor any other created thing!* What more can I ask for on this earth but to be pursued in this heavenly way? Nothing in this life compares to You! Then why, O God, do I tend to run from Your perfect love? And why do I wander from Your path of peace? When I step away, O God, remind me once again of Your vows. Forgive me when I choose not to be held by Your immeasurable grace. Chase me, relentless Pursuer, and catch me one more time. Please *compose and quiet my soul. … Open the eyes of my heart* as I turn the pages of Your unending love letters; and open my ears to Your Spirit's sweet love songs to my soul. Yes, bring me back to Your embrace so that I may rest and then respond to Your beautiful captivation that has set me free.

1 John 4:19; Hosea 2:14; Jeremiah 17:14; John 6:44;
Romans 8:38-39; Psalm 131:2; Ephesians 1:18

One Who Forgives

He will tread our iniquities under foot. Yes, You will cast all their sins into the depths of the sea.

MICAH 7:19

O God, You are the One Who Forgives. Yes, I praise You that through the blood of Christ, I am now *white as snow. Even though my sins were red like crimson, they are now like wool.* I also rejoice when I hear Your words of promise: *As far as the east is from the west, so far have I removed your transgressions from you.* O God, I know complete forgiveness only comes through the power of the cross; thank You, Jesus my Savior, for Your outstretched arms that embraced my sin. Dear Lord, I now ask two things of You. One, please give me the ability to forgive myself. Help me to accept the forgiveness that You have already graciously granted me. Why do I hang onto my heavy sin of guilt and shame? Remind me, again, that You want to take these burdens from me as well. And second, please, O God, give me the capacity to *forgive others as You have forgiven me.* I pray that I *will not take into account a wrong suffered.* O Lord, *You are rich in mercy because of Your great love;* help me to be rich like You! Convict my heart that if I *do not forgive others, You will not forgive me.* Again, through Your loving power help me to *forgive up to seventy times seven!* I know, *with You, O God, all things are possible.* Yes, I owe my life to the One Who Forgives.

**Isaiah 1:18; Psalm 103:12; Matthew 6:12; 1 Corinthians 13:5;
Ephesians 2:4; Matthew 6:15; 18:21-22; 19:26**

Name-Caller

Lift up your eyes on high and see who has created these stars, the One who leads forth their host by number, He calls them all by name.

ISAIAH 40:26

O God, You are the Name-Caller. You have named Your stars in heaven; You have named Your people on earth. Yes, You are a God who is both personal and purposeful! You called *Noah* by name to build a boat. You called *Abraham* by name to birth a nation. You called *Moses* by name to free Your people. You called *Samuel* by name to speak as a prophet. You called *Gideon* by name to fight as a warrior. You called *David* by name to rule as a king. You called *Mary* by name to birth a Savior. You called *Peter* by name to build Your church. You called *Paul* by name to reach the Gentiles. O God, I know that just as You have called these people of the past, *You have also called me by name* today. Yes, in the stillness of my soul, I have heard You call me personally, tenderly, truthfully, intentionally. Invade me with Your love, O God, and involve me with Your ways. Help me every day to fulfill what You require of me: *to do justly, to love mercy, and to walk humbly with You.* Yes, Name-Caller, my heart cries out, *Here I am Lord, send me.*

Genesis 6:13-14; 12:1-2; Exodus 3:4; 1 Samuel 3:10; Judges 6:12-14; 1 Samuel 16:10-12; Luke 1:26-31; Matthew 16:15-18; Acts 9:4-5, 15-20; Isaiah 43:1; Micah 6:8; Isaiah 6:8

God of Understanding

His understanding is inscrutable.

ISAIAH 40:28

O God, You are the God of Understanding. *Who has directed the Spirit of the Lord, or as His counselor has informed Him? With whom did He consult. … and who taught Him in the path of justice and taught Him knowledge?* O God, I have so many questions: Why sorrow? Why conflict? Why struggle? Why pain? Are You there? Do You see? Do You care? Let me trust You, God of love, when You say, *My thoughts are not your thoughts, neither My ways your ways. For as the heavens are higher than the earth, so are My ways higher than Your ways, and My thoughts than your thoughts.* Yes, I will trust You, O High God. *You know my thoughts from afar;* even when I don't understand myself, You understand me. I only *see in a mirror dimly*, but You see clearly every single detail of my life, past, present, and future. *Your understanding is infinite!* For You, Intimate One, *are greater than my heart, and You know all things.* So I will choose to live a life of open-handed faith, not of closed-fisted facts. And with this faith, freedom will come—freedom to watch You bring joy from sorrow, peace from conflict, strength from struggle, and comfort from pain. Yes, God of Understanding, here's my heart, without questions. Help me trust Your higher ways.

Isaiah 40:13-14; 55:8-9; Psalm 139:2; 1 Corinthians 13:12; Psalm 147:5; 1 John 3:20

Lord of All

Therefore behold, I am going to make them know—this time I will make them know My power and My might; and they shall know that My name is the Lord.

JEREMIAH 16.21

O God, You are Lord of All. *Yes, Lord God! Behold, You have made the heavens and the earth by Your great power and Your outstretched arm. … Nothing is too difficult for You. Certainly, You are the Lord, the God of all flesh.* You lovingly warn all people, *Cursed is the man who trusts in mankind and makes flesh his strength, and whose heart turns away from Me. For he will be like a bush in the desert and will not see when prosperity comes, but will live in stony wastes in the wilderness, a land of salt without inhabitant.* But then, You also pleadingly promise, *Blessed is the man who trusts in Me and whose trust is Me. For he will be like a tree planted by the water that extends its roots by a stream, and will not fear when the heat comes; but its leaves will be green, and it will not be anxious in a year of drought nor cease to yield fruit.* So, You have laid it out plainly to my heart, asking, "Which will you choose to be like: A bush in the desert, or a tree by the stream?" O dear God, I want to be *like this tree! Please, plant me deep, and make my roots strong!* Yes, I ask You, Maker of heaven and earth, "Be my Lord of All!"

Jeremiah 32:17, 27; 17:5-8; Psalm 1:3

God of Grace

*And the grace of our Lord was more than abundant, with the faith and love which are
found in Christ Jesus.*

1 TIMOTHY 1:14

O God, You are the God of Grace. Neither any righteous deed of mine, nor any unrighteous deed of mine can keep me from *approaching Your throne with reverent boldness; because there, I know I will receive mercy and find grace to help in time of need.* Yes, *Your gift of grace through faith in Christ Jesus* is the only passageway from darkness to light, from lost to found, from *slave to son.* Thank You for giving this ongoing *grace to the humble.* Therefore, continually convict my heart of unconfessed sin so that I can bring it into Your holy presence on bended knee. Thank You, God and Savior, that the stench of my sin, when laid upon Your altar of sacrifice, becomes a *soothing aroma to You.* Indeed, You have marvelously mingled Your incense of grace with Your fire of love! For *where my sin increased, Your grace abounded all the more.* You have saved me, O God; and furthermore, as I walk through trials on this earth, You sweetly promise to *perfect, confirm, strengthen, and establish me.* Merciful God, I am overwhelmed by this undeserved favor! Indeed, You are the God of Grace.

**Hebrews 4:16; Ephesians 2:8; Galatians 3:26; James 4:6; Exodus 29:18; Romans 5:20;
1 Peter 5:10**

God of Comfort

In His arm He will gather the lambs and carry them in His bosom.
ISAIAH 40:11

O God, You are the God of Comfort. Come close to me, I pray. I need You this moment. How heavy is my sorrow, how weighty is my grief. *Draw near to my heart that is broken; come save my spirit that is crushed.* Hold me, dear Jesus. Help me, O God. Please come—*weep with me.* Your tears will help me bear this loss; I cannot do this alone. Yes, sweet Savior, hold me close. Envelope me in *Your everlasting arms.* Please, *take my groanings that are too deep for words.* Thank You for understanding them; thank You for interpreting them; thank You for answering them. I will lean into You, my Comforter; and with You, I will weep. Soon, and very soon, *You will wipe away every tear;* but at this moment, I ask You to fill me with Your incomprehensible peace.

**Psalm 34:18; John 11:35; Deuteronomy 33:27; Romans 8:26;
Revelation 7:17**

Faithful

And I saw heaven opened, and behold, a white horse, and He who sat upon it is called Faithful and True.

REVELATION 19:11

O God, You are Faithful. Your consistency calms me; Your patterns please me. Just as the sun radiantly rises each morning, my heart, too, quietly anticipates Your life-giving light. And just *as the rain comes down from heaven, and does not return there without watering the earth, and making it bear and sprout, ... neither does Your word return to You empty.* Yes, O God, Your word never ceases to shower my soul with hope. And just as You, year after year, beautifully *change the seasons*, You also, year after year, change me. Help me always remember that every changing season of my life is lovingly wrapped within the parameters of Your faithfulness. You are steady in strength, continuous in care, persistent in power. *You always keep Your promises; ... You will always be with me.* Dear God, as a result of *Your ongoing faithfulness*, my heart is full of faith! So I will continually praise You, and I will repeatedly thank You, day after day, year after year, season after season. O how I love You, my Faithful One.

**Isaiah 55:10-11; Jeremiah 5:24; Hebrews 10:23; Matthew 28:20;
2 Thessalonians 3:3**

Ever-Present

For the LORD your God is with you wherever you go.

JOSHUA 1:9

O God, You are Ever-Present. *If I go up to the heavens, You are there; if I make my bed in the depths, You are there. If I rise on the wings of the dawn, if I settle on the far side of the sea, even there Your hand will guide me, Your right hand will hold me fast.* Thank You, God of my life, for *Your lovingkindness in the daytime, and for Your sweet love songs in the night.* I know that You are my *refuge and strength in times of trouble.* Yes, Your invading presence is my incomprehensible peace. And with You, I have *fullness of joy!* I thank You for *surrounding me like the mountains;* I thank You for *walking with me in the valley;* I thank You for *setting me upon high places.* Dear God of my heart, how I delight in Your promises! I will meditate one more time on Your sweet words, *I am with You always, even to the end of the age.*

Psalms 139:8-10; 42:8; 46:1; 16:11; 125:2; 23:4; 18:33; Matthew 28:20

Miracle Worker

And answering him, Jesus said, "What do you want Me to do for you?" And the blind man said to Him, "Rabboni, I want to regain my sight!"
MARK 10:51

O God, You are the Miracle Worker! I praise You for Your ancient wonders that continue to work today: *You spoke, and the whole earth was birthed*; now, You speak, and *souls are born of the Spirit*. And I have read how You powerfully *parted the seas*; today, I have seen how You have *powerfully parted sin from the hearts of men*. And I have heard that You *sent bread from heaven*; now, I feast on this *Bread of life, Your word, every morning*. Yes, You once came to earth and *healed the sick, the lame, the blind*; O Miracle Worker, You have now come to me and cured my shame, my guilt, my fear! I rejoice in Your wonders of old, O God, and I rejoice in Your wonders today. In my time, I have seen You protect, I have seen You purify, I have seen You provide. You are alive—always working, always wanting to woo and wow my heart with Your power and with Your love. When my eyes grow faithlessly dim, O Lord, cause me to *regain my sight*. I do not want to miss one second of Your awe-inspiring, wonder-working, life-altering miracles!

Genesis 1:31; John 3:8; Exodus 14:21; Psalm 103:12; Exodus 16:14-15; Isaiah 50:4; Matthew 11:5; Mark 10:51

Commander

Have you ever in your life commanded the morning, and caused the dawn to know its place?

Job 38:12

O God, You are Commander! *Whatever is under the whole heaven is Yours.* I am mesmerized by Your defining words to Job, *calling to him from a whirlwind:*

Where were you when I laid the foundations of the earth? ... Who set its measurements ... or laid its cornerstone ... or who enclosed the sea with doors? ... Have you ever entered the storehouses of the snow, or have you seen the storehouses of hail, which I reserve for the time of distress, for the day of war and battle? Where is the way that the light is divided, or the east wind scattered on the earth? ... Can you lead forth a constellation in its season, and guide the Bear with her satellites? Do you know the ordinances of the heavens, or fix their rule over the earth? ... Can you hunt the prey for the lion ... or prepare the raven its nourishment? ... Do you know the time the mountain goat gives birth? ... Do you give the horse his might? ... Is it by Your understanding that the hawk soars? ... Do you have an arm like God, and can you thunder a voice like His?

O Sovereign God, just like Job, I am humbled and awed by Your power and Your might! *How unsearchable are Your judgments and how unfathomable are Your ways!* I will, therefore, praise You when the sun rises, and I will praise You when the stars shine. I will praise You when the wind blows, and I will praise You when the lightning flashes. I will praise You when the horse runs, and I will praise You when the hawk soars. Yes, I will praise You as Commander of heaven and of earth!

Job 41:11; 38:1,4,6,8,22-24,32-33,39,41; 39:1,19,26; 40:9; Romans 11:33

Jealous

For You shall not worship any other god, for the LORD, whose name is Jealous, is a jealous God.

EXODUS 34:14

O God, You are Jealous. Your heartbeat is love itself; Your commitment is to the death, and then, to life forevermore. Incredibly, even in my sin, You sought me and proclaimed to my heart, *I will betroth you to Me forever; Yes, I will betroth you to Me in righteousness and in justice, in lovingkindness and in compassion, and I will betroth you to Me in faithfulness.* I cannot comprehend this love that has been poured into my heart, but I will rejoice in it for the rest of time! O Lord, help me to be acutely aware, however, that this love of Yours cannot tolerate any other god in my life—not pride, not self, not others, not shame. *For You jealously desire the Spirit which You have made to live in me.* Yes, You want all of my heart, soul, mind, and strength so that You can love me fully. *O Jealous God, You are a consuming fire.* Please, burn away any idol in my life that will keep my heart from Your heart. Forgive me when I fail You; in the same breath, thank You for Your covenant that says *You will not fail me.* Yes, *You are compassionate*, full of mercy and grace. I thank You, *my husband and my Maker*, for Your perfect, jealous love. Keep Your strong hold on me, I pray, with Your gentle hands.

Hosea 2:19-20; James 4:5; Deuteronomy 4:24,31; Isaiah 54:5

Light

For You light my lamp; The LORD my God illumines my darkness.
PSALM 18:28

O God, You are Light. Your first spoken, recorded words to mankind were, *Let there be light.* Could it be that light is the attribute which most represents You: Your power, Your presence, Your purity? For without light, nothing would exist; the earth would have remained *formless and void.* And without You, O God, our hearts would be the same—aimless and without purpose. But You knew our plight and saw our condition. You knew we were living in a domain of darkness, and that we were *distressed and downcast like sheep without a shepherd.* So one more time, You powerfully spoke the words, "Let there be Light." And then Jesus, *who was in the beginning with You*, left His throne and came to earth. And *in Him was life, and the life was the light of men.* Yes, Jesus Messiah, You are the *Light of the World.* O God, thank You for separating light from darkness at the painful expense of separating Yourself from Your Son. I am humbled by this act of mercy and love for mankind. Because of You, I am now *light in the Lord. Help me to walk in this manner,* I pray. Cause me to *arise and shine; . . . for the glory of the Lord has risen upon me.* Yes, shine from me, O God. I want to be like a *city set on a hill that cannot be hidden*, steadily pronouncing Your power, Your presence, Your purity. Yes, O God, say to my heart, "Let there be Light."

**Genesis 1:3,2; Matthew 9:36; John 1:2,4; 8:12; Ephesians 5:8;
Isaiah 60:1; Matthew 5:14**

Foundation

For no man can lay a foundation other than the one which is laid, which is Jesus Christ.
1 CORINTHIANS 3:11

O God, You are my Foundation. Yes, You are the rock that is sure and unshakable; everything else is *sinking sand.* And on this rock, O God, I want to build my house. Help me to realize the deeper my foundation in my knowledge of You, the stronger my house will be. Dear Jesus, the desire of my heart is to *know You* deeper still! I thank You for this initial building block of truth: not only are You my firm foundation, but You are also my *precious cornerstone.* Indeed, every other "brick" I lay revolves around *Your love for me that was demonstrated at the cross.* Therefore, I will lay brick upon brick, truth upon truth—You are *my rock. … You are my fortress. … You are my deliverer. … You are my refuge. … You are my shield. … You are my stronghold.* Yes, because of You, Almighty God, I know that *when the rains come, and when the streams rise, and when the winds blow and beat against my house, it will not fall.* And there, within the walls of my home, I will praise You, God and Savior, from the ground up.

**Matthew 7:26; Philippians 3:10; 1 Peter 2:6; Romans 5:8;
Psalm 18:2; Matthew 7:24-25**

Living God

The king spoke and said to Daniel, "Daniel, servant of the living God, has Your God, whom you constantly serve, been able to deliver you from the lions?"

DANIEL 6:20

O God, You are the Living God. *For all the gods of the peoples are idols.* But You say imploringly to Your people, *To whom would you liken Me, and make Me equal and compare Me, that we should be alike? Those who lavish gold from the purse and weigh silver on the scale, hire a goldsmith, and he makes it into a god; they bow down, indeed they worship it. They lift it upon their shoulder and carry it; they set it in its place and it stands there. It does not move from its place. Though one may cry to it, it cannot answer; it cannot deliver him from his distress.* O Lord of life, You are the God who has a heartbeat! You feel, You hear, You see, You speak. You pursue, You contend, You guard, You guide. You act, You fight, You move, You make. And yes, You deliver! Just as You *delivered Daniel from the mouth of the lion ...* You have delivered me from the domain of darkness! So, I will praise You in unison with the ancient words of a king's changed heart: *God is the living God and he endures forever. ... He delivers and rescues, He performs signs and wonders.* Yes, I will bow down to the Living God.

Psalm 96:5; Isaiah 46:5-7; Daniel 6:26-27; Colossians 1:13; Daniel 6:26

Great

*For from the rising of the sun even to its setting, My name will be great among
the nations.*

MALACHI 1:11

O God, You are Great! Yes, *Our Father who art in heaven, hallowed be Your name!*
Without You, there would be complete darkness in our souls; but You have come as light
into the world. Without You, there would be *disorder, confusion, and every evil thing in
our minds; but You are wisdom that comes from above.* Indeed, without You, O God,
there would be NOTHING; *but by You all things were created, both in the heavens and
on earth, visible and invisible, whether thrones or dominions or rulers or authorities—
all things have been created by You and for You.* How great You are, O God! Your power,
Your might, Your goodness, and Your love reign from heaven, falling directly into the
hearts of men. My *face is to the ground in reverence and awe.* To think that I can *touch
the fringe of Your coat*! Yes, cause my trembling heart to embrace the sweet magnificent truth of both Your grandeur and Your grace. And then, help me to proclaim it to the
world! Make these holy words my ongoing heartbeat: *Sing to the Lord, praise His name;
proclaim His salvation day to day. Tell of His glory among the nations, His wonderful
deeds among all peoples. For great is the Lord, and greatly to be praised.* Yes, You, my
King and my Savior, are worthy of all praise. And I will sing as long as I have breath,
"How Great is our God!"

**Matthew 6:9; John 12:46; James 3:16-17; Colossians 1:16;
Daniel 10:15; Mark 5:27-28; Psalm 96:2-4**

Bread of Life

Behold, I will rain bread from heaven for you; and the people shall go out and gather a day's portion every day.

EXODUS 16:4

O God, You are the Bread of Life. Yes, through *Your Son Jesus*, You have rained Your mercy upon my soul. I will eagerly anticipate the promise of my future heavenly feast with You, O King; but until then, while on this earth, I will dine on the bread sent from above—Your holy word. I praise You for Your goodness, O God; just as *Your manna was sweet to the Israelites in the wilderness*, Your word is sweet to me. Indeed, You, Bread of Life, are *sweeter than honey and the drippings of the honeycomb!* I thank You for Your provision every day; and I thank You that You rejoice when I gather Your blessing. Yes, *You long to be gracious to me and You wait on high to have compassion on me.* Here I am, O Lord, fill me once again! Tell my doubtful heart, once again, of Your love; tell my weary soul, once again, of Your strength; tell my forgetful mind, once again, of Your peace. Every day, I am lacking; but, I rejoice because every day, *You sustain me, You satisfy me.* O sweet Bread of Life, I savor Your morsels of mercy sent from heaven. Yes, *morning by morning, morning by morning, through Your word*, I choose to taste heaven while on this earth.

John 6:35; Exodus 16:31; Psalm 19:10; Isaiah 30:18;
Song of Solomon 2:5; Matthew 5:6; Isaiah 50:4

Delightful

Who is a God like You, who pardons iniquity ... (and) delights in unchanging love?
MICAH 7:18

O God, You are Delightful. I love how You love! You don't miss a beat; You are one step ahead; You put surprises in my path. *O how I delight in You, dear Lord! You give me the desires of my heart.* Just the way *You kept the widow's jar full of oil* long ago, You keep *my heart full of joy* today. Each and every day You speak intimately to me in Your word, and You wow me with Your ways. How I love to *drink of the river of Your delights.* Thank You, O God. I am drinking You in. Yes, *there is a river whose streams make glad the city of God, the holy dwelling places of the Most High.* O God, You tell me that Your *dwelling place is in me*! Yes, just like the *woman at the well was filled with true and living water long ago, You have given me a well of water springing up to eternal life.* You are beautiful; You are plentiful; You are wonderful! I thank You for Your joy; I thank You for Your sweet preplanned surprises; and I thank You for Your rivers of gladness, both now and in my eternal home. Indeed, You are Delightful.

Psalm 37:4; 1 Kings 17:14; John 15:11; Psalms 36:8; 46:4; 1 Corinthians 3:16; John 4:14-15

God of My Heart

For the eyes of the Lord move to and fro throughout the earth that He may strongly support those whose heart is completely His.

2 CHRONICLES 16:9

O God, You are God of my Heart. You know the depths of my feelings, and You know the heights of my dreams. You know my struggles, and You know my fears. You know I want to follow You step by step; but You also know that I am unsure of which way You want me to go. I am perplexed instead of peaceful, confused instead of courageous. I ask You to continue to *search me, O God, and know my heart; try me and know my anxious thoughts; and see if there is any hurtful way in me, and lead me in the everlasting way.* Yes, I ask for discernment in the direction You want me to go. For *You are greater than my heart and You know all things.* Help me to *trust in You completely, without leaning on my own understanding; and help me to acknowledge You fully, believing that You will make my paths straight.* And then, please *equip me in every good thing to do Your will. ... Create in me a clean heart, O God, and renew a steadfast spirit within me. ... Make me confident in You.* My utmost desire, day in and day out, is for my heartbeat to match Your heartbeat—same pulse, same rhythm, same blood flow. *You in me, and I in You, and You in me, and I in You.* Yes, God of my Heart, please be bountifully beautiful in and through me.

Psalm 139:23-24; 1 John 3:20; Proverbs 3:5-6; Hebrews 13:21; Psalm 51:10; Proverbs 3:26; John 15:4-5

Caregiver

Humble yourselves….casting all your anxiety on Him, because He cares for you.
1 PETER. 5:6–7

O God, You are my Caregiver. You nourish me with the bread of life; You satisfy me with Your living water; You groom me with Your word of truth. You know exactly what I need, when I need it. When *I am weak, You are my strength.* When I am frail, *You are my fortress.* When I am feeble, *You are my sustainer.* When I am confused, *You are my peace.* As this physical world grows dim, Your heavenly light shines brighter and brighter. Yes, *I will not lose heart; … my inner man is being renewed day by day.* I have no worries, because You care for me. You are my constant companion. Yes, *Your presence gives me much needed rest. … Your presence gives me eternal hope.* Thank You loving Lord, for holding me in Your arms like a *shepherd who tenderly holds his sheep.* I cherish the deep warmth of Your protective embrace. My soul sighs, "I love my Caregiver, and my Caregiver loves me."

**2 Corinthians 12:10; 2 Samuel 22:33; Psalm 145:14; 1 Corinthians 14:33;
2 Corinthians 4:16; Exodus 33:14; Titus 3:7; Isaiah 40:11**

Invisible

And the Spirit of God was moving.

GENESIS 1:2

O God, You are Invisible. *Even though I have not seen You, I love You, and I believe in You, and I greatly rejoice with joy inexpressible.* For You have done great things, O God. You have invaded me with Your peace. You have overcome me with Your hope. You have captured me with Your love. Yes, *just like Moses, You have made my faith-filled heart see You, even though You remain unseen.* Thank You, O God. Please continue this good work in me. I pray for this childlike faith in others as well. You say in Your word that *none of us are without excuse, for since the creation of the world Your invisible attributes, Your eternal power and divine nature, have been clearly seen.* O God, I ask that You would pursue these doubtful unbelieving souls the way You pursued me! Make them see You too. I plead with You, cause *the eyes of their heart to be enlightened, so they may know what is the hope of their calling, and what are the riches of the glory of Your inheritance in the saints, and what is the surpassing greatness of Your power toward those who believe.* O God, who would not want to receive You and Your unseen treasures? *Beside You, I desire nothing on this earth.* Everlasting God, when I choose to *look at the things which are not seen,* I can almost feel the *eternal weight of glory that awaits me in heaven.* You are so good to me! Yes, my unseen God owns my undoubting heart.

1 Peter 1:8; Hebrews 11:27; Romans 1:20; Ephesians 1:18-19; Psalm 73:25; 2 Corinthians 4:17-18

Morning Star

And I will give him the morning star.

REVELATION 2:28

O God, You are the Morning Star. Through Your Son, the Light of the World has come to man. Yes, I love the searching question of the wise men of old: *Where is He who has been born King of the Jews? For we have seen His star in the east, and have come to worship Him.* My heart has come to worship You as well, my King! Indeed, *You, dear Jesus, are the root and offspring of David, the bright morning star.* Come, *shine on me* each new day, I pray. *Yes, satisfy me in the morning with Your lovingkindness.* Cause this *marvelous light of Yours to arise within my heart* so that I, too, can shine like the stars in the heavens. I want to pierce the *darkness of this crooked and perverse generation* with Your glory and grace. Help me to draw others to Your mesmerizing light, Your captivating love. Yes, shine on me, my bright Morning Star.

**Matthew 2:2; Revelation 22:16; Numbers 6:25; Psalm 90:14;
2 Peter 1:19; Philippians 2:15**

Triumphant

He had disarmed the rulers and authorities ... having triumphed over them through Him.
COLOSSIANS 2:15

O God, You are Triumphant. You have known the storyline from the beginning, and good versus evil has always been Your theme. The serpent in the garden and the sin of man was no surprise to You. But again, You had a plan. Satan would have his way for a time; but You promised to *crush him underfoot.* So, the war waged on, good versus evil, evil versus good, through time and history. Until one day, in the streets of Jerusalem, *a large crowd was waving palm branches, shouting, "Hosanna, blessed is He who comes in the name of the Lord."* Jesus Messiah, King of kings, *riding on a donkey.* Savior of the world. Yet one week later, You were crucified, dead, and buried? Did evil win? No! You *rose from the dead* proclaiming, *"Death is swallowed up in victory." Yes, thanks be to God* who has triumphed over evil through the blood of Christ and the power of the cross. But the storyline continues: *flesh versus the Spirit, Spirit versus the flesh.* O God, we are still living in a time where *fleshly lusts war against our soul.* The struggle is real and the pull is strong; but You promise *not to let me be tempted beyond what I am able to bear.* Even so, I do long for the struggle to be over! Yes, I eagerly await the climactic ending of Your strategic story. *You will come in a cloud with power and great glory, ... and You once and for all will slay the evil one and throw him into the everlasting fire.* Good will completely triumph over evil; then, Your Kingdom and Your people will live joyfully ever after.

**Romans 16:20; John 12:13-15; 1 Corinthians 15:54,57; Romans 8:5-6;
1 Peter 2:11; 1 Corinthians 10:13; Luke 21:27; Revelation 20:10**

Awesome

How awesome is this place! This is none other than the house of God, and this is the gate of heaven.

GENESIS 28:17

O God, You are Awesome! Yes, *You are the Lord God of heaven, the great and awesome God.* Hear my heart worship You as I embrace these timeless holy words: *Sing to God, O kingdoms of the earth; sing praises to the Lord, to Him who rides upon the highest heavens, which are from ancient time; behold, He speaks forth with His voice, a mighty voice. Ascribe strength to God; His majesty is over Israel, and His strength is in the skies. O God, You are awesome from Your sanctuary. The God of Israel Himself gives strength and power to the people. Blessed be God!* Dear Lord, thank You that I am considered one of Your people, and that You have come from the high heavens to abide in me. *I am Your sanctuary, Your holy temple. ... You long to fill me with the brightness of Your glory.* What an awesome and incomprehensible act! Your great love brought You to me. Yes, Your lovingkindness has smitten and overtaken my heart. You beautifully baffle me day after day. Dear Lord, through Your strength and through Your power, cause me to pour out this lovingkindness toward others; help me bring Your love to lost and lonely souls! Make me a holy yet approachable reflection of You. Yes, I want others to also be overtaken by Your love and filled with Your glory. O Awesome God, come to me, so I can go to the world.

Nehemiah 1:5; Psalm 68:32-35; 1 Corinthians 3:16; Ezekiel 10:4

Amazing

The sons of Israel went through the midst of the sea on the dry land, and the waters were like a wall to them on their right hand and on their left.

EXODUS 14:22

O God, You are Amazing! How amazing is Your grace; how amazing is Your love. My soul is filled with both awe and wonder as I consider the works of Your hands on behalf of Your people. As Protector, *You closed the door to the ark* long ago; and as Savior, You *have opened the door of salvation forever.* As Judge, *You can withhold rain for years*; but as God of mercy, You promise to provide *rivers in the desert.* Yes, You are Commander of the rain drops and Commander when the rain stops—*You hold the world's water in the hollow of Your hand.* Amazing! As God of Strength, *Your voice is over many waters; You are the God of glory who thunders! Your voice is powerful, Your voice is majestic.* O God, You reign when You rain! And then, God of Comfort, You are also the One who calms the storm. You say with a whisper, *Hush, be still.* Yes, *even the wind and sea obey You.* I praise You for Your power; I praise You for Your peace. I praise You for Your grace; I praise You for Your love. What an awesome privilege to call You, my Amazing God.

**Genesis 7:16; John 10:9; 1 Kings 17:1; Isaiah 43:19; 40:12;
Psalm 29:3-4; Mark 4:39,41**

God of Power

Once God has spoken; Twice I have heard this: That power belongs to God.
PSALM 62:11

O God, You are the God of Power. When I meditate on Your wonders, I am awed once again. I love Your ancient words that speak of Your strength and might. I see You *fighting the enemy while Your people kept silent;* and then I see *You crumbling city walls while Your people shouted. I see You sending fire from heaven while Your people worshipped;* and then I see *You sending manna from above as Your people waited.* O dear God, I also see that underneath this mighty power, there lies Your matchless love. Yes, Your love contrived a plan, and *Your overcoming power caused a baby to be born from a virgin.* Your love sent a Savior to the world, and *Your restraining power held Him on the cross.* Your love forsook Your Son, and *Your surpassing power raised Him from the dead.* Yes, God of Might, Your power *tore the curtain, and the earth shook; and the rocks were split, and the tombs were opened;* and now, Holy One, I can enter into Your presence! O yes, when I meditate on Your wonders, I am awed once again.

Exodus 14:14,19; Joshua 6:20; 2 Chronicles 7:1; Exodus 16:21; Luke 1:35; Isaiah 53:10; Ephesians 1:19-20; Matthew 27:51-52

Indescribable Gift

Thanks be to God for His indescribable gift!
2 CORINTHIANS 9:15

O God, You are the Indescribable Gift. Amazing and true, You freely gave Your perfect life as a gift. Adam sinned, and as a result, we all are fallen and deserving of death; but You, dear Jesus, entered in as the Savior. *For if by the transgression of the one the many died, much more did the grace of God and the gift by the grace of the one Man, Jesus Christ, abound to the many. For if by the transgression of the one, death reigned through the one, much more those who receive the abundance of grace and of the gift of righteousness will reign in life through the One, Jesus Christ.* Again, You say in Your word: *The wages of sin is death, but the free gift of God is eternal life in Christ Jesus our Lord.* Free gift—of God? Am I worthy to reach out and take it? No, absolutely not. But Your steadfast love, O God, implores me to receive it with a whole heart. And when I do, *my sins that were as scarlet will be white as snow,* and my life that *once was dead in my transgressions will be made alive together with Christ,* and my soul that *was formerly far off will be brought near by His blood.* Incredibly, O God, I will be *delivered from the domain of darkness, and transferred to the kingdom of Your beloved Son.* Yes, dear Jesus, because of Your sacrifice, I am changed from wretched to righteous, from prisoner to purchased, from slave to son! Dear Lord Jesus, You are indeed the Indescribable Gift!

Romans 5:15,17; 6:23; Isaiah 1:18; Ephesians 2:5,13; Colossians 1:13

Sovereign

The LORD has established His throne in the heavens, and His sovereignty rules over all.
PSALM 103:19

O God, You are Sovereign. You have complete control over all creation: *You make the dawn and sunset shout for joy. You visit the earth, and cause it to overflow; You greatly enrich it; the stream of God is full of water; You prepare their grain, for You prepare the earth.* You also have absolute authority over all time and history: *The Most High is ruler over the realm of mankind, and bestows it on whom He wishes.* And You have settled supremacy over all good and evil: *You are the One forming light and creating darkness, causing well-being and creating calamity; You are the Lord who does all these.* And we know that what the enemy *means for evil, You mean for good.* And God, You have detailed demand over all my life: *Your eyes have seen my unformed substance; and in Your book they were all written, the days that were ordained for me, when as yet there was not one of them.* Indeed, O God, You are the Sovereign One! Therefore I will praise You with all creation, all history, all happenings, and all my days, singing, *O clap your hands, all peoples; shout to God with the voice of joy. For the Lord Most High is to be feared, a great King over all the earth. He subdues peoples under us, and nations under our feet. He chooses our inheritance for us, the glory of Jacob whom He loves.* Indeed, the Sovereign God reigns over all.

Psalm 65:8-9; Daniel 4:17; Isaiah 45:7; Genesis 50:20; Psalms 139:16; 47:1-4

Advocate

My little children, I am writing these things to you that you may not sin. And if anyone sins, we have an Advocate with the Father, Jesus Christ the righteous.

1 JOHN 2:1

O God, You are the Advocate. Yes, dear Jesus, You came to be like us. You *passed through the heavens,* felt our humanness, conquered our sin, and died our death, so that You could go back in triumph *and sit at the right hand of the Majesty on high.* There, You are our Advocate. Indeed, *You are able to save forever those who draw near to God through You, since You always live to make intercession for us.* Thank You for *knowing our frame.* I am grateful for Your empathy. You understand me in every way. Again, thank You. It also soothes my soul to know this promise: *The Spirit also helps our weakness; for we do not know how to pray as we should, but the Spirit Himself intercedes for us with groanings too deep for words; and He who searches the hearts knows what the mind of the Spirit is, because He intercedes for the saints according to the will of God.* Dear Advocate, You know the right words to say when I do not. You translate my woes and my weaknesses into words that will be best for me in the long run, assuring me that *all things work together for good to those that love God, to those who are called according to Your purpose.* For *this I know, that God is for me.* So I thank You for Your interceding words that will bring hope and healing to my soul. I trust You, dear Friend. Thank You for perfectly understanding, and perfectly speaking on my behalf.

Hebrews 4:14; 1:3; 7:25; Psalm 103:14; Romans 8: 26-27, 28; Psalm 56:9

One Who Catches Our Tears

You have taken account of my wanderings; put my tears in Your bottle. Are they not in Your book?

PSALM 56:8

O God, You are the One Who Catches Our Tears. You took account of the childless Hannah as she wept before You in the temple. The high priest supposed she was drunk, but she said, *No, my lord, I am a woman oppressed in spirit; I have drunk neither wine nor strong drink, but I have poured out my soul before the Lord.* And Lord, You heard the cries of David as he was hiding from his enemies: *How long shall I take counsel in my soul, having sorrow in my heart all the day? How long will my enemy be exalted over me?* And Jesus, You respected humble *Mary at Your feet, weeping, and she began to wet Your feet with her tears, and kept wiping them with the hair of her head.* And also, You took note of Peter, who after his three denials, *went out and wept bitterly.* And yet again, You paid attention to Paul's heartfelt tears when he spoke sadly about his fellow unbelieving Jews: *For many walk, of whom I often told you, and now tell you even weeping, that they are enemies of the cross of Christ.* O God, thank You for catching the tears of Your people: tears of sadness, tears of anguish, tears of humility, tears of remorse, and tears of yearning. They, and those who shed them, do not go unnoticed by You. In fact, the sounds of weeping in these ways are beautiful prayers that touch Your heart. Yes, Merciful One, *Your ears are open to our cries.* Therefore, I humbly ask You to continue to take account of my own tears right now. I am completely spent; I am almost hopeless. Please hold me in Your arms as I weep. Please hold my grief; it is too heavy for me. Let me hear You whisper, *Take courage, it is I, do not be afraid.* And then, dear Lord, allow me to find solace in Your presence.

**1 Samuel 1:15; Psalm 13:2; Luke 7:38; 22:62; Philippians 3:18;
Psalm 34:15; Matthew 14:27**

One Who Wipes Our Tears

And God will wipe every tear from their eyes.

REVELATION 7:17

O God, You are the One Who Wipes Our Tears. You heard the longsuffering cries of the barren Hannah and then blessed her with a child: *And it came about in due time, after Hannah conceived, that she gave birth to a son; and she named him Samuel, saying, "Because I have asked him of the Lord."* And in Your time, You answered the anguished soul of David when he was hiding from his enemies. *You said to him, "You will shepherd My people Israel, and you will be a ruler over Israel."* And Jesus, after humble Mary finished wiping Your feet with her hair and her tears, You said of her, *Truly I say to you, wherever this gospel is preached in the whole world, what this woman has done shall also be spoken of in memory of her.* Also, You saw Peter's repentant cries and soon afterward said of him, *And I say to you that you are Peter, and upon this rock I will build My church; and the gates of Hades shall not overpower it.* And then to Paul and those like him, who longingly weep for the salvation of people's souls, You promise, *Those who sow in tears shall reap with joyful shouting. He who goes to and fro weeping, carrying his bag of seed, shall indeed come again with a shout of joy, bringing his sheaves with him.* Dear God, You are the One who not only catches our tears, but also the One who wipes them away. Yes, in due time, O God, You *save those who are crushed in spirit.* Dear Lord, thank You for not leaving me alone in my sorrow; thank You for coming to my aid in my grief. Give me patience as You answer in Your perfect time and in Your perfect way. And Sovereign One, even if what I long for does not come to me on this side of heaven, I know I can trust You. Yes, even so, my soul will joyfully cling to this everlasting promise: *And He shall wipe away every tear from their eyes; and there shall no longer be any death; there shall no longer be any mourning, or crying, or pain.* Indeed, dear Lord, *weeping may last for the night, but a shout of joy comes in the morning.*

1 Samuel 1:20; 2 Samuel 5:2; Matthew 26:13; 16:18; Psalms 126:5-6; 34:18; Revelation 21:4; Psalm 30:5

Consuming Fire

And many of those who practiced magic brought their books together and began burning them in the sight of everyone; and they counted up the price of them and found it fifty thousand pieces of silver. So the word of the Lord was growing mightily and prevailing.
ACTS 19:19–20

O God, You are a Consuming Fire. You spoke through Moses concerning the Israelites entering the promised land: *Know therefore today that it is the Lord your God who is crossing over before you as a consuming fire. He will destroy them and He will subdue them before you, so that you may drive them out and destroy them quickly, just as the Lord has spoken to you.* Yes, dear Lord, just as You drove out the enemy before Your people of old, You will do the same for me today. I ask You to burn away these adversaries from my heart: fear and foolishness, confusion and carelessness, worry and waywardness. May there be nothing left of each of these, and any other encroaching sins, I pray. Also, O God, You said through Moses as the people entered the land: *So watch yourselves, lest you forget the covenant of the Lord your God, which He made with you, and make for yourselves a graven image in the form of anything against which the Lord your God has commanded you. For the Lord Your God is a consuming fire, a jealous God.* Indeed, O Lord, I see and understand that while Your holy fire unleashes against wickedness and evil, it also radiates passionately for righteousness and good. How You long for us to know You, and follow You. So make my heart willing to place my sin on Your holy altar; then with Your touch, please light it ablaze. Yes, dear Lord, You are the only One who can bring *beauty from ashes.* Thank You, Holy One, for Your righteous ways and Your jealous love. You are a Consuming Fire within my soul.

Deuteronomy 9:3; 4:23-24; Isaiah 61:3

One Who Tries Hearts

You have heard of the endurance of Job and have seen the outcome of the Lord's dealings, that the Lord is full of compassion and is merciful.

JAMES 5:11

O God, You are the One Who Tries Hearts. You say, *The heart is more deceitful than all else and desperately sick; who can understand it? I, the Lord, search the heart, I test the mind, even to give to each man according to his ways, according to the results of his deeds.* Only You, O God, can completely understand what lies inside each one of us. And only You, dear Savior, can heal our sickness. If it were not for You, none of us could stand as holy and pure before Your throne. Dear Lord, I know my eternal salvation is secure, but the battle between good and evil is ongoing within me: *The flesh sets its desire against the Spirit, and the Spirit against the flesh; for these are in opposition to one another, so that I do not do the things that I please.* I ask You to *examine me* gracefully, groom me carefully, and grow me wisely toward You. Yes, continue Your good work of sanctification in me. Daily *search me and know my heart; try me and know my anxious thoughts; and see if there be any hurtful way in me, and lead me in the everlasting way.* I understand and adhere to this truth: *The refining pot is for silver and the furnace is for gold, but the Lord tests the hearts.* So again, dear God, have Your way with me. Remove anything from this earthen vessel that is a hindrance to Your radiant glory. For I long to be described like David, whom You persistently tested, tried, and gracefully declared, *He is a man after My own heart.*

Jeremiah 17:9-10; Galatians 5:17; 1 Thessalonians 2:4; Psalm 139: 23-24; Proverbs 17:3; Acts 13:22

Head

And He put all things in subjection under His feet, and gave Him as head over all things to the church, which is His body, the fullness of Him who fills all in all.
EPHESIANS 1:22–23

O God, You are the Head. Yes, Jesus, it is beautifully said of You: *He is the image of the invisible God, the firstborn of all creation. And He is before all things, and in Him all things hold together. He is also head of the body, the church; and He is the beginning, the firstborn from the dead; so that He Himself might come to have first place in everything.* Indeed, You have power and authority over all creation and mankind. You are the Ruler of heaven and earth, kings and kingdoms. And God, You are Ruler over me! I desire You to have first place in everything that involves me. I pray that I will hear Your voice and follow Your lead. I want to be an effective working entity of Your body, the church: *And He gave some as pastors and teachers, building up of the body of Christ; until we all attain to the unity of the faith, and of the knowledge of the Son of God, to a mature man, to the measure of the stature which belongs to the fullness of Christ.* Please dear Jesus, take command, and allow me to *grow up in all aspects into You.* Let me hear Your truth; let me see Your perspective; let me think Your thoughts; let me speak Your words. This is my earnest prayer: *Teach me Your way, O Lord; I will walk in Your truth; unite my heart to fear Your name. I will give thanks to You, O Lord my God, with all my heart, and will glorify Your name forever.* Yes, Almighty God, Head of the Universe, please be the Head of me.

Colossians 1:15,17-18; Ephesians 4:11-13,15; Psalm 86:11-12

One Whom I Believe

For I know whom I have believed and I am convinced that He is able to guard what I have entrusted to Him until that day.

2 TIMOTHY 1: 12

O God, You are the One Whom I Believe. Yes, Lord, You say, *Without faith it is impossible to please Me. For he who comes to Me must believe that I am, and that I am a rewarder of those who seek Me.* Help me to learn from Thomas, who initially doubted the resurrection, saying, *"Unless I shall see in His hands the imprint of the nails, and put my finger into the place of the nails, and put my hand into His side, I will not believe." And after eight days again His disciples were inside, and Thomas with them, Jesus came, the doors having been shut, and stood in their midst, and said, "Peace be with you." Then He said to Thomas, "Reach here your finger, and see My hands; and reach here your hand, and put it into My side; and be not unbelieving, but believing. Because you have seen Me, have you believed? Blessed are they who did not see, and yet believed."* O Lord, please continue to work in me a deep-rooted faith. Honor this prayer of my heart as You did to the one who spoke it long ago, *I do believe; help my unbelief.* Yes, I want to respond in full unwavering confidence to You and Your promises. Make my faith like Martha's, when You spoke and asked her these words of life-changing truth, saying, *"I am the resurrection and the life; he who believes in Me will live even if he dies, and everyone who lives and believes in Me will never die. Do you believe this?" She said, "Yes, Lord; I have believed that You are the Christ, the Son of God, even He who comes into the world."* Indeed, O God, in my heart of hearts, You are the One Whom I believe! And *even though I haven't seen You, I love You, and though I do not see You now, but believe You, I greatly rejoice with joy inexpressible and full of glory, obtaining the outcome of my faith the salvation of my soul.*

Hebrews 11:6; John 20:24-25; Mark 9:24; John 20:25-29; 1 Peter 1:8-9

Three in One

The grace of the Lord Jesus Christ, and the love of God, and the fellowship of the Holy Spirit, be with you all.

2 CORINTHIANS 13:14

O God, You are the Three In One. Three persons, One God. I confess, this is confusing at times for me. This heavenly concept does not seem humanly possible; but that's just it—You, O God, are not limited by human boundaries. You are God, and You are able to do anything, and all things. So therefore, I will trust You as God. And I will choose to believe You even if my finite mind cannot fully grasp You; for this is faith. I thank You for Your word that speaks of You as God the Father, God the Son, and God the Holy Spirit: *Now it came about when all the people were baptized, that Jesus was also baptized, and while He was praying, heaven was opened, and the Holy Spirit descended upon Him in bodily form like a dove, and a voice came out of heaven, "You are My beloved Son, in You I am well-pleased."* Also, this Scripture speaks truth: *In the beginning was the Word, and the Word was with God, and the Word was God, He was in the beginning with God. And the Word became flesh and dwelt among us, and we beheld His glory, glory as of the only begotten from the Father, full of grace and truth.* Yes, Jesus Son of God, You became flesh and You are *the radiance of God's glory and the exact representation of His nature.* And You came for a purpose: *the love of God has been poured out within our hearts through the Holy Spirit who was given to us. For while we were still helpless, at the right time Christ died for the ungodly.* Jesus, You died and rose again, so that the *Helper, the Holy Spirit, could come.* Ah yes, the work of the Father, Son, and Spirit—how divinely beautiful to the human soul! Jesus, I will cling to Your words, *If anyone loves Me, he will keep My word; and My Father will love him and We will come to him and make Our abode with him.* Yes, Three in One, make Your abode in me.

Luke 3:21-22; John 1:1-2,14; Hebrews 1:3; Romans 5:5-6; John 16:7; 14:23

Chosen One

Behold, My Servant, whom I uphold; My chosen one in whom My soul delights. I have put My Spirit upon Him; He will bring forth justice to the nations.

ISAIAH 42:1

O God, You are the Chosen One. Yes, by faith, I understand the concept of God the Father, God the Son, and God the Holy Spirit. With that being said, I believe *the Father has sent His Son to be the Savior of the world.* Heavenly Father, You said from above, *This is My Son, My Chosen One; listen to Him!* And also, *This is My beloved Son, in whom I am well-pleased.* O God, thank You for Your perfect choice. You knew from the beginning what Jesus came to do, and only He could do it. *In this is love, not that we loved God, but that He loved us and sent His Son to be the propitiation for our sins.* How it must have broken Your heart to turn Your back on Your Son for the sake of Your people, who did not even believe You! At the cross, *the people stood by, looking on. And even the rulers were sneering at Him, saying, "He saved others, let Him save Himself if this is the Christ of God, His Chosen One."* Dear Jesus, I thank You for not saving Yourself. I humbly rejoice in this passage: *But we do see Him who has been made for a little while lower than the angels, namely, Jesus, because of the suffering of death, crowned with glory and honor, that by the grace of God He might taste death for everyone. For it was fitting for Him, for whom are all things, and through whom are all things, in bringing many sons to glory, to perfect the author of their salvation through sufferings.* Chosen One, Perfect One, You suffered and died for my sin; and You purchased for me a present and eternal glory. Hallelujah, I will thank You forever!

1 John 4:14; Luke 9:35; Matthew 3:17; 1 John 4:10; Luke 23:35; Hebrews 2:9-10

Steadfast

The LORD's lovingkindnesses indeed never cease, for His compassions never fail.
LAMENTATIONS 3:22

O God, You are Steadfast. Your unfailing love is evident as You pursue Your people all through Scripture. You spoke to Moses saying, *I have surely seen the affliction of My people who are in Egypt, and have given heed to their cry because of their taskmasters, for I am aware of their sufferings. So I have come down to deliver them from the power of the Egyptians.* And then, You spoke through David saying, *He sent from on high, He took me; He drew me out of many waters. He delivered me from my strong enemy, and from those who hated me, for they were too mighty for me. They confronted me in the day of my calamity, but the Lord was my stay. He brought me forth also into a broad place; He rescued me, because He delighted in me.* And later, You spoke through Jeremiah saying, *I have loved you with an everlasting love; therefore I have drawn you with lovingkindness.* Also, You said through Hosea, *I will betroth you to Me forever; yes, I will betroth you to Me in righteousness and in justice, in lovingkindness and in compassion, and I will betroth you to Me in faithfulness. Then you will know the Lord.* And Jesus, You spoke these words, *I am the good shepherd; and I know My own, and My own know Me, even as the Father knows Me and I know the Father; and I lay down My life for the sheep.* O God, You are steadfast—steadfast in Your deliverance, steadfast in Your rescue, steadfast in Your lovingkindness, steadfast in Your commitment, and steadfast in Your plan, even to the death. Thank You for Your relentless pursuit; thank You for never giving up on me. Messiah, I humbly thank You for Your eternal embrace.

**Exodus 3:7-8; Psalm 18:16-19; Jeremiah 31:3; Hosea 2:19-20;
John 10:14-15**

God of the Mundane

Is this not the carpenter's son? Is not His mother called Mary, and His brothers, James and Joseph and Simon and Judas?

MATTHEW 13:55

O God, You are the God of the Mundane. I love how Your wonders are birthed from the ordinary routine of Your people. I see this in Moses' life when *he was pasturing the flock: He led the flock to the west side of the wilderness, and came to Horeb, the mountain of God. And the angel of the Lord appeared to him in a blazing fire from the midst of a bush.* And I see this in Gideon's life when *he was beating out wheat in the wine press in order to save it from the Midianites. And the angel of the Lord appeared to him and said to him, "The Lord is with you, O valiant warrior."* And I also see this in Ruth's life when *she went and gleaned in the field after the reapers: She happened to come to the portion of the field belonging to Boaz, who was of the family of Elimelech,* a kinsmen redeemer. And then, You moved in the mundane of Lydia's life: *On the Sabbath day we (Paul and his followers) went outside the gate to a riverside, where we were supposing that there would be a place of prayer; and we sat down and began speaking to the women who had assembled. And a certain woman named Lydia, from the city of Thyatira, a seller of purple fabrics, a worshiper of God, was listening; and the Lord* opened *her heart to respond to the things spoken by Paul.* O God, I pray I will learn from these men and women of old. Help me to do my daily routine with joy, knowing that You are in my midst. During the ordinary, I can choose to pray to You all day long, inviting Your divine power into my repetitive labor, turning it into a *spiritual service of worship.* And I can also listen to You, and then choose to joyfully obey Your voice, doing the next thing in front of me, whether small or great. Yes, Lord, *teach me to number my days.* I want to make them count for Your glory, no matter the task at hand. May I not miss the truth that You are beautifully present within the mundane; and there, Your wonders are birthed.

Exodus 3:1-2; Judges 6:11-12; Ruth 2:2; Acts 16:13-14; Romans 12:1;
Psalm 90:12

God of Form and Function

The earth was formless and void, and darkness was over the surface of the deep, and the Spirit of God was moving over the surface of the waters.

GENESIS 1:2

O God, You are the God of Form and Function. When *You created the heavens and the earth,* it was not random. You had a plan, and You had order to that plan. *And You saw that it was good.* Likewise, when You created man You said, *"Let Us make man in Our image, according to Our likeness." God created man in His own image, in the image of God He created him; male and female he created them.* Wow, this is an amazing thought: our form is "in You"; we bear Your image! I pray this truth will humble me as I live out each of my days. And dear Lord, I also see that our function is "of You." You said to Adam, *Be fruitful and multiply, and fill the earth, and subdue it; and rule over the fish of the sea and over the birds of the sky, and over every living thing that moves on the earth.* You gave Adam purpose. So Lord, help me to take these truths to heart. You have created me, and You have a plan for me, and there is order to this plan. You, O God, are not random with my life. Indeed, *You formed my inward parts; You weaved me in my mother's womb.* And You say to me, *You are My workmanship, created in Christ Jesus for good works, which I prepared beforehand that you should walk in them.* Yes, God of Form and Function, thank You for not leaving me to my own hopeless demise. I will humbly bow before You as my Maker, and courageously follow You as my Master.

Genesis 1:1; 1:25-28; Psalm 139:13; Ephesians 2:10

God Who Silences the Enemy

Then Daniel spoke to the king, "O king, live forever! My God sent His angel and shut the lions' mouths, and they have not harmed me."
DANIEL 6:21–22

O God, You are the One Who Silences the Enemy. God, I ask You to do this very thing in my life right now. Why do I adhere to the same lies? And why do I cower to the same fears? I know better. Really, my faith is stronger than this, isn't it? I ask for Your help. Please, *lead me to the rock that is higher than I. For You have been a refuge for me, a tower of strength against the enemy.* Yes, remind me of the truths found in Your word; they are *living and active and sharper than any two-edged sword.* O God, I pray that I will then use this powerful sword to fight my enemies. Jesus Himself did this very thing in the wilderness when His enemy approached Him. And as a result, *the devil left Him, and behold, angels came and began to minister to Him.* So therefore, I must regain my faith, and fight in this same way. Yes, I *will take up the shield of faith, with which I will be able to extinguish all the flaming missiles of the evil one. And I will take the helmet of salvation, and the sword of the Spirit, which is the word of God.* Thank You for reminding me that no lies, nor tactics, nor schemes of the enemy can stand in the presence of Your truth. You promise, *No weapon formed against me shall prosper.* Most certainly then, through Your word and by Your power, You are the Silencer of my Enemy.

Psalm 61:2-3; Hebrews 4:12; Matthew 4:11; Ephesians 6:16-17; Isaiah 54:17

God of the Low Whisper

He leads me beside quiet waters.

PSALM 23:2

O God, You are the God of the Low Whisper. *Save me, O God, for the waters have threatened my life. I have sunk in deep mire, and there is no foothold; I have come into deep waters, and a flood overflows me. I am weary with my crying; my throat is parched.* I need You to come to my rescue, O God. Right now, my days are chaotic and out of control. My strength is nearly gone. My courage is next to nothing. I have no idea how to handle the days ahead. O Lord, keep me attentive to Your voice in the midst of this storm. Help me to hear and embrace the sound of Your low whisper. Let me rise above the clamor and hear You say to my heart, *Come to Me. Listen, that you may live.* Yes, God, Your whisper is full of hope. You say with compassion, *Do not be afraid ... I will give you rest ... I know the plans I have for you ... I am the good shepherd ... Come, follow Me.* O dear Lord, Your tender voice calms me; Your quiet words soothe me. Keep me attentive, for Your low whisper is my delight. Yes, You calm the storm within me while it continues to rage about. Thank You, Gentle One, for firmly steadying my soul.

Psalm 69:1-3; Isaiah 55:3; Matthew 14:27; 11:28; Jeremiah 29:11; John 10:14; Matthew 4:19

God of the Mighty Wind

As they were going along and talking, behold, there appeared a chariot of fire and horses of fire which separated the two of them. And Elijah went up by a whirlwind to heaven.

2 Kings 2:11

O God, You are God of the Mighty Wind. Yes, dear Lord, I love this story of old: *The hand of the Lord was upon me and, He brought me out by the Spirit of the Lord and set me down in the middle of the valley; and it was full of bones. And He caused me to pass among them round about, and behold, there were very many on the surface of the valley; and lo, they were very dry. Then He said to me, "Prophesy to the breath, prophesy, son of man, and say to the breath, 'Thus says the Lord God, "Come from the four winds, O breath, and breathe on the these slain, that they come to life."'" So I prophesied as He commanded me, and the breath came into them, and they came to life, and stood on their feet, an exceedingly great army.* O God, what a picture of Your grace and might! This story also portrays those attributes: *And when the day of Pentecost had come, they were all together in one place. And suddenly there came from heaven a noise like a violent, rushing wind, and it filled the whole house where they were sitting. And there appeared to them tongues as of fire distributing themselves, and they rested on each one of them. And they were all filled with the Holy Spirit and began to speak with other tongues, as the Spirit was giving them utterance.* Dear Lord, Your Mighty Wind represents Your Holy Spirit that gives each one of us new and refreshing life. *Bless the Lord, O my soul! O Lord my God, You are very great; You are clothed with splendor and majesty. You make the clouds Your chariot; You walk upon the wings of the wind; You make the winds Your messengers, flaming fire Your ministers.* Come, O God, catch me in Your whirlwind, I pray. Renew me with Your Spirit, so that I, too, can stand mightily and speak beautifully of Your great name.

Ezekiel 37:1-2,9-10; Acts 2:1-4; Psalm 104:1,3-4

One Who Softens Hearts

And I will remove the heart of stone from your flesh and give you a heart of flesh.
EZEKIEL 36:26

O God, You are the One Who Softens Hearts. In Your word, You tell us why our hearts can become hard: *Take care, brethren, lest there should be in any one of you an evil, unbelieving heart, in falling away from the living God. But encourage one another day after day, as long as it is still called "Today," lest any one of you be hardened by the deceitfulness of sin.* O Lord, I pray against these things in my daily walk with You: against evil, against unbelief, against falling away, and against deceit. Convict me in these areas, O God. Forgive me when my heart becomes brittle and cold. Pull me back toward You, I pray. Continue Your molding work, even when I wrestle against You. Ultimately, I want Your way, not mine. Yes, bend my stiff neck, O God. I will cling to Your good promise: *And I will give them a heart to know Me, for I am the Lord; and they will be My people, and I will be their God, for they will return to Me with their whole heart.* Yes, dear Lord, make me pliable once more. For *Your hands have made me and fashioned me; give me understanding that I may learn Your commandments.* Indeed, I want to say without reservation, *I delight to do Your will, O my God; Your Law is within my heart. With my mouth I will give thanks abundantly to the Lord; and in the midst of many I will praise Him. I will run the way of Your commandments, for You will enlarge my heart.*

Hebrews 3:12-13; Jeremiah 24:7; Psalm 119:73; 40:8; 109:30; 119:32

Great High Priest

Therefore, since then we have a great high priest who has passed through the heavens,
Jesus the Son of God, let us hold fast our confession.

HEBREWS 4:14

O God, You are the Great High Priest. In the days of old, before Jesus' fulfillment of Scripture, the *priests were continually entering the outer tabernacle, performing the divine worship, but into the second (the holy of holies) only the high priest entered, once a year, not without taking blood, which he offered for himself and for the sins of the people committed in ignorance. But when Christ appeared as a high priest of the good things to come, He entered through the greater and more perfect tabernacle, not made with hands, that is to say, not of this creation, and through the blood of goats and calves, but through His own blood, He entered the holy place once for all, having obtained eternal redemption. When He had made purification of sins, He sat down at the right hand of the Majesty on high.* Because of this completed act, we now live with the good news! Once and for all, the perfect High Priest offered the perfect sacrifice. He who had no sin conquered sin. God the Son, You opened the way to God the Father! And this is the beautiful truth: *For we do not have a high priest who cannot sympathize with our weaknesses, but One who has been tempted in all things as we are, yet without sin. Let us therefore draw near with confidence to the throne of grace, that we may receive mercy and may find grace to help in time of need.* Great High Priest, thank You. In Your throne room, I hear the angels singing, *Holy, holy, holy, is the Lord God, the Almighty, who was, and who is, and who is to come.*

Hebrews 9:6-7,11-12; 1:3; 4:15-16; Revelation 4:8

One Who Stands By Me

Nevertheless I am continually with You; You have taken hold of my right hand. With Your counsel You will guide me.

PSALM 73:23–24

O God, You are the One Who Stands by Me. You stood beside *Shadrach, Meshach and Abed-nego, when they fell into the midst of the furnace of blazing fire still tied up.* Your word says that King Nebuchadnezzar *was astounded and stood up in haste, and said, Look! I see four men loosed and walking about in the midst of the fire without harm, and the appearance of the fourth is like a son to the gods!* And then, You stood beside Peter when *he got out of the boat, and walked on the water and came toward You. But seeing the wind, he became afraid, and beginning to sink, he cried out, saying, "Lord, save me!" And immediately You stretched out Your hand and took hold of him.* And also, You encouraged the apostle Paul in prison: *And as a great dissension was developing, the commander was afraid Paul would be torn to pieces by them and ordered the troops to go down and take him away from them by force, and bring him into the barracks. But on the night immediately following, the Lord stood at his side and said, "Take courage; for as you have solemnly witnessed to My cause at Jerusalem, so you must witness at Rome also."* O God, just as You stood beside these men of old, I know You will stand by me today! Therefore, I will proclaim with confidence, *I have set the Lord continually before me; because He is at my right hand, I will not be shaken. Therefore my heart is glad, and my glory rejoices; my flesh also will dwell securely.* Yes, Protector and Friend, thank You for being the one Who Stands by Me.

Daniel 3:23-25; Matthew 14:29-31; Acts 23:10-11; Psalm 16:8-9

Shadowing God

Keep me as the apple of the eye; hide me in the shadow of Your wings.

PSALM 17:8

O God, You are the Shadowing God. I claim this beautiful promise: *He who dwells in the shelter of the Most High will abide in the shadow of the Almighty. I will say to the Lord, "My refuge and my fortress, my God, in whom I trust!"* Yes, O Lord, *You are my keeper; You are my shade at my right hand. The sun will not smite me by day, nor the moon by night.* I will trust You completely, and I will stay close to Your side; for Your protection is my peace. And Lord, as I walk with You, I will praise You for Your fulfilled promise both now and eternally: *Behold, a king will reign righteously, and princes will rule justly. And each will be like a refuge from the wind, and a shelter from the storm, like streams of water in a dry country, like the shade of a huge rock in a parched land.* Thank You, Jesus, King of kings! *For You have been a defense for the helpless, a defense for the needy in his distress, a refuge from the storm, a shade from the heat. Like heat by the shadow of a cloud, the song of the ruthless is silenced.* Most certainly O God, *in the shadow of Your wings I will sing for joy.*

Psalms 91:1-2; 121:5-6; Isaiah 32:1-2; 25:4-5; Psalm 63:7

One Who Brings Good from Calamity

And we know that God causes all things to work together for good to those who love God, to those who are called according to His purpose.

ROMANS 8:28

O God, You are the One Who Brings Good from Calamity. Joseph's brothers betrayed him; but years later he rose to be ruler of Egypt, second-in-command to Pharaoh. In doing so, Joseph saved the nation from famine, saying to his brothers, *And as for you, you meant evil against me, but God meant it for good in order to bring about this present result, to preserve many people alive.* And Paul spoke of his suffering in this way: *Now I want you to know, brethren, that my circumstances have turned out for the greater progress of the gospel, so that my imprisonment in the cause of Christ has become well known throughout the whole praetorian guard and to everyone else, and that most of the brethren, trusting in the Lord because of my imprisonment, have far more courage to speak the work of God without fear.* And it is said of Jesus concerning His persecution and death: *He was pierced through for our transgressions, He was crushed for our iniquities; the chastening for our well-being fell upon Him, and by His scourging we are healed. As a result of the anguish of His soul, He will see it and be satisfied, by His knowledge the Righteous One, My Servant, will justify the many, as He will bear their iniquities.* O God, I see that You are always at work on the behalf of Your children even when things seem so bleak. I pray that in this dark place surrounding me right now, I will boldly shine Your light for all to see. The hope I cling to is that my suffering will not be in vain; indeed, You will bring good from it. Yes, right now, in the midst of the uncertainty, I ask You to *put a new song in my mouth, a song of praise to You, so that many will see and fear, and will trust in the Lord.*

Genesis 50:20; Philippians 1:12-14; Isaiah 53:5,11; Psalm 40:3

My Anchor

This hope we have as an anchor of the soul, a hope both sure and steadfast and one which enters within the veil, where Jesus has entered as a forerunner for us.

HEBREWS 6:19–20

O God, You are my Anchor. Without Your word, I would be *tossed here and there by waves, and carried about by every wind of doctrine, by the trickery of men, by craftiness in deceitful scheming.* Indeed, I am stable because *the sum of Your word is truth.* Dear Jesus, I love how You prayed this principle over those who believe in You: *Father, I do not ask You to take them out of the world, but to keep them from the evil one. They are not of the world, even as I am not of the world. Sanctify them in the truth; Your word is truth.* And You promise, *those who love Your law have great peace, and nothing causes them to stumble.* Yes, O God, I want the absolute truth of *Christ to dwell in my heart through faith, so that I may be rooted and grounded in His love.* And when I do need clarity in my daily walk with You, let me hear Your words of instruction: *But if any of you lacks wisdom, let him ask of God, who gives to all men generously and without reproach, and it will be given to him. But let him ask in faith without any doubting, for the one who doubts is like the surf of the sea driven and tossed by the wind. For let not that man expect that he will receive anything from the Lord, being a double-minded man, unstable in all his ways.* O God, by faith, I will hold on to You securely with both hands; for You are my Rock, You are my Mainstay, You are my Anchor.

Ephesians 4:14; Psalm 119:160; John 17:15-17; Psalm 119:165; Ephesians 3:17; James 1:5-8

Father Who Sees in Secret

Beware of practicing your righteousness before men to be noticed by them; otherwise you have no reward with your Father who is in heaven.

MATTHEW 6:1

O God, You are the Father Who Sees in Secret. Let me take these convicting questions to heart: *For am I now seeking the favor of men, or of God? Or am I striving to please men?* O dear Lord, my heart's desire is to please You and You alone. It is clear, *if I were trying to please men, I would not be a bond-servant of Christ.* So please help me not to be swayed by men, or crave their approval. Instead, help me to hear You clearly, and obey You completely, even if it means that I'm standing alone, or going unnoticed. Let me adhere to these words of truth: *When therefore you give alms, do not sound a trumpet before you, as the hypocrites do in the synagogues and in the streets, that they may be honored by men. Truly I say to you, they have their reward in full. But when you give alms, do not let your left hand know what your right hand is doing that your alms may be in secret; and your Father who sees in secret will repay you. But you, when you pray, go into your inner room, and when you have shut your door, pray to your Father who is in secret, and your Father who sees in secret will repay you.* Yes, O God, while I walk quietly by Your side, I will look for the secret blessings that You hand out each and every day. Your nod of approval is more gratifying to me than the applause of many. For *the reward of humility and the fear of the Lord are riches, honor and life.*

Galatians 1:10; Matthew 6:2-6; Proverbs 22:4

God of New Life

How can a man be born when he is old? He cannot enter a second time into his mother's womb and be born, can he?

JOHN 3:4

O God, You are the God of New Life. Physically, *You formed man of the dust from the ground, and breathed into his nostrils the breath of life; and man became a living being.* Likewise, Jesus, You spoke these words concerning us spiritually: *Truly, truly, I say to you, unless one is born again, he cannot see the kingdom of God. Unless one is born of water and the Spirit, he cannot enter into the kingdom of God. That which is born of the flesh is flesh, and that which is born of the Spirit is spirit. Do not marvel that I said to you, "You must be born again." The wind blows where it wishes and you hear the sound of it, but do not know where it comes from and where it is going; so is everyone who is born of the Spirit.* Thank You, dear Jesus; through Your death, and resurrection, I can now have Your Holy Spirit living inside of me—this is amazing grace! I rejoice in this truth: *If any man is in Christ, he is a new creature, the old things passed away; behold, new things have come.* Yes, I continually long for the new things! So *breathe on me,* O God, and through Your powerful Spirit, cause me to trust You; and may I daily *walk in newness of life.*

Genesis 2:7; John 3:3,5-8; 2 Corinthians 5:17; John 20:22; Romans 6:4

Master Architect

For every house is built by someone, but the builder of all things is God.
HEBREWS 3:4

O God, You are the Master Architect. The garden of Eden was designed exactly as You planned, and nothing was in error. And You gave Moses instruction in the wilderness *when he was about to erect the tabernacle; for You said, "See that you make all things according to the pattern which was shown you on the mountain."* And likewise, Your holy temple in Jerusalem also had a specific floor plan that You gave to King David. *"All this,"* said David, *"the Lord made me understand in writing by His hand upon me, all the details of this pattern."* And to think, both of these God-designed, but man-made temples are a mere *copy and shadow of the heavenly things.* Indeed, everything built in the physical temples reflect the heavenly reality: *We have such a high priest, who has taken His seat at the right hand of the throne of the Majesty in the heavens, a minister in the sanctuary, and in the true tabernacle, which the Lord pitched, not man.* Master Architect, thank You for giving us a glimpse of what is to come! Heaven is full of Your fulfilled promises and Your perfect plans. You have things waiting for us, *things which eye has not seen and ear has not heard, and which have not entered the heart of man, all that You have prepared for those who love You.* Author of Eden, earth, and ever-after, I will wait with expectant joy. Yes, I will be *looking for the city which has foundations, whose architect and builder is God.*

Hebrews 8:5; 1 Chronicles 28:19; Hebrews 8:5,1; 1 Corinthians 2:9; Hebrews 11:10

God of the Hopeless

Where now is my hope? And who regards my hope?
JOB 17:15

O God, You are God of the Hopeless. Thank You for the lessons of Job who, by Your sovereign plan, was greatly afflicted. Your word allows us to see his struggling heart as he cried out in physical and emotional pain: *He breaks me on every side, and I am gone; and He has uprooted my hope like a tree.* But Job also says determinedly, *Though He slay me, I will hope in Him.* O God, the same struggle is so real for each of us when trying times come our way. Deep down, we know You are *an ever present help in time of trouble;* but at the same time, our hearts tend to cry out, *Teacher, do You not care that we are perishing?* Please speak into our hopeless hearts when they are being tossed about like waves in a mighty storm. *Answer me, O Lord, for Your lovingkindness is good; according to the greatness of Your compassion, turn to me, and do not hide Your face from Your servant, for I am in distress; answer me quickly. Oh draw near to my soul and redeem it.* Yes, Lord, come to me as You did so profoundly to Job. For You showed him *things too wonderful for him, which he did not know.* Yes, set my heart straight and remind me both of who You are and what You are able to do. Keep my eyes fixed on You, and refill me with Your truth. And then, with a renewed heart and mind I will confidently say, *And now, Lord, for what do I wait? My hope is in You.*

**Job 19:10; 13:15; Psalm 46:1; Mark 4:38; Psalm 69:16-18; Job 42:3;
Psalm 39:7**

One Who Inaugurates

The Holy Spirit is signifying this, that the way into the holy place has not yet been disclosed while the outer tabernacle is still standing, which is a symbol for the present time. ... But when Christ appeared...

HEBREWS 9:8–9:11

O God, You are the One Who Inaugurates. Dear Lord, give me understanding concerning Your truths of old: *For where a covenant is, there must of necessity be the death of the one who made it. For a covenant is valid only when men are dead, for it is never in force while the one who made it lives. Therefore even the first covenant was not inaugurated without blood. Moses took the blood of the calves and the goats, with water and scarlet wool and hyssop, and sprinkled both the blood itself and the people, saying, "This is the blood of the covenant which God commanded you."* Likewise, O God, You ushered in Your new covenant with a living sacrifice: *Since therefore, brethren, we have confidence to enter the holy place by the blood of Jesus, by a new and living way which He inaugurated for us through the veil, that is, His flesh.* Because of the shedding of Your perfect blood, dear Jesus, the new has fulfilled the old once and for all. Yes, Jesus, You are the last and final sacrifice! *For Christ did not enter a holy place made with hands, a mere copy of the true one but into heaven itself, now to appear in the presence of God for us; nor was it that He should offer Himself often, as the high priest enters the holy place year by year with blood not his own. Otherwise, He would have needed to suffer often since the foundation of the world; but now once at the consummation of the ages He has been manifested to put away sin by the sacrifice of Himself.* Hallelujah, dear Jesus, thank You! Your temporary death inaugurated eternal life for many. Indeed, the veil has been torn, and we can enter Your throne room!

Hebrews 9:16-18,19-20; 10:20; 9:24-26

My Protector

The angel of the LORD encamps around those who fear Him, and rescues them.

PSALM 34:7

O God, You are my Protector. Yes, *You are faithful, and You will strengthen and protect me from the evil one.* You promise that *You will give Your angels charge concerning me, to guard me in all my ways.* Thank You for truths I can cling to during challenging circumstances. By faith, help me to believe You are always by my side, doing things for me that I am not even aware of. I will cling to this story of old: *Behold, an army with horses and chariots was circling the city. And (Elisha's) servant said to him, "Alas, my master! What shall we do?" So he answered, "Do not fear, for those who are with us are more than those who are with them." Then Elisha prayed and said, "O Lord, I pray, open his eyes that he may see." And the Lord opened the servant's eyes, and he saw; and behold, the mountain was full of horses and chariots of fire all around Elisha.* Yes, O God, surround me with Your invisible, yet invincible presence. And help me to hear the same words that You spoke to Joshua just before crossing the Jordan River with the entire Israelite nation, *Have I not commanded you? Be strong and courageous. Do not tremble or be dismayed, for the Lord your God is with you wherever you go.* Indeed, You are with me in my own journey, holding my hand, watching over me with diligence, encouraging me as I go. Thank You for Your protective presence. Because of You, my heart and soul can rest as my mind and body move forward. In the midst of my challenge, I will hear You say, *I will be with you; I will not fail you or forsake you.* So as I march on, I will proclaim with assurance, *You are my lovingkindness and my fortress, my stronghold and my deliverer; my shield and the One in whom I take refuge;* my Protector and my peace.

**2 Thessalonians 3:3; Psalm 91:11; 2 Kings 6:15-17; Joshua 1:9,5;
Psalm 144:2**

Merciful

But the tax collector, standing some distance away, was even unwilling to lift up his eyes to heaven, but was beating his breast, saying, "God, be merciful to me, the sinner!"
LUKE 18:13

O God, You are Merciful. I marvel at this truth written in Peter's letter. He begins, *Blessed be the God and Father of our Lord Jesus Christ, who according to His great mercy has caused us to be born again to a living hope through the resurrection of Jesus Christ from the dead, to obtain an inheritance which is imperishable and undefiled and will not fade away, reserved in heaven for you.* Dear Savior, because of Your great mercy, I have new life now and forever. I have done nothing to deserve this heaven-sent gift! Your word makes this very clear: *For we also once were foolish ourselves, disobedient, deceived, enslaved to various lusts and pleasures, spending our life in malice and envy, hateful, hating one another. But when the kindness of God our Savior and His love for mankind appeared, He saved us, not on the basis of deeds which we have done in righteousness, but according to His mercy, by the washing of regeneration and renewing of the Holy Spirit, whom He poured out upon us richly through Jesus Christ our Savior.* I am rich indeed! You have washed my sins away, You have instilled me with Your Spirit, and You have given me eternal life. This sinner-turned-saint humbly rejoices in Your lavish love. Indeed, I will proclaim, *The Lord is gracious and merciful; slow to anger and great in lovingkindness. The Lord is good to all, and His mercies are over all His works.*

1 Peter 1:3-4; Titus 3:3-6; Psalm 145:8-9

God of the Lonely

God makes a home for the lonely; He leads out the prisoners into prosperity, only the rebellious dwell in a parched land.

PSALM 68:6

O God, You are God of the Lonely. You took notice of the young dreamer Joseph when he was maliciously *thrown into the pit by his brothers.* And You saw the little boy Samuel and his faithful mother Hannah: When she *had weaned him, she took him up with her, with a three-year-old bull and one ephah of flour and a jug of wine, and brought him to the house of the Lord in Shiloh, although the child was young.* And You kept Your eye on the submissive prophet Hosea when You commanded him, *Go again, love a woman who is loved by her husband, yet an adulteress.* O God, these people of Yours, and many more like them throughout Your word, experienced such deep loneliness. David cries out for each of us, *Turn to me and be gracious to me, for I am lonely and afflicted. The troubles of my heart are enlarged; bring me out of my distresses, look upon my affliction and my trouble, and forgive all my sins. Look upon my enemies, for they are many; and they hate me with violent hatred. Guard my soul and deliver me; do not let me be ashamed, for I take refuge in You. Let integrity and uprightness preserve me, for I wait for You.* Yes, Lord, as I wait quietly, I will remember this: in my loneliness, I am not alone. In the midst of the darkness I will say, *But as for me, the nearness of God is my good.* You came to Joseph in the pit and in the prison cell; You spoke to Hannah's boy Samuel in the middle of the night; and You encouraged Hosea with Your redeeming love. Likewise, in Your personal way, You will comfort me. *For You will satisfy the thirsty soul, and the hungry soul You will fill with what is good.*

Genesis 37:23-24; 1 Samuel 1:24; Hosea 3:1; Psalms 25:16-21; 73:28; 107:9

God of the Mind

For who has known the mind of the LORD, that he should instruct Him? But we have the mind of Christ.

1 CORINTHIANS 2:16

O God, You are God of the Mind. Your word says: *In reference to your former manner of life, lay aside the old self, which is being corrupted in accordance with the lusts of deceit, and be renewed in the spirit of your mind, and put on the new self, which in the likeness of God has been created in righteousness and holiness of the truth.* O God, I pray You will help me to think Your divine thoughts, not my fleshly ones! The battle rages within me and the struggle to *take every thought captive to the obedience of Christ* is ongoing. Your word through Paul implores, *Do not be conformed to this world, but be transformed by the renewing of your mind, that you may prove what the will of God is, that which is good and acceptable and perfect.* Dear Lord, I understand that what I think about directs me either toward You or away from You. Again, give me the desire and ability to *set my mind on the things above, not on the things that are on earth.* I know from past experience, if I *let the word of Christ dwell within me richly,* then Your peace and direction will follow. Yes, Lord, I love Your word and I love Your ways. Help me to meditate *on whatever is true, whatever is honorable, whatever is right, whatever is pure, whatever is lovely, whatever is of good repute, if there is any excellence and if anything worthy of praise, let my mind dwell on these things.* O God of the Mind, become Master of mine.

**Ephesians 4:22-24; 2 Corinthians 10:5; Romans 12:2;
Colossians 3:2,16; Philippians 4:8**

God of the Will

Father, if You are willing, remove this cup from Me; yet not My will, but Yours be done.
LUKE 22:42

O God, You are God of the Will. You gracefully give us the option to obey or disobey, to be humble or proud, to be submissive or stubborn. O God, how often I choose the latter! I hear myself in Paul's words of frustration, *For I know nothing good dwells in me, that is, in my flesh; for the wishing is present in me, but the doing of the good is not. For the good that I wish, I do not do; but I practice the very evil that I do not wish.* Dear Jesus, I need Your help! Please come and take over my flesh so that I will walk according to Your ways. Your word says, *But if the Spirit of Him who raised Jesus from the dead dwells in you, He who raised Christ Jesus from the dead will also give life to your mortal bodies through His Spirit who indwells you. For if you are living according to the flesh, you must die; but if by the Spirit you are putting to death the deeds of the body, you will live.* Ah yes, Jesus, You are the only answer to replacing my stubborn will with Your heavenly one. I must confess and *die daily.* You tell us, *For those who belong to Christ Jesus have crucified the flesh with its passions and desires.* Dear Lord, I ask You to come in and take over so that I can genuinely say, *I delight to do Your will, O my God; Your law is within my heart.* Indeed, dear Lord, in and through me, I ask, *Your kingdom come, Your will be done.*

**Romans 7:18-19; 8:11,13; 1 Corinthians 15:31; Galatians 5:24;
Psalm 40:8; Matthew 6:10**

God of the Emotions

*Seeing the people, He felt compassion for them, because they were distressed and dispirit-
ed like sheep without a shepherd.*

MATTHEW 9:36

O God, You are God of Emotions. This truth is explicitly portrayed throughout Your life, dear Jesus. You showed Your great love when *You gathered the children in Your arms and began blessing them, laying Your hands upon them.* And You exhibited Your righteous anger when *You entered the temple and cast out all those who were buying and selling in the temple, overturning the tables of moneychangers and the seats of those who were selling doves, saying, "My house shall be called a house of prayer, but you are making it a robbers' den."* And You felt great fatigue *when You, being wearied from Your journey, sat down by the well.* And You felt great sorrow concerning Your friends w*hen You saw Mary weeping, and the Jews who came with her, also weeping. You were deeply moved in spirit, and were troubled, and You wept.* And You knew and lived out great joy saying, *These things I have spoken to you, that My joy may be in you, and that your joy may be made full.* And You portrayed great anguish when *You were praying very fervently; and Your sweat became like drops of blood, falling to the ground.* And You experienced great humiliation and intense pain when *they stripped You, and put a scarlet robe on You, and spat on You, and took the reed and began to beat You on the head.* Dear Jesus, there is not one emotion that You did not experience and then respond to perfectly. And there is nothing humdrum or robotic about the way You walked this earth. Because of this truth, I will run to You, my Savior, and I will laugh, and cry, and wrestle; and I will be angry, and love, and have compassion; and I will be burdened, and be afflicted, and be joyful; yes, I will be moved mightily from within. And I know that You, Feeling God, will meet me in each turn, showing me how to play out my emotions accurately, rather than being overtaken by them dramatically. You are my Teacher, please hold my hand; I want to live *life abundantly* like You.

**Mark 10:16; Matthew 21:12-13; John 4:6; 11:33,35; 15:11; Luke 22:44;
Matthew 27:28,30; John 10:10**

Fruitful God

A good tree cannot produce bad fruit, nor can a bad tree produce good fruit. So then, you will know them by their fruits.

MATTHEW 7:18,20

O God, You are Fruitful. This is true with Your people both now and long ago: *The sons of Israel were fruitful and increased greatly, and multiplied, and became exceedingly mighty, so that the land was filled with them.* And this is true of Your beautiful creation: *You send forth springs in the valleys; they flow between the mountains; they give drink to every beast of the field. You cause the grass to grow for the cattle, and vegetation for the labor of man, so that he may bring forth food from the earth.* And this is true of Your word: *And the word of God kept on spreading; and the number of the disciples continued to increase greatly in Jerusalem.* And this is true of Your Spirit: *the fruit of the Spirit is love, joy, peace, patience, kindness, goodness, faithfulness, gentleness, self-control; against such things there is no law.* O God, just as You cause Your people and Your creation to consistently multiply throughout all of time and history, I pray that Your word and Your Spirit will expound abundantly through me today. Your analogy concerning spiritual growth is so clear; for You say, *How blessed is the man who does not walk in the counsel of the wicked, nor stand in the path of sinners, nor sit in the seat of scoffers! But his delight is in the law of the Lord, and in His law he meditates day and night, and he will be like a tree firmly planted by streams of water, which yields its fruit in its season, and its leaf does not wither; and in whatever he does, he prospers.* Yes, Fruitful God, plant me deep into the rich soil of Your word, and cause Your Spirit to blossom and bear fruit.

Exodus 1:7; Psalm 104:10-11,14; Acts 6:7; Galatians 5:22-23; Psalm 1:1-3

God of Life in the Womb

When Elizabeth heard Mary's greeting, the baby leaped in her womb; and Elizabeth was filled with the Holy Spirit. And she cried out with a loud voice and said, "Blessed are you among women, and blessed is the fruit of your womb!"

LUKE 1:41-42

O God, You are God of Life in the Womb. You guard and nurture each detail of this fascinating journey, and You make no mistakes. Your word affirms that I have always been special to You, even when I was only a thought. For You say, *Before I formed you in the womb I knew you.* Indeed, *my frame was not hidden from You, when I was made in secret, and skillfully wrought in the depths of the earth. Your eyes have seen my unformed substance.* With joy and anticipation, *You formed my inward parts; You weaved me in my mother's womb.* Yes, You designed the color of my eyes, the complexion of my skin, the contour of my lips, the shape of my nose, the shade of my hair. You knew the beat of my heart and the print on my thumb. From the beginning, You knew my strengths, and You were very aware of my frailties. And with creative affirmation throughout Your miraculous work, You say with pleasure, *With Me nothing is impossible.* Indeed, Creator of all Life, *I will give thanks to You, for I am fearfully and wonderfully made; wonderful are Your works, and my soul knows it very well.* Yes, my soul knows it very well. For I am *Your workmanship* uniquely created to bring You glory. *I am made in Your image, according to Your likeness.* And now, I will enter the world with a shout, and then be received with joy.

Jeremiah 1:5; Psalms 139:15-16,13; Luke 1:37; Psalm 139:14; Ephesians 2:10; Genesis 1:26

Guilt Offering

When I kept silent about my sin, my body wasted away through my groaning all day long. For day and night Your hand was heavy upon me; my vitality was drained away as with the fever heat of summer.

PSALM 32:3-4

O God, You are the Guilt Offering. In the days of old, *You spoke to Moses, saying, "Speak to the sons of Israel, 'When a man or woman commits any of the sins of mankind, acting unfaithfully against the Lord, and that person is guilty, then he shall confess his sins which he has committed, and he shall make restitution in full for his wrong.'"* And, *He shall also bring his guilt offering to the Lord for his sin which he has committed, a female from the flock, a lamb or a goat as a sin offering. So the priest shall make atonement on his behalf for his sin.* Year after year, the blood of goats and rams were offered to cover the sins of Your people. All of this bloodshed pointed to the final sacrifice: Your perfect Son, Jesus. At the cross, He was crucified for our sins and He bore our guilt. Your word says: *The Lord was pleased to crush Him putting Him to grief; if He would render Himself as a guilt offering, He will see His offspring, He will prolong His days, and the good pleasure of the Lord will prosper in His hand.* God the Father, thank You for Your plan; God the Son, thank You for Your willingness to implement it; God the Spirit, thank You for reassuring me that I no longer need to bear the weight of my guilt. My wrongs have been righted. The deep crimson stain of my sin is washed away, and I am pure and clean in Your sight. Yes, *I acknowledged my sin to You, and my iniquity I did not hide; I said, "I will confess my transgressions to the Lord"; and You forgave the guilt of my sin.* Merciful Savior, I cherish these words of truth: *If therefore the Son shall make you free, you shall be free indeed.* Therefore, may the cords of guilt never entangle my heart again.

Numbers 5:5-7; Leviticus 5:6; Isaiah 53:10; Psalm 32:5-6; John 8:36

Sin Offering

Let him offer to the LORD a bull without defect as a sin offering for the sin he has committed.

LEVITICUS 4:3

O God, You are the Sin Offering. In ancient history, over and over again, unblemished animals were slain to offer appeasement for the sins of Your people. This sacrificial ritual kept Your children aware of their wrongdoings, as well as their desperate need of a Savior. And then, the promised Messiah came. Jesus, You are the God-Man who gave Yourself as the final sacrifice. You fulfilled every prophecy, and You wiped away all sins. Yes, this is the good news: *There is therefore now no condemnation for those who are in Christ Jesus. For the law of the Spirit of life in Christ Jesus has set you free from the law of sin and of death. For what the Law could not do, weak as it was through the flesh, God did: sending His own Son in the likeness of sinful flesh and as an offering for sin, He condemned sin in the flesh, in order that the requirement of the Law might be fulfilled in us, who do not walk according to the flesh, but according to the Spirit.* And again, Your word proclaims: *He Himself bore our sins in His body on the cross, that we might die to sin and live to righteousness; for by His wounds you were healed.* And one more time: *He made Him who knew no sin to be sin on our behalf, that we might become the righteousness of God in Him.* O God, thank You, thank You, thank You. You gave Yourself. You laid down Your life. You defeated sin. And *it is finished.*

Romans 8:1-4; 1 Peter 2:24; 2 Corinthians 5:21; John 19:30

Burnt Offering

He shall lay his hand on the head of the burnt offering, that it may be accepted for him to make atonement on his behalf. … And the priest shall offer it up in smoke on the altar on the wood which is on the fire; it is a burnt offering, an offering by fire of a soothing aroma to the LORD.

LEVITICUS 1:4,17

O God, You are the Burnt Offering. I understand that everything in the Old Testament points toward Jesus the Messiah. So when You said to Abraham, *Take now your son, your only son, whom you love, Isaac, and go to the land of Moriah; and offer him there as a burnt offering,* You had the prophetic future of Your own Son in mind. The story unfolds: Abraham obeyed, and in faith he bound up his son, and just as *he stretched out his hand, and took the knife to slay his son, the angel of the Lord called to him from heaven and said, "Abraham, Abraham! Do not stretch out your hand against the lad, and do nothing to him; for now I know that you fear God, since you have not withheld your son, your only son, from Me." Then Abraham raised his eyes and looked, and behold, behind him a ram caught in the thicket by his horns; and Abraham went and took the ram, and offered him up for a burnt offering in the place of his son.* God, I do see how this story reveals the truth concerning the sacrifice of Your only Son, the One whom You dearly loved. When John the Baptist saw the Messiah, he proclaimed, *Behold, the Lamb of God that takes away the sins of the world.* And it was prophesied of Jesus; *Blessed is the one who comes in the name of the Lord; we have blessed you from the house of the Lord. The Lord is God, and He has given us light; bind the festival sacrifice with cords to the horns of the altar.* O God, You did not withhold Your Son from becoming the appropriate offering for the sins of mankind. He stayed bound, so that we could go free. Yes, He was offered in my place. I can only repeat what Your people sang long ago in response to Your mercy, *You are my God, and I give thanks to You; You are my God, I extol You. Give thanks to the Lord, for He is good; for His lovingkindness is everlasting.*

Genesis 22:2,10-13; John 1:29; Psalm 118:26-29

Peace Offering

Now if his offering is a sacrifice of peace offerings, if he is going to offer out of the herd, whether male or female, he shall offer it without defect before the LORD.

LEVITICUS 3:1

O God, You are the Peace Offering. Thank You, Jesus, once again. You came forward as the perfect and final sacrifice in order to bring us peace. Holy God, You are a wrathful God concerning sin. I know I cannot stand in Your presence; my heart is too deceitful. But You, merciful Savior, were the satisfactory offering of appeasement; nothing else and no one else would do. Scripture says: *But now in Christ Jesus you who formerly were far off have been brought near by the blood of Christ. For He Himself is our peace.* Because of Your sacrificial offering, my sin has been forgiven; now, I can approach Your throne. And not only do I have sweet and holy communion with You, but I am also unified with my brothers and sisters in Christ. *He came and preached peace to you who were far away, and peace to those who were near; for through Him we both have our access in one Spirit to the Father. So then we are no longer strangers and aliens, but we are fellow citizens with the saints, and are of God's household.* Thank You, Jesus, for being *the propitiation for our sins; and not for ours only, but also for those of the whole world!* Again, I will rejoice in this truth: my soul has been saved from holy wrath and has now been transferred into divine communion. I hear and embrace Your words of promise, *In that day you shall know that I am in My Father, and you in Me, and I in you.* Indeed, dear Jesus, because You became the final Peace Offering, my soul can finally have peace.

Ephesians 2:13-14,17-19; 1 John 2:2; John 14:20

Wave Offering

Speak to the sons of Israel, and say to them, "When you enter the land which I am going to give to you and reap its harvest, then you shall bring in the sheaf of the first fruits of your harvest to the priest. He shall wave the sheaf before the LORD for you to be accepted."

LEVITICUS 23:10–11

O God, You are the Wave Offering. In the spring harvest of old, the first sheaf of grain was waved before You by the priest; this was the offering of the first fruits, given in thanks and praise for Your abundant provision. Dear Jesus, I know that You, too, are called the "first fruits." *But now Christ is risen from the dead, the first fruits of those who have fallen asleep.* Indeed You, dear Jesus, are the *firstborn of all creation* and also the *firstborn from the dead.* Therefore, it is appropriate that You are the final Wave Offering in which we can give thanks and praise; for You have provided abundant life for Your children forever! I love this picture of Mary and Joseph as they brought You, dear Jesus, to the Simeon the priest: *And this man was righteous and devout, looking for the consolation of Israel; and the Holy Spirit was upon him. And it had been revealed to him by the Holy Spirit that he would not see death before he had seen the Lord's Christ. And he came in the Spirit into the temple; and when the parents brought in the child Jesus, to carry out for Him the custom of the Law, then he took Him into his arms, and blessed God.* Ah yes, the priest received their firstborn Son. And Simeon, holding Him with adoration and praise, said, *For my eyes have seen Your salvation, which You have prepared in the presence of all peoples, a light of revelation to the Gentiles, and the glory of Your people Israel.* And You, Provider God, accepted the final Wave Offering with delight.

1 Corinthians 15:20; Colossians 1:15,18; Luke 2:25-28,30-32

One Betrayed

Then Judas Iscariot, who was one of the twelve, went off to the chief priests in order to betray Him to them. They were glad when they heard this, and promised to give him money. And he began seeking how to betray Him at an opportune time.

MARK 14:10–11

O God, You are the One Betrayed. The story unfolds: *And when it was evening He came with the twelve. And as they were reclining at the table and eating, Jesus said, "Truly I say to you that one of you will betray Me—one who is eating with me." And as they began to be grieved and to say to Him one by one, "Surely not I?" And He said to them, "It is one of the twelve, one who dips with Me in the bowl."* Then Judas got up from the table and left them. Then in the garden: *While He was still speaking, behold, a multitude came, and the one called Judas, one of the twelve, was preceding them; and he approached Jesus to kiss Him. But Jesus said to him, "Judas, are you betraying me with a kiss?"* O Savior God, this betrayal led You to the cross. In Judas' kiss, You experienced the deep hurt of a friend's disloyalty. How abandoned and alone You must have felt on that night when each of Your close friends ran from Your side. In fact, all of mankind *hid their face from You.* O God, forgive me for my abandonment! I humbly thank You for remaining faithful to me in spite of my running away. I also want to thank You for Your empathy when I, too, feel betrayed by the ones I love. Like the palmist says, *My heart throbs, my strength fails; and the light of my eyes, even that has gone from me. My loved ones and my friends stand aloof from my plague; and my kinsmen stand afar off.* O God, sometimes I feel so alone, so misunderstood, so judged. But, it is always in this place that I reestablish my faith in You. You understand me, and You realign me. Yes, instead of crying out in defense toward others, I will cry out to You, *The Lord is my light and salvation; whom shall I fear? The Lord is the defense of my life; whom shall I dread?* Indeed, in times of betrayal, You know exactly how I feel, and You know exactly how to comfort me. In Your unmatched loyalty, You will hear my cry. And then You will come to me, and *You will surround me with favor as with a shield.*

Mark 14:17-20; Luke 22:47-48; Isaiah 53:3; Psalms 38:10-11; 27:1; 5:12

One Despised

He was despised and forsaken by men, a man of sorrows and acquainted with grief; And like one from whom men hide their face, He was despised, and we did not esteem Him.
ISAIAH 53:3

O God, You are the One Despised. Dear Jesus, when You walked the earth, You had many who loved You and believed in You, as well as many who hated You and rejected You. This truth was prophesied: *"Behold I lay a stone in Zion, a precious corner stone, and He who believes in Him shall not be disappointed."* This value then is for those who believe. But for those who disbelieve, *"The stone which the builders rejected, this became the Corner stone,"* and *"A stone of stumbling and a rock of offense."* Yes, the Jews in Your day, dear Jesus, could not accept You as the Messiah; therefore, they could not handle the power and popularity that You were gaining among the people. *The chief priests and the Pharisees convened a council, and were saying, "What are we doing? For this man is performing many signs. If we let Him go on like this, all men will believe in Him and the Romans will come and take away both our place and our nation."... So from that day on they planned together to kill Him. ... And He was delivered up because of envy.* Dear Jesus, You know what it is to be despised! And You know what it is to be falsely accused. And You know what it is to be *oppressed and afflicted, yet You did not open Your mouth.* You silently suffered and willingly died for a greater purpose than saving Yourself. With amazing grace, You died for those who crucified You. For in Your last breath, You cried out, *Father, forgive them; for they do not know what they are doing.* O God, to love like You! How did You do it? Help me to follow Your example. Please give me a softened heart that will obey Your voice when You say strong words such as these, *You have heard that it was said, 'You shall love your neighbor, and hate your enemy.' But I say to you, love your enemies, and pray for those who persecute you.* Yes, Forgiving One, please help me to love like You.

**1 Peter 2:6-8; John 11:47-48, 53; Matthew 27:18; Isaiah 53:7;
Luke 23:34; Matthew 5:43-44**

Forsaken One

By oppression and judgment He was taken away; and as for His generation, who considered that He was cut off out of the land of the living.

ISAIAH 53:8

O God, You are the Forsaken One. Dear Jesus, You spoke these words to Your disciples while in the garden: *"My soul is deeply grieved, to the point of death; remain here and keep watch with Me."* And He went a little beyond them, and fell on His face and prayed, saying, *"My Father, if it is possible, let this cup pass from Me; yet not as I will, but as Thou wilt."* And then after being taken into custody, and tried, and beaten, and nailed to a cross for hours, *You cried out with a loud voice, saying, "ELI, ELI, LAMA SABACHTHANI?" that is, "MY GOD, MY GOD, WHY HAVE YOU FORSAKEN ME?"* And also the prophetic psalm speaks Your words, *Far from my deliverance are the words of my groaning, O my God, I cry by day, but You do not answer; and by night, but I have no rest … I am a worm, and not a man, a reproach of men, and despised by the people. All who see me sneer at me … I am poured out like water, and all my bones are out of joint; my heart is like wax; it is melted within me. My strength is dried up like a potsherd, and my tongue cleaves to my jaws; and You lay me in the dust of death. For dogs have surrounded me; a band of evildoers has encompassed me; they pierced my hands and my feet.* God, how it must have pained You to turn Your face away from Your beloved Son as He cried out to You. But at the same time, *You were pleased to crush Him, putting Him to grief,* because You knew the final outcome. And Jesus, as an outpouring of Your great love for mankind, You chose this route as well—sin needed to be forgiven, and death needed to be conquered. Yes, O God, Your temporary forsaking of Your Son has brought eternal glory to Your children. So I will forever praise You and I will always thank You, God the Father and God the Son, for the immeasurable love that was spilled out at the cross. Because You rose from the dead, the Forsaken One has guaranteed *to never leave or forsake me.*

**Matthew 26:38-39; 27:46; Psalm 22:1-2,6-7,14-16;
Isaiah 53:10; Hebrews 13:5**

One Who Tasted Death

But we do see Him who has been made for a little while lower than the angels, namely, Jesus, because of the suffering of death crowned with glory and honor, so by the grace of God He might taste death for everyone.

HEBREWS 2:9

O God, You are the One Who Tasted Death. Yes, dear Jesus, Your purpose in coming to earth as the God-Man was to die. You said, *The Son of Man did not come to be served, but to serve, and to give His life a ransom for many.* And on several occasions You told Your disciples, *Behold, we are going to Jerusalem, and the Son of Man will be delivered to the chief priests and the scribes; and they will condemn Him to death, and will deliver Him to the Gentiles. And they will mock Him and spit upon Him, and scourge Him, and kill Him, and three days later He will rise again.* And You said of Mary who wiped Your feet with her hair and costly perfume, *Let her alone, in order that she may keep it for the day of My burial.* So from the beginning, You knew. Your prophetic word also spoke: *He poured out Himself to death, and was numbered with the transgressors; yet He Himself bore the sin of many, and interceded for the transgressors.* And giving up Your life was Your choice. You said, *For this reason the Father loves Me, because I lay down My life that I may take it again. No one has taken it away from Me, but I lay it down on My own initiative. I have authority to lay it down, and I have authority to take it up again. This commandment I received from My Father.* O dear Jesus, thank You for choosing to taste death for me! It all happened just as You said. You came, You died, and You were buried. *And when it was evening, there came a rich man from Arimathea, named Joseph ... and he took the body and wrapped it in a clean linen cloth, and laid it in his own new tomb, which he had hewn out in the rock; and he rolled a large stone against the entrance of the tomb and went away.* And there in that tomb, You not only tasted death, You conquered it, once and for all.

Mark 10:45,33-34; John 12:7; Isaiah 53:12; John 10:17-18;
Matthew 27:57,59-60

One Who Raises the Dead

Why is it considered incredible among you people if God does raise the dead?
ACTS 26:8

O God, You are the One Who Raises the Dead. Your word says: *The last enemy that will be abolished is death.* And Jesus, You set this truth in motion. Peter the apostle defended Your resurrection so accurately to the opposing Jews: *Men of Israel, listen to these words: Jesus the Nazarene, a man attested to you by God with miracles and wonders and signs which God performed through Him in your midst, just as you yourselves know—this Man, delivered up by the predetermined plan and foreknowledge of God, you nailed to a cross by the hands of godless men and put Him to death. And God raised Him up again, putting an end to the agony of death, since it was impossible for Him to be held in its power.* Indeed, O God, *You did not allow Your Holy One to undergo decay.* As a result, this is the beautiful truth: *But now Christ has been raised from the dead, the first fruits of those who are asleep. For since by a man came death, by a man also came the resurrection of the dead. For as in Adam all die, so also in Christ all shall be made alive.* O God, *by the appearing of our Savior Christ Jesus, death was abolished!* Therefore, *I will give thanks to You, O Lord my God, with all my heart, and will glorify Your name forever. For Your lovingkindness toward me is great, and You have delivered my soul from the depths of Sheol.*

1 Corinthians 15:26; Acts 2:22-24; Psalm 16:10; 1 Corinthians 15:20-22;
2 Timothy 1:10; Psalm 86:12-13

Director

And (Ruth) happened to come to the portion of the field belonging to Boaz.
RUTH 2:3

O God, You are the Director. You know that I choose to *walk by faith, not by sight.* And You also know that this is sometimes unsettling for me. Which way do I take, which road do I walk down? *Show me the way I should go, for to You I lift up my soul ... Teach me to do Your will, for You are my God; may Your good Spirit lead me on level ground.* Yes, Lord, please *lead me not into temptation, but deliver me from evil.* I want Your way, even if it's a road of patience, or perseverance, or trial. I ask for Your divine wisdom to override any of my potential wayward decisions. Reroute my heart and mind back to You, O God. Thank You that *in my heart I plan my course, but You, O Lord, determine my steps.* Keep me close to You, and continue to *direct my heart into Your love and into the steadfastness of Christ.* Through the guidance of Your word, let me hear You say, *This is the way, walk in it.* Yes, be the Director of my path, O God; for I am confident that the seemingly unknown road to me is completely and clearly known to You. *And no good thing do You withhold from those whose walk is blameless.*

**2 Corinthians 5:7; Psalm 143:8,10; Matthew 6:13; Proverbs 16:9;
2 Thessalonians 3:5; Isaiah 30:21; Psalm 84:11**

Conductor

There is an appointed time for everything.
ECCLESIASTES 3:1

O God, You are the Conductor. *You laid the earth's foundation and marked off its dimensions.* You cause *the rivers to clap their hands, and the mountains to sing together for joy.* At the appointed time, You open *the storehouses of the snow ... and cut a channel for the torrents of rain, and a path for the thunderstorm.* Yes, *even the wind and the waves obey You.* You, O God, have commanding authority over all the earth! And *You make everything beautiful in its time.* Therefore, *praise the Lord all the earth, you great sea creatures and all ocean depths, lightning and hail and snow and clouds, stormy winds that do His bidding, you mountains and hills, fruit trees and all cedars, wild animals and all cattle, small creatures and flying birds, kings of the earth and all nations, you princes and all rulers on the earth, young men and maidens, old men and children. Let them praise the name of the Lord, for His name alone is exalted.* I too will join in the chorus of all these sights and sounds; and may You, O Conductor, be pleased with Your glorious bidding.

**Job 38:4-5; Psalm 98:8-9; Job 38:22,25; Mark 4:41;
Ecclesiastes 3:11; Psalm 148:7-13**

Worthy

Worthy is the Lamb that was slain to receive power and riches and wisdom and might and honor and glory and blessing.

REVELATION 5:12

O God, You are Worthy. All power is Yours; all riches are Yours; all wisdom is Yours; all might is Yours; all honor is Yours; all glory is Yours; and all blessing is Yours. If all this is true (and my heart knows it is) then, why were You *the Lamb that was slain?* My soul cries, "Why this tragic slaughter of the One who has done no wrong—the One who is all pure and righteous and holy?" It is so hard for my mind to comprehend that You, the unblemished Worthy One, chose to *take on the form of a bond servant … You humbled Yourself by becoming obedient to the point of death, even death on a cross.* Again, why this tragic death? The incomprehensible answer can only be because of Your great love. *For You, O God, so loved the world that You gave Your only begotten Son, that whoever believes in Him should not perish but have eternal life.* Thank You, dear Jesus, for absorbing the wrath that my sin deserves! *You knew no sin but chose to be sin on my behalf, that I might become the righteousness of God.* Hear me praise You from my inmost being, *To Him who sits on the throne, and to the Lamb, be blessing and honor and glory and dominion forever and ever.* You indeed, O God, are Worthy of all my praise.

Revelation 5:12; Philippians 2:7,8; John 3:16; 2 Corinthians 5:21; Revelation 5:13

One Who Surprises

Great are the works of the LORD; they are studied by all who delight in them.

PSALM 111:2

O God, You are the One Who Surprises. Abraham was surprised by *the ram caught in the bush.* Pharaoh's daughter was surprised by the baby in *the basket among the reeds.* And the people of Israel were surprised by the *thin flakes like frost that appeared on the desert floor.* Also, Naomi was surprised by her *kinsman-redeemer.* King Nebuchadnezzar was surprised by the *fourth man in the fire.* And the shepherds were surprised by the *great company of heavenly hosts* that brought the message of the Messiah. God, it is Your delightful desire to surprise Your people. Thank You for Your breath-taking wonders! What You have planned from the beginning, Your people rejoice in the moment it's revealed. I choose to embrace each of these timeless surprises mentioned above as my own, because they all point to the greatest Surprise of all—Jesus my Savior.

Genesis 22:13; Exodus 2:5; 16:14; Ruth 2:20; Daniel 3:25; Luke 2:13

Sweet

Then (Moses) cried out to the LORD, and the LORD showed him a tree; and he threw it into the waters, and the waters became sweet.

EXODUS 15:25

O God, You are Sweet. Your words to my heart both soothe and satisfy. When life gets me down, You know exactly what to say. Thank You for Your timely *gentle whisper.* Indeed, *how sweet are Your words to my taste! Yes, sweeter than honey to my mouth!* Not just Your words, but Your actions are cherished as well. Dear Savior of mine, I am *one of Your sheep and I follow You because I know Your voice.* But sometimes I just need to collapse in Your embrace and melt in Your love. Life is hard and I need Your tender, loving care. *Like a shepherd You tend Your flock, in Your arms You gather them and carry them.* Thank You for the way You hold me so close, reassuring me that all is going to be okay, and that You are at work even now. Help me to believe Your sincere words of promise in this very moment: *I will never desert You, nor will I ever forsake you.* Yes, Sweet One, *I am Yours and You are mine.*

**1 Kings 19:12; Psalm 119:103; John 10:4; Isaiah 40:11; Hebrews 13:5;
Song of Solomon 6:3**

Loyal

So let us know, let us press on to know the LORD. His going forth is as certain as the dawn; and He will come to us like the rain watering the earth.

HOSEA 6:3

O God, You are Loyal. You are the *friend who sticks closer than a brother.* I can trust You with my secrets and bring You all my questions because Your name is *Faithful and True.* You sort out my thinking, You calm down my wrestling, You readjust my planning; then You lead me *beside quiet waters.* Thank You for the consistency of Your character and the steadfastness of Your love; it makes my heart full of assurance that I belong to You. Yes, I rejoice that *lovingkindness and truth have met together; righteousness and peace have kissed each other. Truth springs from the earth; and righteousness looks down from heaven. Indeed Lord, You give what is good.* Again, I give thanks to Your great name and for Your great love. Your loyalty lifts me to a better place, a place of confidence, a place of peace. And in this place I will, in turn, lift up Your name and say to all who can hear, *I will put my trust in You. In God, whose word I praise, in God I have put my trust.* Yes, Loyal One, thank You for sticking ever so close to me.

Proverbs 18:24; Revelation 19:11; Psalms 23:2; 85:10-11; 56:3-4

Flame Starter

And there appeared to them tongues as of fire distributing themselves, and they rested on each one of them.

ACTS 2:3

O God, You are the Flame Starter. You burn with purpose and passion for all mankind, and You long to ignite the flicker in each of our hearts. Show us Your glory like the days of old: *When Solomon finished praying, fire came down from heaven and consumed the burnt offering and the sacrifices, and the glory of the Lord filled the temple. The priests could not enter the house of the Lord because the glory of the Lord filled the Lord's house. All the sons of Israel, seeing the fire come down and the glory of the Lord upon the house, bowed down on the pavement with their faces to the ground, and they worshiped and gave praise to the Lord, saying, "Truly He is good; truly His lovingkindness is everlasting."* Remind me, dear Lord, that today You no longer dwell in a man-made structure, but that *my body is a temple of the Holy Spirit.* So, *King of Glory, come in!* For *You are the One who lights my lamp and illumines my darkness.* Yes, Lord, the same way Your flame filled the ancient temple structure, please fill me. Ignite Your Flame ablaze in my heart and set me on Your path of passion and purpose.

2 Chronicles 7:1-3; 1 Corinthians 6:19; Psalms 24:7; 18:28

Pure

The commandment of the LORD is pure, enlightening the eyes.
PSALM 19:8

O God, You are Pure. Indeed, You are altogether lovely, honorable, and undefiled. Dear Jesus, You are the *lamb without blemish* offered on my behalf. You are the *one pearl of great value* that my heart seeks. You are the *living water*—perfectly clean, crystal clear, and eternally refreshing. You are the true *light, and in You there is no darkness at all.* You are the standard of everything righteous and holy and good. In You, there is no flaw. Because of Your nature, it is impossible for me, in my sin, to stand in Your presence! So I come to You, and humbly ask You to *sit as a smelter and purifier of silver, and purify me and refine me like gold and silver, so that I may present to You offerings of righteousness.* Yes, just as one *takes away the dross from the silver,* please take away the sin from my heart. By Your Son's precious blood, make me pure, because You are pure; and through Your invading Spirit, cause me *to be holy, because You are holy.* As a result of Your great work in me, I will both claim and cling to Your promise: *Blessed are the pure in heart, for they shall see God.*

1 Peter 1:19; Matthew 13:46; John 4:10; 1 John 1:5; Malachi 3:3;
Proverbs 25:4; 1 Peter 1:16; Matthew 5:8

Divine

In the year of King Uzziah's death I saw the Lord sitting on a throne, lofty and exalted,
with the train of His robe filling the temple.

ISAIAH 6:1

O God, You are Divine. *You are in Your holy temple.* Yes, *heaven is Your throne and the earth is Your footstool.* In this place, O God, You are both great and grand! Isaiah himself witnessed the incredible sight: *Seraphim stood above Him, each having six wings; with two he covered His face, and with two he covered His feet, and with two he flew. And one called out to another and said, "Holy, Holy, Holy, is the Lord of hosts, the whole earth is full of His glory."* My mind cannot contain Your magnificence! And John witnessed Your splendor as well: *His head and His hair were white like white wool, like snow; and His eyes were like a flame of fire; and His feet were like burnished bronze, when it has been caused to glow in a furnace, and His voice was like the sound of many waters. And in His right hand He held seven stars; and out of His mouth came a sharp two-edged sword; and His face was like the sun shining in its strength.* These glimpses of You, O God, are spectacular! But what baffles me the most is that You, God of Glory, chose to become a mere man—fully human, and yet still fully divine. You exchanged a robe that filled the heavenly temple for a cloak that dragged the streets of Jerusalem. To think that I can even dare to *touch the fringe of it.* And yet, that's why You came, for broken people like me. You declare, *The afflicted and needy are seeking water, but there is none. And their tongue is parched with thirst; I, the Lord, will answer them Myself, as the God of Israel I will not forsake them.* Thank You for turning and looking my way; for Your Divine touch has put heaven in my heart.

Psalm 11:4; Isaiah 66:1; 6:2-3; Revelation 1:14-16; Matthew 9:20;
Isaiah 41:17

Protector

In that day this song will be sung in the land of Judah: "We have a strong city; He sets up walls and ramparts for security."

ISAIAH 26:1

O God, You are the Protector. *As the mountains surround Jerusalem, so the Lord surrounds His people from this time forth and forever.* Thank You for Your strong hand that covers me. Because of You, even in the midst of great struggle, I have peace. Yes, when I choose to keep my eyes on You, *Your peace, which surpasses all comprehension, guards my heart and my mind in Christ Jesus.* I will cling to Your words of truth: *My sheep hear My voice, and I know them, and they follow Me; and I give eternal life to them, and they shall never perish; and no one shall snatch them out of My hand.* Hallelujah, thank You, Jesus, for Your present safety; thank You, Jesus, for Your future security. I have confidence *that no weapon formed against me will prosper...* because *You, Lord, are faithful, and You will strengthen and protect me from the evil one.* Again, hallelujah! I praise Your name for both fortifying my steps and safeguarding my soul. Because of You, I will sing these words as I daily walk by Your side: *My shield is with God, He saves the upright in heart.*

Psalm 125:2; Philippians 4:7; John 10:27-28; Isaiah 54:17; 2 Thessalonians 3:3; Psalm 7:10

Showstopper

Two men suddenly stood near them in dazzling clothing; and as the women were terrified and bowed their faces to the ground, the men said to them, "Why do you seek the living One among the dead? He is not here, but He has risen."

LUKE 24:4–6

O God, You are the Showstopper. You have done great and impossible things that leave me without words. Please listen to my prolonged applause as I list only some of Your astounding wonders: In the beginning, *the Lord God formed man of the dust from the ground, and breathed into his nostrils the breath of life* ... Then, in the days of Noah, *they went into the ark, by twos of all flesh* ... And then, in the days of Moses, *the Lord swept the sea back by a strong east wind all night, and turned the sea into dry land, so the waters were divided* ... And in the days of Joshua, *the people shouted, and the priests blew the trumpets and the wall of Jericho fell down flat* ... And then there's young Mary, listening to the angel's words: *The Holy Spirit will come upon you, and power of the Most High will overshadow you, and for that reason the holy offspring shall be called the Son of God.* And Jesus was born, *Immanuel, God with us!* And through His divine hands *the blind received sight and the lame walked, the lepers were cleansed, and the deaf could hear; and the dead were raised up, and the poor had the gospel preached to them.* Yes, God, for these great works and many thousands more, You stop me in my tracks! I am awed by Your power. My applause is not enough. Here, with humbled praise, I offer You my heart.

Genesis 2:7; 7:15; Exodus 14:21; Joshua 6:20; Luke 1:35; Matthew 1:23; 11:5

Game Changer

For He rescued us from the domain of darkness, and transferred us to the kingdom of His beloved Son.

COLOSSIANS 1:13

O God, You are the Game Changer. You work in ways that both move our stiff necks and override our stubborn hearts. You *opened the mouth of a donkey* in order to redirect angry Balaam ... You caused Joseph's jealous and defiant brothers to *bow down to him with their faces to the ground* ... And You *appointed a great fish to swallow Jonah* so he would then turn around and obey Your voice. Loving God, in Your grace and mercy, which sometimes hurts, You will have Your way with Your people! Yes, *like channels of water in Your hand, You can turn a man's heart wherever You wish.* Again, You work mightily; You work intentionally. You caused the *rooster to crow* so Peter could really hear, and *You blinded Saul's his eyes* so he could truly see, and *You gave Your life as a ransom* that many will truly live. Continue to redirect our hearts toward You, O God. For Your desire is for our *eyes to be open so that we may turn from darkness to light and from the domain of Satan to God, in order that we may receive forgiveness of sins and an inheritance among those who have been sanctified by faith in You.* Yes, please be the sovereign Game Changer in each of our paths, for our own good and for Your ultimate glory.

Numbers 22:28; Genesis 42:6; Jonah 1:17; Proverbs 21:1; Luke 22:34; Acts 9:8-9,17-18; Mark 10:45; Acts 26:18

Able

Now to Him who is able to keep you from stumbling, and to make you stand in the presence of His glory blameless with great joy, to the only God our Savior, through Jesus Christ our Lord, be glory, majesty, dominion and authority, before all time and now and forever. Amen.

JUDE 24-25

O God, You are Able. *Wisdom and power belong to You.* Yes, by Your intelligent design, You are able to *change the times and the seasons, to remove kings and establish kings, to give wisdom to wise men, and knowledge to men of understanding.* Indeed, You are able to *uphold all things by the word of Your power.* You speak into situations, and it is done: as God of Compassion, You are able to *heal the brokenhearted;* as God of Mercy, You are able to *pardon all my iniquities;* and as *Lawgiver and Judge, You are able to both save and destroy.* Thank You, Jesus, for taking on the condemnation and death that I deserve. I am humbled by this truth: *He made Him who knew no sin to be sin on our behalf, so that we might become the righteousness of God.* For Your ability to take on the sin of the world, and conquer it, has brought eternal life to all those who trust in You. Hallelujah! Yes, God, You indeed are *able to do exceedingly abundantly beyond all that I ask or think.*

**Daniel 2:20-21; Hebrews 1:3; Psalms 147:3; 103:3; James 4:12;
2 Corinthians 5:21; Ephesians 3:20**

Near

And He made from one man every nation of mankind… that they would seek God, if perhaps they might grope for Him and find Him, though He is not far from each one of us; for in Him we live and move and exist.

ACTS 17:26–28

O God, You are Near. Thank You for these ancient words of truth that I can claim as my own today: *I have loved you with an everlasting love; therefore I have drawn you with lovingkindness.* Jesus, You are the lovingkindness that draws me to God. For Scripture says: *But now in Christ Jesus you who were formerly far off have been brought near by the blood of Christ.* Thank You for pulling me close to You; thank You for *the right to become Your child;* thank You for *taking me in Your arms and blessing me.* With You, I can both sing with gladness as well as weep with sorrow. I am so thankful that You understand me, and that You walk with me through all my physical and emotional highs and lows. Yes, *You are in my midst, a victorious warrior. You exult over me with joy, and quiet me in Your love.* I Thank You for Your celebration songs as well as your compassionate whispers. Because of Your loyalty, I can undoubtedly say, *As for me, the nearness of God is my good; I have made the Lord God my refuge, that I may tell of all Your works.*

**Jeremiah 31:3; Ephesians 2:13; John 1:12; Mark 10:16;
Zephaniah 3:17; Psalm 73:28**

Enough

Whom have I in heaven but You? And besides You, I desire nothing on earth.
Psalm 73:25

O God, You are Enough. *For all that is in the world, the lust of the flesh and the lust of the eyes and the boastful pride of life, is not from You, but the world.* I have tried this wayward path, and I was left wanting. And I have tasted this false fruit and it does not satisfy; on the contrary, it left my heart bitter and my soul sick. Thank You, O God, for coming to me in my depravity and offering me a rich and a real life. Your ancient words soothe my soul: *The Lord will comfort Zion; He will comfort all her waste places. And her wilderness He will make like Eden. And her desert like the garden of the Lord; joy and gladness will be found in her, thanksgiving and sound of a melody.* Yes, because of You, my heart sings. I now rejoice in this reality each and every day: *God, being rich in mercy, because of His great love with which He loved us, even when I was dead in my transgressions, made me alive together with Christ; by grace I have been saved.* From empty to full, from poor to rich, from death to life, God of Blessing, my soul declares, "You are more than Enough!"

1 John 2:16; Isaiah 51:3; Ephesians 2:4-5

Persistent

Behold, I stand at the door and knock; if anyone hears My voice and opens the door,
I will come in to him and will dine with him and he with Me.

REVELATION 3:20

O God, You are Persistent. Yes, You are resolute in Your love for us. Jesus, You left Your throne and came to earth *to seek and to save that which was lost.* With determination, You spoke these words on our behalf: *The Spirit of the Lord is upon Me, because He anointed Me to preach the gospel to the poor. He has sent Me to proclaim release to the captives, and recovery of sight to the blind, to set free those who are oppressed.* Thank You, Persistent One, for coming to the lost, to the poor, to the captives, to the blind, and to the oppressed. Your steadfast love is beautiful: *You sat with and gave freedom to the woman at the well ... You forgave and challenged the woman caught in adultery ... and You touched and healed the blind man's eyes ... Your lovingkindness, O Lord, extends to the heavens, Your faithfulness reaches to the skies! Your righteousness is like the mountains of God; Your judgments are like a great deep. O Lord, You preserve man and beast.* God, I thank You for both relentlessly pursuing me and reliably preserving me. Now, dear Lord, make me a conduit of Your love, a vessel of Your light. This radical love is not just for me! Put Your persistence inside me, so that I, too, can knock on doors of people's hearts and tell them the good news. May I mimic Your servants of old: *And daily in the temple, and in every house, they kept right on teaching and preaching Jesus as the Christ.* Yes, make me as lovingly persistent to others as You have been to me.

Luke 19:10; 4:18; John 4:4-15; 8:3-11; 9:1-7; Psalm 36:5-6; Acts 5:42

Available

On the day I called, You answered me; You made me bold with strength in my soul.

PSALM 138:3

O God, You are Available. Yes, *God is our refuge and strength, a very present help in trouble. Therefore we will not fear, though the earth should change and the mountains slip into the heart of the sea; though its waters roar and foam, though the mountains quake at its swelling pride.* Nothing escapes You; You know our plight, and You answer us when we call. May we learn from the disciples: *And there arose a fierce gale of wind, and the waves were breaking over the boat so much that the boat was already filling up. And He Himself was in the stern, asleep on the cushion; and they awoke Him and said to Him, "Teacher, do You not care that we are perishing?" And being aroused, He rebuked the wind and said to the sea, "Hush, be still." And the wind died down and it became perfectly calm. And He said to them, "Why are you so timid? How is it that you have no faith?"* God, forgive me when I think You are unavailable or unconcerned about my struggles. Give me a fearless faith that You are able to calm any storm, be it on the outside with diverse circumstances, or more likely, inside my troubled heart. For *You are near to all who call upon You, to all who call upon You in truth. You will fulfill the desire of those who fear You; You will also hear their cry and save them.* I humbly thank You, Awesome God, Lord of the mountains and the seas, the wind and the waves, circumstances and hearts—thank You for being Available to me. In every situation, I cling to Your promise: *My presence will go with you, and I will give you rest.*

Psalm 46:1-3; Mark 4:37-40; Psalm 145:18-19; Exodus 33:14

Colorful

I set my rainbow in the cloud, and it shall be for a sign of a covenant between Me and the earth.

GENESIS 9:13

O God, You are Colorful. *O Lord, how many are Your works! In wisdom You have made them all; the earth is full of Your possessions.* Indeed, summer brings baby blue skies, plush green grass, and plentiful flowers; and then, fall foliage bursts full of vibrant red, orange, and gold; and next, winter pronounces a wonderland of white, brown, and evergreen; and finally, spring births beautiful pinks, purples, and yellows at every turn. God, Your seasonal artistry is breathtaking. *Shout joyfully to God, all the earth; sing the glory of His name; make His praise glorious. Say to God, "How awesome are Your works!"* I love that Your eye-catching creation also has purpose: *I shall give you rains in their season, so that the land will yield its produce and the trees of the field will bear their fruit.* Thank You for Your vivid beauty that accompanies Your intentional provision. Your divine handiwork convicts our human hearts that You indeed are the Maker of heaven and earth: *For since the creation of the world His invisible attributes, His eternal power and divine nature, have been clearly seen, being understood through what has been made, so that we are without excuse.* So God, I acknowledge You: in the summer, I will walk with You in rich thankfulness; in the fall, I will sing, "Glory!" to match the incredible scene around me; then as the snow blankets the earth, I will quietly adore Your presence; in the spring, I will blossom with praise once again as I observe Your bright budding all around. Colorful God, You have captivated me! *Let the glory of the Lord endure forever; let the Lord be glad in His works ... let my meditation be pleasing to Him; as for me, I shall be glad in the Lord.*

Psalms 104:24; 66:1-3; Leviticus 26:4; Romans 1:20; Psalm 104:31,34

God of Wisdom

The fear of the LORD is the beginning of wisdom, and the knowledge of the Holy One is understanding.

PROVERBS 9:10

O God, You are the God of Wisdom. And *the wisdom from above is first pure, then peaceable, gentle, reasonable, full of mercy and good fruits, unwavering, and without hypocrisy.* God, You are able to be all of these attributes at the same time! So, because of who You are, I seek You and only You. The world misleads, the culture teaches falsely. Therefore, I come to You asking for Your heavenly wisdom as I walk this earth because You sweetly promise to *give it to all men generously and without reproach ...* I will ask *in faith without doubting, so that I will not be like the surf of the sea driven and tossed by the wind.* Yes, the clear direction that I hear from You in Your word and through Your Spirit, I will not hesitatingly doubt; instead, I will resolutely obey. For You say: *Everyone who hears these words of Mine and acts on them, may be compared to a wise man who built his house on the rock. And the rain fell, and the floods came, and the winds blew and slammed against that house; and yet it did not fall, for it had been founded on the rock.* Thank You for fortifying me with Your foundational truths. Yes, I believe Your promise that as I seek You, *wisdom will enter my heart, and knowledge will be pleasant to my soul; discretion will guard me, and understanding will watch over me.* I will choose You, Wise God, not the way of the world, even if I have to stand or walk alone.

James 3:17; 1:5-6; Matthew 7:24-25; Proverbs 2:10-11

King of Ages

Now to the King eternal, immortal, invisible, the only God, be honor and glory forever and ever. Amen.

1 TIMOTHY 1:17

O God, You are the King of Ages. You proclaim to all mankind past, present, and future: *"I, even I am the Lord; and there is no savior besides Me. It is I who have declared and saved and proclaimed, and there was no strange god among you; so you are My witnesses," declares the Lord, "and I am He; and there is none who can deliver out of My hand; I act and who can reverse it?"* Yes, King of time and history and rulers, there will be a day that all *nations will fear Your name, and all the kings of the earth Your glory.* Because *You reign, You are clothed with majesty; You have clothed and girded Yourself with strength; indeed, the world is firmly established, it will not be moved. Your throne is established from of old; You are from everlasting.* King of Ages, I humbly bend my knee to You today. You are holy and sovereign, present and eternal. I will join in and sing the *song of Moses the bond-servant of God and the song of the Lamb, saying, "Great and marvelous are Your works, O Lord God, the Almighty; righteous and true are Your ways, King of the nations. Who will not fear, O Lord, and glorify Your name? For all the nations will come and worship before You, for Your righteous acts have been revealed. Indeed, You are the Kings of Ages."*

Isaiah 43:11-13; Psalms 102:15; 93:1-2; Revelation 15:3-4

Fighter

The LORD will fight for you while you keep silent.

EXODUS 14:14

O God, You are a Fighter. In the battle long ago, You caused *Jericho's massive city walls to fall down flat while Your people shouted Your great name.* And in King Jehoshaphat's day, You performed Your mighty work as Your people praised You: *And when they began singing and praising, the Lord set ambushes against the sons of Ammon, Moab, and Mount Seir, who had come against Judah; so they were routed.* And again, You showed up through David the shepherd boy as *he ran quickly to the battle line and defeated Goliath with a sling and a stone.* God, in Your arsenal, You even have *storehouses of hail, which You have reserved for the time of distress, for the day of war and battle.* Yes, God You are a Fighter, and You prevail over the enemies of your people. So I ask You, Almighty One, to fight for me. Indeed O God, *fight against those who fight against me.* I have one distinct enemy, Satan himself, who uses all kinds of tactics to keep me down: shame, anger, pride, doubt, and dismay. When he approaches, remind me of this truth: *Greater is He who is in me than he who is in the world.* Yes rise up in me, surround me, work through me. And I will *take up my shield of faith with which I will be able to extinguish all the flaming missiles of the evil one.* And because of You, Fighting God, I will prevail.

Joshua 6:15-20; 2 Chronicles 20:22; 1 Samuel 17:46-52; Job 38:22-23; Psalm 35:1; 1 John 4:4; Ephesians 6:16

One Who Equips

(David) took his stick in his hand and chose for himself five smooth stones from the brook, and put them in the shepherd's bag which he had, even in his pouch, and his sling was in his hand; and he approached the Philistine.

I SAMUEL 17:40

O God, You are the One Who Equips. I confess, dear Lord, the task that You have set before me seems impossible! And then, before I even get these words out of my mouth, I hear You say to my doubting heart, Remember, *with Me, nothing is impossible.* And I also hear You say, *My word is a lamp to your feet and a light to your path.* Indeed, Your word is my instruction manual; You will tell me what to do and how to do it. For *all Scripture is inspired by You and profitable for teaching, for reproof, for correction, for training in righteousness; that I may be adequate, equipped for every good work.* Yes, Lord, strengthen my faith, not in myself, but in You and in Your word. Working without You is striving; working in submission to You is power. So as I push forward in obedient faith, I trust Your promises: You will both *supply all my needs according to Your riches in glory in Christ Jesus* as well as *perfect, confirm, strengthen and establish me* through the enduring process. Yes, I will trust You as You equip me. I now hear You say to my reassured heart, *Faithful am I who calls you, and I also will bring it to pass.*

**Luke 1:37; Psalm 119:105; 2 Timothy 3:16; Philippians 4:19;
1 Peter 5:10; 1 Thessalonians 5:24**

Mainstay

But you are to cling to the LORD your God, as you have done to this day.

JOSHUA 23:8

O God, You are my Mainstay. Yes, *I have impressed Your words on my heart and my soul; and I have bound them as a sign on my hand and they have become as frontals on my forehead. And I have taught them to my sons, talking of them when I sit in my house and when I walk along the road and when I lie down and when I rise up. And I have written them on the doorposts of my house.* Indeed, *my soul clings to You; Your right hand upholds me.* Thank You for Your promises; thank You for Your strength; thank You for Your might. *For apart from You, I can do nothing.* Yes, Lord Jesus, *You are the costly cornerstone for the foundation, firmly placed. And because I believe in it, I will not be disturbed.* I have confidence that is greater than myself. Indeed, You are the backbone of my life! Because of You, I will stand firm in all circumstances and shout with victorious assurance: *He only is my rock and my salvation, my stronghold; I will not be shaken. On God my salvation and my glory rest; the rock of my strength, my refuge is in God.* Thank You for Your soul protection; thank You for Your divine power; thank You for Your permanent presence. Yes, my heart knows You are my Mainstay.

Deuteronomy 11:18-20; Psalm 63:8; John 15:5; Isaiah 28:16; Psalm 62:6-7

First Place

*He is before all things, and in Him all thing hold together. He is also head of the body,
the church; and He is the beginning, the firstborn from the dead, so that He Himself
might come to have first place in everything.*

COLOSSIANS 1:17–18

O God, You are First Place. I hear You say with strong warning, *You shall have no
other gods before Me. You shall not make for yourself an idol, or any likeness of what
is in heaven above or on the earth beneath or in the water under the earth. You shall
not worship them or serve them; for I, the Lord your God, am a jealous God, visiting the
iniquity of the fathers on the children, on the third and the fourth generations of those
who hate Me, but showing lovingkindness to thousands, to those who love Me and
keep My commandments.* O God, forgive me when I stray from You; forgive me when I
bow to other gods and worship various idols. The world creeps in, shouting, "Success!
Comfort! Possessions! Pleasure! Self!" and on and on. Yes, Lord, *I have left my first
love.* Why am I pulled? Why do I wander? Why do I give in? Please Lord, come, renew,
refresh, and remind me once more. My heart knows that You are best for me. Clean
house, I pray. *Teach me Your way, O Lord; I will walk in Your truth; unite my heart to
fear Your name.* Help me not to be distracted or swayed by so many things; rather, help
me to focus on *the one thing that is needed:* a relationship with You. You know what is
good for me, and You know what is not good for me. Help me to trust You all over again.
Make me strong. Yes, I will reclaim Your promise that has proven beautifully true over
and over in my life: *Seek first My kingdom and My righteousness; and all these things
shall be added to you.* O God, take First Place in my life, this day, this moment.

Exodus 20:3-6; Revelation 2:4; Psalm 86:11; Luke 10:41; Matthew 6:33

Supreme

The Most High is ruler over the realm of mankind.
DANIEL 4:17

O God, You are Supreme. *For You are a great God, and a great King above all gods, in Your hand are the depths of the earth; the peaks of the mountains are Yours also. The sea is Yours, for it was You who made it; and Your hands formed the dry land.* Indeed, by Your power, through the working of Your Son, *all things were created, both in the heavens and on the earth, visible and invisible, whether thrones or dominions or rulers or authorities—all things have been created by You and for You. And You are before all things, and in You all things hold together.* Thank You, Supreme One, for calling the universe into existence, as well as caring for me. It baffles me that You can simultaneously run this vast world and tend to my minute problems. *For You are our God, and we are the people of Your pasture, and the sheep of Your hand.* Yes, You are predominant in Your power, and preeminent in Your love. Again, thank You. I pray that I would allow You to reign first and foremost in my life. I know You are the King of heaven and earth, but I ask You to be King of me. When You say to me, *Seek my face,* may my heart reply, *Your face, O Lord, I shall seek.* Indeed, in my allegiance to You I want to say, *My heart is steadfast, O God, my heart is steadfast.* O Supreme One, my knee is bent, my head is bowed, my heart is Yours. Yes, *I shall run the way of Your commandments, for You will enlarge my heart. Teach me, O Lord, the way of Your statutes, and I will observe it to the end.*

Psalm 95:3-5; Colossians 1:16-17; Psalms 95:7; 27:8; 57:7; 119:32-33

Just

Rejoice greatly, O daughter of Zion! Shout triumph, O daughter of Jerusalem! Behold,
your king is coming to you; He is just and endowed with salvation, humble, and mounted
on a donkey, even on a colt, the foal of a donkey.

ZECHARIAH 9:9

O God, You are Just. *The heavens declare Your righteousness, for You Yourself are*
judge. It is certain that *with You, there is no partiality.* Yes, Holy One, Your wrathful
judgment of sin is for all people, but Your gracious salvation from this judgment is
offered to all people as well. Thank You, loving Lord, for providing the way: *For Christ*
also died for sins once for all, the just for the unjust, so that He might bring us to God,
having been put to death in the flesh, but made alive in the spirit. Yes, thank You,
fairest Lord Jesus, for making a way for each one of us. *For the same Lord is Lord of*
all, abounding in riches for all who call upon Him. Indeed I am rich in my inheritance!
Who is a God like You, who pardons iniquity and passes over the rebellious act of the
remnant of His possession? You do not retain Your anger forever, because You delight
in unchanging love. You will again have compassion on us; You will tread our iniquities
under foot. Yes, You will cast all our sins into the depths of the sea. From my humbled
and forgiven heart I will *give thanks to the God of heaven, for His lovingkindness is*
everlasting. O Righteous Judge, I do rejoice, for You are more than Just!

Psalm 50:6; Romans 2:11; 1 Peter 3:18; Romans 10:12;
Micah 7:18-19; Psalm 136:26

Man of Sorrows

He was despised and forsaken of men, a man of sorrows, and acquainted with grief.
ISAIAH 53:3

O God, You are a Man of Sorrows. Yes, *Jesus Son of God, You are the great high priest who has passed through the heaven.* In so doing, You became a man *who can sympathize with our weaknesses.* Every emotion that I have experienced, You have endured as well, yet without sin. Right now, dear Lord, You know the depth of my sorrow, not from the outside, but from within. Please make sense of this mess. This grief is too much for me. *Save me, O God, for the waters have threatened my life. I have sunk in deep mire, and there is no foothold; I have come into deep waters, and the flood overflows me. I am weary with my crying; my throat is parched; my eyes fail while I wait for my God.* Come Lord Jesus, comfort me; hold me; hear me. Help me not to push You away in anger. Help me not to blame You for this chaos. Help me not to become bitter with this loss. Help me to trust in You. Help me to *cling to You.* Help me to hear You weeping with me. The only answer is the cross. *Surely our grief He Himself bore, and our sorrows He carried; yet we ourselves esteemed Him stricken, smitten of God, and afflicted.* Jesus, in Your life You experienced grief of Your own, in Your death You experienced mine, and in Your resurrection You promise to walk with me step by step. Yes, Man of Sorrows, I am not alone. I have to trust You because You are my only hope. Please help me carry this load; please enter my grief. *Blessed be the Lord, who daily bears my burden, the God who is my salvation.*

Hebrews 4:14-15; Psalms 69:1-3; 63:8; Isaiah 53:4; Psalm 68:19

Invincible

The LORD said to my Lord: "Sit at My right hand until I make Your enemies a footstool for Your feet."

PSALM 110:1

O God, You are Invincible. You have never been, nor will You ever be defeated. You have shown Your power against other gods and enemies throughout time and history. In Adam's day, You punished Satan, the deceiver, saying, *Because you have done this, cursed are you.* In Moses' day, by his hand, You proved Yourself stronger than each of the gods of Egypt. You said, *And the Egyptians shall know that I am the Lord, when I stretch out My hand on Egypt and bring out the sons of Israel from their midst.* In Elijah's day, You proved to the desperate prophets of Baal, whose god remained silent, that You were the Almighty One by sending fire from heaven that *fell and consumed the burnt offering, the wood and the stones and the dust, and it licked up the water that was in the trench.* And in Jesus' day, You continued to prove Yourself invincible. What seemed like certain defeat at the cross was instead absolute victory. The words spoken in Jesus' last breaths, *It is finished,* were words of overwhelming triumph. Both at the cross, and at the resurrection, sin was absorbed and death was defeated. Yes, *death is swallowed up in victory. O death, where is your victory? O death, where is your sting? The sting of death is sin, and the power of sin is the law; but thanks be to God, who gives us the victory through our Lord Jesus Christ.* You are the Overcomer of enemies, gods, sin, and death; therefore there is hope both for the present day and for the days to come! For we know this too: when the end of time draws near, You will throw the devil *into the lake of fire* by Your Invincible hand; then finally, Your people will live in perfect peace with You forever.

**Genesis 3:14; Exodus 7:5; 1 Kings 18:38; John 19:30;
1 Corinthians 15:54-57; Revelation 20:10**

Immortal

He who is the blessed and only Sovereign, the King of kings and the Lord of lords, who alone possesses immortality and dwells in unapproachable light, whom no man has seen or can see. To Him be honor and eternal dominion! Amen.

1 Timothy 6:15–16

O God, You are Immortal. In earthly terms, You were before the beginning and You will be after the end. Yes, *before the mountains were born, or before You gave birth to the earth and the world, even from everlasting to everlasting, You are God.* Indeed, *You are the Alpha and the Omega, who is and who was and who is to come, the Almighty.* To think, Your desire is to give us this same everlasting life. *God… who has saved us, and called us with a holy calling, not according to our works, but according to His own purpose and grace which was granted us in Christ Jesus from all eternity, but now has been revealed by the appearing of our Savior Christ Jesus, who abolished death, and brought immortality to light through the gospel*—amazing love from an Eternal Father! Thank You for the incredible gift of unending life through Your Son. *And just as we have borne the image of the earthly, we shall also bear the image of the heavenly.* Yes, by Your divine grace, my soul is deemed ceaseless. Your word says: *We will all be changed, in a moment, in the twinkling of an eye, at the last trumpet; for the trumpet will sound, and the dead will be raised imperishable, and we will be changed.* Therefore, Immortal One, with both awe and gratitude, *every day I will bless You, and I will praise Your name forever and ever.*

Psalm 90:2; Revelation 1:8; 2 Timothy 1:9-10; 1 Corinthians 15:49,51-52; Psalm 145:2

One Who Empties

Have this attitude in yourselves which was also in Christ Jesus, who, although He existed in the form of God, did not regard equality with God a thing to be grasped, but emptied Himself, taking the form of a bond-servant.

PHILIPPIANS 2.5-7

O God, You are the One Who Empties. You emptied Yourself of Your kingly throne and Your royal robe, and then traded it for a *manger bed and swaddling clothes.* And, You emptied Yourself of Your immense wealth and traded it in for extreme poverty: *Though You were rich, yet for our sake You became poor that we, through Your poverty, might become rich.* And You emptied Yourself of Your power by restraining it, saying, *I do nothing on My own initiative, but I speak these things as the Father taught Me.* Yes, You emptied Yourself and became like us: *For we do not have a high priest who cannot sympathize with our weaknesses, but One who has been tempted in all things as we are, yet without sin.* And Living God, You emptied Yourself of life! On the cross You proclaimed, *"It is finished!"* And You bowed Your head and gave up Your spirit. Dear God, the emptying of Yourself on my behalf brings me to my knees. What kind of love is this? I am overwhelmed at Your resolute plan to purchase and pardon Your people. I am now filled with abundant life in You. Yes, thank You, God of heaven, for coming to earth, and emptying Yourself for me.

Luke 2:7; 2 Corinthians 8:9; John 8:28; Hebrews 4:15; John 19:30

One Who Fills

And they were all filled with the Holy Spirit.

ACTS 2:4

O God, You are the One Who Fills. I praise You with a humbled heart that I have begun to know *the love of Christ that surpasses knowledge, that I may be filled up to all the fullness of God.* Yes, *Your love has been poured out within my heart through the Holy Spirit who was given to me. ...* And *from this fullness of Your grace I have received one blessing after another!* Your Spirit beautifully yields Your *love, joy, peace, patience, kindness, goodness, faithfulness, gentleness and self-control.* Thank You generous One! I have done nothing to deserve Your grace. I pray that I will keep in step with Your Spirit each day. I am yours, dear Lord. Take charge over me; for *in Christ I have been made complete. You are the head over every power and authority.* Yes, You are the One *who fills everything in every way.* So have Your way with me, O God; may Your Spirit overcome my flesh. Yes, Lord, continually remind me that the purpose of being filled up is to then be poured out. Cause my heart to be still enough to receive Your word and give me faith enough to believe it, so that I may then *be filled with an inexpressible and glorious joy* to share with the desperate world around me.

**Ephesians 3:19; Romans 5:5; John 1:16; Galatians 5:22-23;
Colossians 2:10; Ephesians 1:23; 1 Peter 1:8**

One Who Unites

For God, who said, "Light shall shine out of darkness," is the One who has shown in our hearts to give the Light of the knowledge of the glory of God in the face of Christ.

2 CORINTHIANS 4:6

O God, You are the One Who Unites. *Yet for us there is but one God, the Father, from whom are all things and we exist for Him; and one Lord, Jesus Christ, by whom are all things, and we exist through Him.* Father God, You looked from heaven and spoke, *This is my Son, My Chosen One; listen to Him.* And, Jesus, You stood in our midst and said, *I and the Father are one.* And amazingly, You prayed that we, Your chosen people, would soon join in Your communion; I humbly receive Your words: I pray *that all of them may be one, Father, just as You are in Me and I am in You. May they also be in us so that the world may believe that You have sent Me.* Thank You, God, that You desire to be in fellowship with me! I am humbled by the price that was paid to make this happen: *For Christ also died for sins once for all, the just for the unjust, in order that He might bring us to God.* Yes, Jesus, Your perfect sacrifice erased sin and death so that I can now step into the holy presence of God. You are the only One who can bring about this union! So I hear Your words now, dear Jesus, *If anyone loves Me, he will keep My word; and My Father will love him, and We will come to him and make Our abode with him.* Yes, God the Father, Jesus the Son, through your Holy Spirit, make Your abode with me; for You are the One who Unites!

1 Corinthians 8:6; Luke 9:35; John 10:30; 17:21-22; 1 Peter 3:18; John 14:23

One Who Gives Boldness

On the day I called, You answered me; You have made me bold with strength in my soul.
PSALM 138:3

O God, You are the One Who Gives Boldness. *You have not given me a spirit of timidity, but of power and love and discipline.* Thank You. With this empowered resolve, I pray that I would mimic Your servants of old: *Caleb quieted the people before Moses, and said, "We should by all means go up and take possession of the land, for we shall surely overcome it."* And also Esther, who on behalf of her nation said, *And thus I will go in to the king, which is not according to the law; and if I perish, I perish.* And David as well, he *ran quickly toward the battle line to meet the Philistine* giant. Yes, Lord, rise up in me as Your present-day servant and make me bold for the sake of Your name. Let me respond to Your command that says, *Get yourself up on a high mountain, O Zion, bearer of good news, lift up your voice mightily, O Jerusalem, bearer of good news; lift it up, do not fear. Say to the cities of Judah, "Here is your God!"* Yes, I pray that life giving words *may be given to me in the opening of my mouth, to make known with boldness the mystery of the gospel* because the world needs to hear my fearless proclamation … the world needs You!

2 Timothy 1:7; Numbers 13:30; Esther 4:16; 1 Samuel 17:48;
Isaiah 40:9; Ephesians 6:19

Revealed Mystery

He made known to us the mystery of His will.
EPHESIANS 1:9

O God, You are the Revealed Mystery. I recall Your prophetic words: *A voice is calling, "Clear the way for the Lord in the wilderness; make smooth in the desert a highway for our God. Let every valley be lifted up, and every mountain and hill be made low; and let the rough ground become a plain, and the rugged terrain a broad valley; then the glory of the Lord will be revealed, and all flesh will see it together; for the mouth of the Lord has spoken."* And I praise You for the fulfillment when John, the forerunner, spoke: *Behold the Lamb of God who takes away the sin of the world!* Jesus, You are the One my soul seeks. You are the One for whom my heart beats. You are the *way, the truth and the life.* Indeed, You are the great Mystery Revealed! I rejoice in these words of truth, *Arise, shine; for your light has come, and the glory of the Lord has risen upon you.* Yes, I cling to this incredible thought, *Christ in me, the hope of glory!* Therefore, I will sing because of Your light, I will shout because of Your love, I will stand because of Your security, and I will speak because of Your truth. Yes, hear me proclaim with all my fellow believers, Jesus, *He was revealed in the flesh, was vindicated in the Spirit, beheld by angels, proclaimed among the nations, believed on in the world, taken up in glory.* Dear Savior, You are the perfect answer; You are the disclosed treasure; You are the fulfilled prophecy. O God and Messiah, thank You for Revealing Your Mystery to me.

Isaiah 40:3; John 1:29; 14:6; Isaiah 60:1; Colossians 1:27; 1 Timothy 3:16

One Who Prepares

You prepare a table before me in the presence of my enemies.

PSALM 23:5

O God, You are the One Who Prepares. *By faith I understand that the worlds were prepared by Your word, so that what is seen was not made out of things which are visible.* I also understand that You designed me to both know You and to make You known. And in this design, You promised to be my help by *giving me a heart to know You* and by giving me unique gifts to make You known. You even call me Your *workmanship created in Christ Jesus for good works, which You prepared beforehand, that I should walk in them.* God, I pray that I will diligently use my appropriated gifts for the building of Your kingdom. And, sweet Savior, I love that not only have You plotted out my life's work on this earth, but You are faithful in my inheritance as well. You say to my sometimes wavering faith, *Let not your heart be troubled; believe in God, believe also in Me. In My Father's house are many dwelling places; if it were not so, I would have told you; for I go to prepare a place for you. And if I go and prepare a place for you, I will come again, and receive you to Myself; that where I am, there you may be also.* Yes, thank You God, that You *formed my inward parts,* that You constructed my lifelong days, and You are making ready a heavenly home in which I can be with You forever.

Hebrews 11:3; Jeremiah 24:7; Ephesians 2:10; John 14:1-3; Psalm 139:13

Only One

And the LORD will be king over all the earth; in that day the LORD will be the only one, and His name the only one.

ZECHARIAH 14:9

O God, You are the Only One. *To whom then will you liken God? Or what likeness will you compare with Him?* Indeed, *lift up your eyes on high and see who has created the stars, the One who leads forth their host by number, He calls them all by name.* Yes, *there is none like You, O Lord; You are great, and great is Your name in might.* You are the One who parts the seas, who shuts lions' mouths, and who breaks down walls; and You are the One who forgives terrible sins, who saves lost souls, and who redeems broken hearts. So God, help me worship You and only You. I pray, give me an unwavering heart because I know I am so prone to wander. Please help me not to *worship any other god;* rip them from my hands, tear them from my heart. *Turn my eyes from looking at vanity, and revive me in Your ways.* Indeed, my heart is resolved: *I will follow You and fear You; and I will keep Your commandments, listen to Your voice, serve You, and cling to You.* You and You alone, *I will worship with reverence, and rejoice with trembling.* Because my heart knows that You, my God, are the Only One for me.

Isaiah 46:5; 40:26; Jeremiah 10:6; Exodus 34:14; Psalm 119:37; Deuteronomy 13:4; Psalm 2:11

Curse Breaker

But we do see Him who has been made for a little while lower than the angels, namely, Jesus, because of the suffering of death crowned with glory and honor, so that by the grace of God He might taste death for everyone.

HEBREWS 2:9

O God, You are the Curse Breaker. You said to Adam, *Because you have listened to the voice of your wife, and have eaten from the tree about which I commanded you, saying, "You shall not eat from it"; Cursed is the ground because of you; in toil you shall eat of it all the days of your life.* Yes, *creation was subjected to futility, not of its own will, but because of Him who subjected it.* And not only has creation lived under a curse, but so has man. We have been plagued by the inability to keep Your laws. We are slaves to self and sin. You have spoken, *Cursed is the man who trusts in mankind and makes flesh his strength, and whose heart turns away from the Lord.* But in spite of ourselves and our circumstances, remarkably, there is hope! For You, O God, are the Curse Breaker! You have not forgotten us in our depravity; You have not left us in our imperfections. For these words are truth: *But when the fullness of the time came, God sent forth His Son, born of a woman, born under the Law, in order that He might redeem those who were under the Law, that we might receive the adoption as sons. And because you are sons, God has sent forth the Spirit of His Son into our hearts, crying, "Abba! Father!"* Indeed, the story is too good to be true, and yet it is true! *Christ redeemed us from the curse of the Law, having become a curse for us—for it is written, "Cursed is everyone who hangs on a tree"—in order that the blessing of Abraham might come to the Gentiles, so that we might receive the promise of the Spirit through faith.* Only because of You have I gone from slave to son, from sinner to saint, from death to life. Thank You, Curse Breaker; my chains are off, I am free!

Genesis 3:17; Romans 8:20; Jeremiah 17:5; Galatians 4:4-6; 3:13-14

Pleased

And walk in love, just as Christ also loved you and gave Himself up for us, an offering and a sacrifice to God as a fragrant aroma.

EPHESIANS 5:2

O God, You are Pleased. I hear You say to my heart, *For I delight in loyalty rather than sacrifice, and in the knowledge of God rather than burnt offerings.* And in the same heartbeat I respond, *The sacrifices of God are a broken spirit; a broken and contrite heart, O God, You will not despise.* And I also understand that *without faith it is impossible to please You.* So God, here is my humbled heart of faith. Help me to believe in all of who You are, so that I can live a life in which You find pleasure. I want to *present my body as a living and holy sacrifice, acceptable to You, which is my spiritual service of worship;* not out of duty to You, O God, but out of a deep love for You. From this state of dependence and obedience, I know You are pleased with me. Thank You for Your guidance on how to live this out. You say to Your people, *Is this not the fast which I choose, to loosen the bonds of wickedness, to undo the bands of the yoke, and to let the oppressed go free, and break every yoke? Is it not to divide your bread with the hungry and bring the homeless poor into the house; when you see the naked, to cover; and not to hide yourself from your own flesh?* Yes, God, You are pleased with a faithful and fruitful heart. Empty words or obligatory gifts are a stench to You. So please, set my heart right to first receive Your love, and then make it my ambition to pour it out on others. For this is the kind of sacrifice You greatly reward: *Then your light will break out like the dawn, and your recovery will speedily spring forth; and your righteousness will go before you; the glory of the Lord will be your rear guard.* Thank You, O God, for Your promises. You are Pleased to be a *rewarder of those who diligently seek You.*

Hosea 6:6; Psalm 51:17; Hebrews 11:6; Romans 12:1; Isaiah 58:6-7,8; Hebrews 11:6

Leader

He leads me beside quiet waters.

PSALM 23:2

O God, You are my Leader. I remember the story of Your people in the wilderness: *And the Lord was going before them in a pillar of cloud by day to lead them on the way, and in a pillar of fire by night to give them light, that they might travel by day and by night. He did not take away the pillar of cloud by day, nor the pillar of fire by night, from before the people.* O God, just the way You were with these sojourners back then, You are with me right now. I may not physically see Your existence, but my eyes of faith are open wide to the truth. For I know *You have enclosed me behind and before, and You have laid Your hand upon me.* And not only have you surrounded me with Your presence, You have also invaded me with Your Spirit. Your Spirit helps me, comforts me, convicts me, and corrects me. Thank You for this promise: *For all who are being led by the Spirit of God, these are the sons of God.* So as Your child, dear Lord, I choose to play Follow-the-Leader. Each day I wake up, these are my words that I will raise up to You in prayer: *Let me hear Your lovingkindness in the morning; for I trust in You; teach me the way in which I should walk; for to You I lift up my soul. Deliver me, O Lord, from my enemies; I take refuge in You. Teach me to do Your will, for You are my God; let Your good Spirit lead me on level ground.* Each evening I will rest peacefully thinking, "Oh how I love my Leader." *For it is good to give thanks to the Lord, and to sing praises to His name, O Most High; to declare His lovingkindness in the morning, and His faithfulness by night.*

Exodus 13:21-22; Psalm 139:5; Romans 8:14; Psalms 143:8-10; 92:1-2

One Who Commissions

You are the light of the world. … Let your light shine before men in such a way that they may see your good works, and glorify your Father who is in heaven.
MATTHEW 5:14,16

O God, You are the One Who Commissions. You commissioned Abraham saying, *Go forth from your country, and from your relatives and from your father's house, to the land which I will show you; and I will make you a great nation, and I will bless you, and make your name great; and so you shall be a blessing.* And You commissioned David through your prophet Samuel saying, *Fill your horn with oil, and go; I will send you to Jesse the Bethlemite, for I have selected a king for Myself among his sons.* And You commissioned Your servant Ezekiel saying, *Son of man, take into your heart all My words which I have shall speak to you, listen closely, and go to the exiles, to the sons of your people, and speak to them and tell them, whether they listen or not.* And You commissioned Paul saying, *You are a chosen instrument of Mine to bear My name before the Gentiles and kings and the sons of Israel.* And Father God, I know You also commission me. You say to my heart, *Go therefore and make disciples of all nations, baptizing them in the name of the Father, and the Son, and the Holy Spirit, teaching them to observe all that I commanded you; and lo, I am with you always, even to the end of the age.* O God, *may I walk in a manner worthy of the calling with which I have been called.* For I am humbled to shine Your light. I am honored to speak Your name. Yes, You have Commissioned me to bear the good news to the world. Therefore I will *press on toward the goal.*

**Genesis 12:1-2; 1 Samuel 16:1; Ezekiel 3:10-11; Acts 9:15;
Matthew 28:19-20; Ephesians 4:1; Philippians 3:14**

One Who Edifies

All Scripture is inspired by God and profitable for teaching, for reproof, for correction, for training in righteousness; so that the man of God may be adequate, equipped for every good work.

2 TIMOTHY 3:16–17

O God, You are the One Who Edifies. You challenge me to grow up in my knowledge and understanding of You, and not to be complacent with *the elementary principles of the oracles of God,* which is like milk for a newborn. *For everyone who partakes only of milk is not accustomed to the word of righteousness, for he is a babe. But solid food is for the mature, who because of practice have their senses trained to discern good and evil.* Yes, Lord, You say again, *Do not be children in your thinking; yet in evil be babes, but in your thinking be mature.* Just as I age physically, I want to also age spiritually, so that I can truthfully say, *When I was a child, I used to speak as a child, think as a child, reason as a child; when I became a man, I did away with childish things.* Continue to teach me in Your word, and train me in Your ways, even if that means firm correction. For I know that *You discipline me for my good, that I may share in Your holiness. All discipline for the moment seems not to be joyful, but sorrowful; yet if I have been trained by it, afterwards it yields the peaceful fruit of righteousness.* Yes, Lord, I welcome Your loving hand of discipline so that I will slowly but surely become more like You. Therefore, through Your instructional word and Your training hand, continue to edify me. *Let the words of my mouth and the meditation of my heart be acceptable in Your sight, O Lord, my rock and my Redeemer.*

Hebrews 5:12-14; 1 Corinthians 14:20; 13:11; Hebrews 12:10-11;Psalm 19:14

Hand-Holder

Because He is at my right hand, I will not be shaken.
PSALM 16:8

O God, You are my Hand-Holder. *When I consider Your heavens, the work of Your fingers, the moon and the stars, which You have set in place, what is man that You are mindful of him?* And yet, it is by this same powerful hand that You *lead me beside quiet waters.* You even say that *my name is engraved upon Your palm.* How intimate is Your care for me, O God of the universe! I hear You proclaiming to me, *I have chosen you and not rejected you. Do not fear, for I am with you; do not anxiously look about you, for I am your God. I will strengthen you, surely I will help you. Surely I will uphold you with My righteous right hand.* And You also say, *I will lead the blind by a way they do not know, in paths they do not know I will guide them. I will make darkness into light before them and rugged places into plains. These are the things I will do, and I will not leave them undone.* Thank You for these promises that will not fail. Put my hand in Yours and hold it tight, so that *even when I fall I will not be hurled headlong.* Your care is complete; Your touch is sweet. Yes, I will put my hand in Yours and walk with You forever.

Psalms 8:3-4; 23:2; Isaiah 49:16; 41:9-10; 42:16; Psalm 37:24

Sufficient

Do you not yet understand or remember the five loaves of five thousand, and how many baskets full you picked up?

MATTHEW 16:9

O God, You are Sufficient. *Like manna in the morning,* Your word gives me exactly what I need. It's there for the taking. Likewise, Your word fills my cup each day, and every day. It's there for the drinking. Yes, thank You for *pouring Your love into my heart through the Holy Spirit who has been given to me.* I don't deserve this ample love! God, please forgive me when I don't eat from Your manna of mercy or drink from Your cup of confidence. Instead, I choose to feast on the past and become bitter, or I drink of the future and become anxious. These unhealthy habits only rob me of *Your grace that is sufficient* for me today. Dear Lord, help me to obey You and *not ponder on things of the past,* nor *worry about tomorrow.* Fill me up today with Your peace, Your strength, Your wisdom. You are more than capable to manage my present. Please walk with me in my temporal weaknesses, so that I may be completely reliant on Your eternal power. For my heart knows, *my sufficiency is from You.*

**Exodus 16:16-18; Romans 5:5; 2 Corinthians 12:9; Isaiah 43:18;
Matthew 6:34; 2 Corinthians 3:5**

Kind

Love is kind.

O God, You are Kind. My heart asks, "Why have You chosen to be *kind to ungrateful and evil men?"* ... *There is no one who does good, not even one* ... *For we also once were foolish ourselves, disobedient, deceived, enslaved to various lusts and pleasures, spending our life in malice and envy, hateful, hating one another. But when Your kindness, O God our Savior, and Your love for mankind appeared, You saved us.* Thank You, Lord, for this undeserving gift of mercy; thank You for Your lovingkindness that cost You Your Son; thank You for this sacrificial act of grace displayed upon the cross. Again, I thank You with my whole heart! For it was in my desperate state that You *turned Your anger away from me, and loved me freely.* I am forever changed. Please Lord, I now ask You to make me a vessel of Your kindness; I want to reach others who are also in need of a Savior. Daily fill my heart so that I too can exhibit *this fruit of Your Spirit.* Yes, make my hands and feet become Your hands and feet; cause me to run to the weary, the broken, the lonely, and the lost. When I touch others, may they understand it's really You. Yes, I ask that Your kindness would pour from me into their hearts. Again and again, thank You, Father, thank You, Son, thank You, Holy Spirit for Your invading and involving work that is initiated by Your lovingkindness.

Luke 6:35; Psalm 14:3; Titus 3:3-5; Hosea 14:4; Galatians 5:22

Praiseworthy

Enter His gates with thanksgiving and His courts with praise. Give thanks to Him, bless His name.

PSALM 100:4

O God, You are Praiseworthy. *I will give thanks to You according to Your righteousness, and will sing praise to Your name, O Lord Most High.* Yes, *I will give thanks to You with all my heart. I will tell of all Your wonders. I will be glad and exult in You.* You are King over all creation, You are Commander over all creatures, and *You care for me*—incredible! You are Ruler of all the nations, You are Righteous in all Your deeds, and *You redeemed my soul from the pit*—beautiful! Yes, hear me praise Your name, O God of my salvation. I will praise You for *hearing my cry; I will praise you for pulling me out of the miry clay. I will praise You for setting my feet upon a rock. I will praise you for making my footsteps firm. And I will praise You for putting a new song in my mouth!* In Your courts, I will sing my joyful song to You, O God my Savior. Indeed, I will join the holy chorus: *Praise the Lord from the heavens, praise Him in the heights above. Praise Him, all His angels, praise Him, all his heavenly hosts. Praise Him sun and moon, praise Him, all you shining stars. Praise Him, you highest heavens and you waters above the skies. Let them praise the name of the Lord.* Yes, *I will sing to the Lord as long as I live; I will sing praise to my God while I have my being.*

Psalms 7:17; 9:1-2; 1 Peter 5:7; Job 33:28; Psalms 40:1-3; 148:1-5; 104:33

Contender

Contend, O LORD, with those who contend with me.

PSALM 35:1

O God, You are my Contender. Draw out Your whole arsenal, Mighty One. *It's time for You to act.* Yes, *gird Your sword on Your thigh, in Your splendor and Your majesty, and fight for the cause of truth and meekness and righteousness.* ... You, *King of Glory,* are *strong and mighty,* You are *the Lord mighty in battle.* I cry to You for help because my *enemy steals, my enemy kills, and my enemy destroys;* he plagues my heart and mind with confusion, falsehood, and doubt. Please, O my King, send *Your sharp arrows into the heart of this enemy;* crush this discourager; pierce through this liar. Let him and his tactics not have their way with me, O God—not one thought, not one emotion, not one heartbeat. Yes, *fight against those who fight against me. Take hold of Your buckler and Your shield and rise up for my help. Draw also Your spear and Your battle axe to meet those who pursue me.* Thank You, God of Might. *You are the defense of my life, whom shall I be afraid?* Of this I am confident: *You will fight for me while I keep silent.* ... *I will put my trust in You,* and I will rejoice in You as *You crush my enemy under my feet.* Indeed, how I love the One Who Contends for me.

Psalms 119:126; 45:3-4; 24:8; John 10:10; Psalms 45:5; 35:1-3; 27:1; Exodus 14:14; Psalm 56:3; Romans 16:20

Intentional

When Jesus came to the place, He looked up and said to him, "Zacchaeus, hurry come down, for today I must stay at your house."

LUKE 19:5

O God, You are Intentional. Just as you sent Noah a *rainbow in the sky,* and just as You *sent Elijah bread in the mouths of ravens,* You sweetly send Your love to me. Likewise, just as You *waited by the well for the woman,* and just as You *called for the blind man to come,* You also presented Yourself to me. Thank You, O God, for Your pursuing love. You guide me like a Shepherd through Your word, allowing me to graze on just what I need for each circumstance. And then, You send me reminders throughout the day letting me know that *You are ever present.* Yes, Your peaceful presence makes me smile; Your absolute action makes me laugh. I am awed that *You are intimately acquainted with all my ways;* and I am overwhelmed by Your lovingkindness. Because of all of this, *I will watch expectantly for You,* O God. Your Intentional love has become my inexpressible joy. Yes, my soul delights *that You call me by name, and that I am Yours.*

Genesis 9:8-9,13; 1 Kings 17:6; John 4:4,6-7; Mark 10:46-49; Psalms 46:1; 139:3; Micah 7:7; Isaiah 43:1

Lovely

I remember the days of old; I meditate on all Your doings; I muse on the work of Your hands.

PSALM 143:5

O God, You are Lovely. *One thing I have asked from the Lord, that shall I seek; that I may dwell in the house of the Lord all the days of my life, to behold the beauty of the Lord, and meditate in His temple.* Indeed, *how lovely are Your dwelling places, O Lord of hosts! My soul longs and even yearns for the courts of the Lord.* As I come into Your holy presence, O God, my heart is enthralled by Your matchless mercy. For in this place of worship, *lovingkindness and truth have met together; righteousness and peace have kissed each other.* To think, You have allowed my soul to be sweetly intertwined between this embrace: I have been wrapped with Your love, truth, righteousness, and peace. So *I will stand in the house of the Lord, in the courts of the house of my God! And I will praise the Lord, for the Lord is good; I will sing praises to His name, for it is lovely.* For You are *the portion of my inheritance and my cup. ... The lines have fallen to me in pleasant places; indeed, my heritage is beautiful to me.* Thank You, O God. I will drink from Your cup with gratitude, and I will enjoy my inheritance forever. Indeed, how Lovely You are to me.

Psalms 27:4; 84:1-2; 85:10; 135:2-3; 16:5-6

One Who Restores

O God, restore us, and cause Your face to shine upon us, and we will be saved.
PSALM 80:3

O God, You are the One Who Restores. I need You, O God, please come. I am down on my knees, completely broken. I can't make sense of the past, and I don't know how to stand in the present. Again, I cry out to You, "Please come, Lord Jesus." I ask You to put these shattered pieces back together—Your hands know how; and Your hands are gentle. I pray You will *restore me to the joy of Your salvation, and sustain Me with a willing spirit. . . . Yes, restore me to You, O Lord, that I may be restored; renew my days as of old.* I ask You to set me back on my feet again. Have Your way with me, dear Savior. Rebuild me to mirror You. And as You wrap Your righteousness around me, I will recall this to mind: *I am a new creature in Christ; old things have passed away, and new things have come.* So, I will rejoice! For Your matchless mercy has moved into the midst of my mess. *You have given me a new heart and a new spirit*—now hear my heart beat for You, and see my spirit worship You. Indeed, I love the *One who restores my soul.*

**Psalm 51:12; Lamentations 5:21; 2 Corinthians 5:17;
Ezekiel 36:26; Psalm 23:3**

Lovingkindness

"But let him who boasts boast of this, that he understands and knows Me, that I am the
LORD *who exercises lovingkindness, justice, and righteousness on earth; for I delight in*
these things," declares the LORD.

JEREMIAH 9:24

O God, You are Lovingkindness. I have finally come *to know and now believe the love*
which You have for me. I feel it every breath I take, and *it is better than life.* You have
rescued me, You have redeemed me, and You continue to reward me with Yourself. My
soul will forever testify that *You are gracious, and righteous; yes, O God, You are com-*
passionate. You preserve the simple; for I was brought low, and You saved me. Indeed,
how precious is Your lovingkindness, O God. I will savor You, as You *richly pour into me.*
But tell me this, how can I contain this *love that is as high as the heavens are above*
the earth? I simply cannot; I must overflow in praise of Your name. So hear my heart
sing to the world, *Praise the Lord! Praise the Lord, O my soul! I will praise the Lord*
while I live; I will sing praises to my God while I have my being. ... For His lovingkind-
ness is everlasting.

1 John 4:16; Psalms 63:3; 116:5-6; 36:7; Titus 3:6;
Psalms 103:11; 146:1-2; 118:1

One Who Knows Me

O LORD, You have searched me and known me.

PSALM 139:1

O God, You are the One Who Knows Me. I feel at times, no one "gets me," not even the ones who love me most. What a sorrow it is for my heart to seemingly be unheard or even pushed aside. I am hurting, dear Lord, but I will sit with You and *I will pour out my heart out to You* and I will remember You. Yes, You are the understanding One. *You know me, O Lord ...* and *all my desire is before You.* With this truth, You know my motives, whether they are selfish or pure, over the top or right on. Therefore, I will *trust You with all of my heart.* And I will trust You to *plead my case* if I am in line with You, or to set me straight if I am not. And I will trust You *to meet my every need according to the riches in glory in Christ Jesus.* Thank You. I will wait for You. Indeed, *I would have despaired unless I had believed that I would see the goodness of the Lord in the land of the living. I will wait for the Lord; I will be strong, and my heart will take courage. I will wait for the Lord.* Yes, today, right now, I choose to peacefully rest in the arms of the One Who Knows Me from the inside-out.

Psalm 62:8; Jeremiah 12:3; Psalm 38:9; Proverbs 3:5; Jeremiah 51:36; Philippians 4:19; Psalm 27:13-14

Overseer

"For I know the plans that I have for you," declares the LORD, "plans for welfare and not for calamity to give you a future and a hope."

JEREMIAH 29:11

O God, You are the Overseer. *For You are a great God, and a great King above all gods; in Your hands are the depths of the earth; the peaks of the mountains are Yours also. The sea is Yours; for it is You who made it; and Your hands formed dry land.* Yes, You own and oversee it all—every star that shines, every raindrop that falls, and every flower that blooms. *You established the earth upon its foundations, so that it will not totter for ever and ever. ... You send forth springs in the valleys; they flow between the mountains; they give drink to every beast of the field. ... You cause the grass to grow for the cattle, and the vegetation for the labor of man.* Indeed, You are the Creator, Provider, and Sustainer of all Your creatures both great and small. I thank You, O God, that this truth includes me! I know *You have numbered my days on this earth,* and each one has been pre-planned by You. I thank You for consistently *meeting me morning by morning* in order to fill me with confidence; I do not have to worry about the day, for You have already laid it out. Yes, I praise You, Overseer of all creation, for *watching over every path I take.*

Psalms 95:3-5; 104:5,10-11,14; 139:16; Isaiah 50:4; Proverbs 5:21

Problem Solver

And Jonah was in the stomach of the fish three days and three nights.
JONAH 1:17

O God, You are the Problem Solver. You know all things. *Nothing is too difficult for You.* You see the beginning, and You see the end. But here I am again, in the middle of another mess. Dear Lord, I do admit, so often, I am at the root of the problem! I confess my sin before You: my attitude is odious, my mindset is muddled, and my perspective is plagued with pride. I am like a tight and tangled ball of string. Untwist me with Your Master-mind, I pray. Start at the beginning and just keep pulling, even if it's humbling and uncomfortable. I ask You to decipher my *inmost thoughts and judge the intentions of my heart.* Only You, O God, can *make my paths straight,* and only You can bring sweet peace back into my distorted disposition. So come again, I pray, and do Your lovely work in me. Please continue to strengthen me in Your ways, as You gingerly straighten me out of mine. Thank You, sweet Savior, for faithfully loving this problem-child. *You are gracious and compassionate. ... Your understanding is infinite;* therefore, I can thankfully say, my knots are not knots to You.

Jeremiah 32:27; Hebrews 4:12; Proverbs 3:6; Psalms 111:4; 147:5

God of Wonders

Oh give thanks to the LORD, call upon His name; make known His deeds among the peoples. Sing to Him, sing praises to Him; speak of all His wonders.
1 CHRONICLES 16:8–9

O God, You are a God of Wonders. Yes, *by Your word the heavens were made, and by the breath of Your mouth all their host. You gather the waters of the sea together as a heap; You lay up the deeps in storehouses. Let all the earth fear You; let all the inhabitants of the world stand in awe of You. For You spoke, and it was done; You commanded, and it stood fast.* O God, when I *stand and consider Your wonders,* I marvel at Your handiwork from smallest entity to greatest mass, from deepest ocean to highest peak, from darkest night to brightest day. On and on, Your creation declares Your marvelous name. You also speak wisdom into my heart through all that You have designed. With beautiful imagery, You challenge me to *be like a tree firmly planted by streams of water.* You also point to the stars and say, *Shine like these in the midst of a crooked and perverse generation.* And You direct me to be *like a house who has laid its foundation on a rock, not sand.* Indeed, *great are Your works; they are studied by all who delight in them. Splendid and majestic is Your work; and Your righteousness endures forever. You have made Your wonders to be remembered.*

Psalm 33:6-9; Job 37:14; Psalm 1:3; Philippians 2:15;
Matthew 7:24-27; Psalm 111:2-4

God of those who Wait

Wait for the LORD; Be strong and let your heart take courage; Yes, wait for the LORD.
PSALM 27:14

O God, You are the God of those who Wait. *Abraham waited for 25 years to receive his promised son. … Joseph waited in Potiphar's house and then in prison for a total of 11 years before he became the promised leader. … Moses waited 40 years in the desert before he went back to rescue his people from slavery. … David waited close to 15 years before he was finally the reigning king of Israel. … And God, You waited patiently for the exact and appropriate hour to send the Savior of the world.* Dear Lord, I confess, I hate to wait; I feel so useless and misplaced at times. Help me to learn from Your servants of old. Give me a steadfast heart even in the midst of silence or suffering. Remind me that You are at work even in what seems like the darkest, loneliest hour. You promise that *tribulations bring about perseverance; and perseverance, proven character; and proven character hope, and hope does not disappoint.* Yes, God, I do know, You are in the midst of my waiting; and I do know during this time You are refining me for the purpose of Your kingdom. You see my potential, and in the quiet, You are building new and beautiful things into me. So therefore, I will say again to myself, *My soul, wait in silence for God only, for my hope is from Him. He only is my rock and my salvation, my stronghold; I will not be shaken.* And while I am waiting, I will praise You. And while I am waiting, I will trust You. And while I am waiting, I will obey You. And while I am waiting, I will pray to You. And while I am waiting, I will love well. And while I am waiting, I will declare Your name to the world.

Genesis 18:10-14; 41:39-41; Exodus 3:7-10; 2 Samuel 5:1-4; John 17:1-3; Romans 5:3-5; Psalm 62:5-6

Sun of Righteousness

But for you who fear My name, the sun of righteousness will rise with healing in its wings; and you will go forth and skip about like calves from the stall.

MALACHI 4:2

O God, You are the Sun of Righteousness. Because of You, dear Jesus, *the day dawns and the morning star arises in my heart.* I love these ancient words of truth that I can daily live by: *The God of Israel said, "The Rock of Israel spoke to me, He who rules over men righteously, who rules in the fear of God, is as the light of morning when the sun rises, a morning without clouds, when the tender grass springs out of the earth, through sunshine after rain."* Yes, Lord, You make my path clear and right; *You are light and in You, there is no darkness at all.* Your brilliance shines on Your people today on earth; but wait—You will shine even greater on us in heaven: *And the light of the moon will be as the light of the sun, and the light of the sun will be seven times brighter, like the light of seven days, on the day the Lord binds up the fracture of His people and heals the bruise He has inflicted.* Your word also says this of our future home with You: *And in His right hand He held seven stars; and out of the mouth came a sharp two-edged sword; and His face was like the sun shining in its strength.* Yes, Lord, You promise someday soon, *we shall see Your face, and Your name shall be on our foreheads. And there shall no longer be any night; they shall not have need of the light of a lamp nor the light of the sun, because You shall illumine us; and we shall reign forever and ever.* Jesus, You indeed, are the Sun of Righteousness now and forever!

**2 Peter 1:19; 2 Samuel 23:3-4; 1 John 1:5; Isaiah 30:26;
Revelation 1:16; 22:5**

Glorified

Jesus spoke these things; and lifting up His eyes to heaven, He said, "Father, the hour has come; glorify Your Son, that the Son may glorify You."

JOHN 17:1

O God, You are Glorified. Dear Jesus, You spoke these words at the last supper concerning Your pathway to the cross: *Now is the Son of Man glorified, and God is glorified in Him.* Indeed dear God, the climax of Your glory was the sacrifice of Your *only Son for the sake of the world that You so loved.* There at the cross, the dark evil of this world was placed on You. Indeed, *You who knew no sin became sin on our behalf, that we might become the righteousness of God.* I marvel at Your sacrifice, Your extraordinary sacrifice. Finally and forever, *the veil of the temple was torn in two.* Dear God, Your grace touched me and pulled me in. I am awed at Your presence, Your holy presence. *For Your lovingkindness toward me is great, and You have delivered my soul from the depths of Sheol.* Thank You! Show me, now, how to live as a result of this undeserved favor! Dear Jesus, I hear Your instruction, *By this is My Father glorified, that you bear much fruit, and so prove to be My disciples.* Therefore, I will carry Your gift of love inside me and give it to others. Yes, *I will give thanks to You, O Lord my God, with all my heart, and will glorify Your name forever.* Indeed, I am humbled and changed by Your redeeming love. And I will be marked by this truth forever: You were Glorified, awe-fully Glorified, for me.

**John 13:31; 3:16; 2 Corinthians 5:21; Matthew 27:51; Psalm 86:13;
John 15:8; Psalm 86:12**

One Who Scatters

After singing a hymn, they went out to the Mount of Olives. Then Jesus said to them,
"You will all fall away because of Me this night, for it is written, 'I will strike down the
shepherd, and the sheep of the flock shall be scattered.'"

MATTHEW 26:30–31

O God, You are the One Who Scatters. You reach out to Your children and long to bless
Your people, but we are a stiff-necked and stubborn lot. Why do we turn from You?
Why do we resist Your ways? Help us to learn from Your people of old, who deliberately
choose to worship other gods instead of trusting in Your lovingkindness. You spoke
these words of warning to them if they decided to go their own way: *You, however, I will*
scatter among the nations and will draw out a sword after you, as your land becomes
desolate and your cities become waste. And these things certainly came to pass due to
their willful disobedience. You were forced to lovingly discipline Your children in order to
bring them back to You. Again, dear Lord, may we learn from their errors and intentionally choose to *take refuge in the shadow of Your wings.* In Your protective care, we find
safety from our enemies, and peace in Your presence. Let us each stand before You and
hear what You offer to all people: *Behold, I am laying in Zion a stone, a tested stone,*
a costly cornerstone for the foundation, firmly placed; he who believes in it will not be
disturbed. You, dear Jesus, are that cornerstone. You will bring protection and peace
to those who call on Your name. But, again, You warn all those who turn away: *And he*
who falls on the stone will be broken to pieces; but on whomever it falls, it will scatter
them like dust. Dear God, You make the choice so clear. May I *choose this day whom I*
will serve.

Leviticus 26:33; Psalm 57:1; Isaiah 28:16; Matthew 21:44; Joshua 24:15

One Who Gathers

And He took them in His arms and began blessing them, laying His hands on them.
MARK 10:16

O God, You are the One Who Gathers. I hear Your words to Your city, dear Jesus, and receive them as my own: *O Jerusalem, Jerusalem, who kills the prophets and stones those who are sent to her! How often I wanted to gather your children together, the way a hen gathers her chicks under her wings, and you were unwilling.* Forgive me, O God, when I resist Your embracing arms of love. I am so prone to stray into unknown territory. Thank You for gracefully coming to my rescue each time. I will cling to this powerful promise that You made to Your people of old, as well as to me today: *For I will take you from the nations, gather you from all the lands, and bring you into your own land. Then I will sprinkle clean water on you, and you will be clean; I will cleanse you from all your filthiness and from all your idols. Moreover, I will give you a new heart and put a new spirit within you; and I will remove the heart of stone from your flesh and give you a heart of flesh. I will put My Spirit within you and cause you to walk in My statutes, and you will be careful to observe My ordinances. And you will live in the land that I gave to your forefathers; so you will be My people, and I will be your God.* Dear God, thank You for Your abundant blessing when I have done nothing to deserve it. I will humbly run to You! There, *You will gather me in Your arms like a shepherd.* I am safe, I am loved, I am cared for. I am restored, I am fed, I am content. I am a recipient of Your unending grace. Finally, I am resting.

Matthew 23:37; Ezekiel 36:24-28; Isaiah 40:11

Vinedresser

I am the true vine, and My Father is the vinedresser.
JOHN 15:1

O God, You are the Vinedresser. First of all, I want to thank You that I am even considered *a branch on the vine*. For I know that I was once considered a *wild olive, and was grafted in among the original branches, and that I became a partaker with them of the rich root of the olive tree*. Again, I humbly thank You for this act of grace on my behalf. Now, dear Jesus, I hear You say to me, *Every branch in Me that does not bear fruit, My Father takes away; and every branch that bears fruit, He prunes it, that it may bear more fruit.* O God, I want to be a fruitful bearer of Your *love, joy, peace, patience, kindness, goodness, faithfulness, gentleness, and self-control;* but, I must confess, sometimes Your pruning hurts. I know Your intentions are for my good and for Your glory, and in the long run, I will most certainly bear more fruit under Your knowledgeable care; but right now, Your pruning hand has afflicted me. You have taken away things that I thought I needed. I do realize, because of these losses, I have had to become more dependent upon You. Indeed, You now have become my All in all. And through this enduring process, I am learning to say from a sincere heart of faith, *I count all things to be loss in view of the surpassing value of knowing You as my Lord.* Therefore, let me hear again Your beautiful words of assurance as I continually submit to Your shaping, *You did not choose Me, but I chose you, and appointed you, that you should go and bear fruit, and that your fruit should remain.* Yes, wise Vinedresser, please continue Your good work in me.

**John 15:5; Romans 11:17; John 15:2; Galatians 5:22-23;
Philippians 3:8; John 15:16**

Vine

I, Jesus, ... am the root and the descendant of David.
REVELATION 22:16

O God, You are the Vine. Jesus, You spoke these words, *I am the true vine, and My Father is the vinedresser.* What a beautiful picture that exemplifies the working relationship between God the Father and God the Son. Thank You, Jesus, for being God Incarnate, for being *Immanuel, which means "God with us."* Indeed, You are the *exact representation of God's nature.* By Your extraordinary plan, You are the *root of Jesse,* the long-awaited Messiah that came to earth to save people from their sins. And You are the *tender shoot that grew up before God, like a root out of parched ground.* Again, thank You for coming. Your perfect presence was born into our mess; Your sinless nature grew up in our chaos. Thank You for becoming one of us, for wanting to be near us, for supplying our every need. You brought hope, You brought light, You brought love. You, indeed, are the Vine that brings bountiful life to all who call You Savior. I hear You say, *Abide in Me, and I in you. As the branch cannot bear fruit of itself, unless it abides in the vine, so neither can you, unless you abide in Me. I am the vine, you are the branches; he who abides in Me and I in him, he bears much fruit; for apart from Me you can do nothing.* Yes, dear God, I will abide in the Vine. And there I will be nourished with Your goodness and sustained with Your strength.

John 15:1; Matthew 1:23; Hebrews 1:3; Isaiah 11:10; 53:2; John 15:4-5

Expected One

Now when John, while imprisoned, heard of the works of Christ, he sent word by his disciples, and said to Him, "Are You the Expected One, or shall we look for someone else?"
MATTHEW 11:2-3

O God, You are the Expected One. Long ago the promised Messiah was foretold: *For a child will be born to us, a son will be given to us; and the government will rest on His shoulders; And His name will be called Wonderful Counselor, Mighty God, Eternal Father, Prince of Peace.* And also it was written: *But as for you, Bethlehem Ephrathah, too little to be among the clans of Judah, from you One will go forth for Me to be ruler in Israel. His goings forth are from long ago, from the days of eternity. Therefore, He will give them up until the time when she who is in labor has borne a child. Then the remainder of His brethren will return to the sons of Israel. And He will arise and shepherd His flock in the strength of the Lord, in the majesty of the name of the Lord His God. And they will remain, because at that time He will be great to the ends of the earth. And this One will be our peace.* Then the prophecy was fulfilled at Your appointed time: *The angel said to the shepherds, "Do not be afraid; for behold, I bring you good news of great joy which shall be for all the people; for today in the city of David there has been born for you a Savior, who is Christ the Lord. And this will be a sign for you; you will find a baby wrapped in cloths, and lying in a manger."* Then years later, You, dear Jesus, spoke these words with affirmation: *Go and report to John what you hear and see; the blind receive sight and the lame walk, the lepers are cleansed and the deaf hear, and the dead are raised up, and the poor have the gospel preached to them. And blessed is he who keeps from stumbling over Me.* Yes, Immanuel, from prophecy to fulfillment to present, You indeed are the Expected One.

Isaiah 9:6; Micah 5:2-5; Luke 2:10-12; Matthew 11:4-6

Honorable

He who offers a sacrifice of thanksgiving honors Me; and to him who orders his way aright I shall show the salvation of God.

PSALM 50:23

O God, You are Honorable. Your word says, *Finally, brethren, whatever is true, whatever is honorable, whatever is right, whatever is pure, whatever is lovely, whatever is of good repute, if there is any excellence and if anything worthy of praise, let your mind dwell on these things.* O God, You are all these things at the same time! Yes, *hallowed be Your name.* You are worthy of all praise. Keep my heart and mind in line with who You are, O God. May my prayers never become meaningless or spoken with mere repetition. For You say concerning Your people of old, *"A son honors his father, and a servant his master. Then if I am a father, where is My honor? And if I am a master, where is My respect?" says the Lord of hosts.* And also, *This people honors Me with their lips, but their heart is far away from Me.* Dear Lord, again, You are worthy to receive all my allegiance, coming from a sincere heart of adoration. Hear me say from the depths of my soul, "You are beautiful, You are strong, You are compassionate, You are good. You are holy, You are righteous, You are great, You are wise. You are kind, You are love, You are just, You are eternal." Every day, I will lift Your name on high. And every day, I will respect You with my life. And from my whole heart, I will sing with the angels, *To Him who sits on the throne, and to the Lamb, be blessing and honor and glory and dominion forever and ever.*

Philippians 4:8; Matthew 6:9; Malachi 1:6; Matthew 15:8; Revelation 5:13

Detailed

In the beginning, God created the heavens and the earth.

GENESIS 1:1

O God, You are Detailed. You spoke the world into existence giving unique attributes to all creatures great and small. Indeed, the detail in Your earthly design is both vast and various: mountains and valleys, sunshine and stars, man and beast. But what is just as wonderful to me is the specificity of Your detail found throughout Your word in Your dealings with men. You gave Noah the exact measurements of the ark: *The length of the ark shall be three hundred cubits, its breadth fifty cubits, and its height thirty cubits. You shall make a window for the ark, and finish it to a cubit from the top; and set the door of the ark in the side of it; you shall make it with lower, second, and third decks.* And later, You gave David explicit plans for the temple for his son Solomon to build, from the *porch of the temple, its buildings, its storehouses, its upper rooms, its inner rooms, and the room for the mercy seat. ... And the golden utensils, the weight of gold for all utensils for every kind of service; for the silver utensils, the weight of silver for all utensils for every kind of service.* And even later, You showed John the beautiful detail of our future home: *The foundation stones of the city wall were adorned with every kind of precious stone. The first foundation was jasper; the second, sapphire; the third, chalcedony; the fourth, emerald; the fifth, sardonyx; the sixth, sardius; the seventh, chrysolite; the eighth, beryl; the ninth, topaz; the tenth, chrysoprase; the eleventh, jacinth; the twelfth, amethyst. And the twelve gates were twelve pearls; each one of the gates was a single pearl. And the street of the city was pure gold, like transparent glass.* O God, Your intentional design is fascinating and purposeful; there is meaning behind every inch and every article and every masterpiece that You have put together. Indeed, Your glory is in the midst of Your detail, from the beginning to the end.

Genesis 6:15-16; 1 Chronicles 28:11,14; Revelation 21:19-21

Diligent

Blessed is the man who listens to me, watching daily at my gates, waiting at my doorposts. For he who finds me finds life and obtains favor from the LORD.

PROVERBS 8:34–35

O God, You are Diligent. You never give up; You never let up. Thank You. Your care for me is continuous. I hear Your sweet words, dear Jesus: *Are not two sparrows sold for a cent? And yet not one of them will fall to the ground apart from Your Father but the very hairs of your head are all numbered. Therefore do not fear; you are of more value than many sparrows.* And Your word promises: *He who began a good work in me will perfect it until the day of Christ Jesus.* Yes, and again, Your word encourages me of Your active concern in my life: *For it is God who is at work in you, both to will and to work for His good pleasure.* Thank You, O God, for Your day-and-night diligence with regard to my ongoing and ever-changing circumstances. Help me to listen to You and then respond in obedience to Your word. Make me a diligent servant as I seek to mirror Your image. May I learn this quality through examples given in Your guiding word: *Suffer hardship with me, as a good soldier of Christ Jesus. No soldier in active service entangles himself in the affairs of everyday life, so that he may please the one who enlisted him as a soldier. And also if anyone competes as an athlete, he does not win the prize unless he competes according to the rules. The hard-working farmer ought to be the first to receive his share of the crops.* Your word is beautiful, instructional, and challenging. May I heed it, never giving up, never letting up, so that I may become Diligent like You.

Matthew 10:29-31; Philippians 1:6; 2:13; 2 Timothy 2:3-6

Personal God

The word of the LORD came expressly to Ezekiel the priest, son of Buzi, in the land of the Chaldeans by the river Chebar; and there the hand of the LORD came upon him.

EZEKIEL 1:3

O God, You are a Personal God. Your word says: *There is no creature hidden from Your sight, but all things are open and laid bare to Your eyes.* Yes, dear Lord, You personally summoned Jeremiah: *Before I formed you in the womb I knew you, and before you were born I consecrated you; I have appointed you a prophet to the nations.* And also, You personally rescued Jonah: *And the Lord appointed a great fish to swallow Jonah, and Jonah was in the stomach of the fish three days and three nights.* And You personally anointed David: *Then Samuel took the horn of oil and anointed him in the midst of his brothers; and the Spirit of the Lord came mightily upon David from that day forward.* And You personally commissioned Peter: *Blessed are you, Simon Barjona, because flesh and blood did not reveal this to you, but My Father who is in heaven. And I also say to you that you are Peter, and upon this rock I will build My church; and the gates of Hades shall not overpower it.* You, O God, know each one of us by name. You know who we are, where we are, and what we are called to do. Today, I ask You to summon us, rescue us, anoint us, and commission us. Let each of our hearts hear Your personal promise from Your perspective: *Do not fear, for I have redeemed you; I have called you by name; you are Mine!* Yes, Lord, You are Personal in Your love to me, so that I can be purposeful with Your love through me. I pray I will rise to Your bidding.

**Hebrews 4:13; Jeremiah 1:5; Jonah 1:17; 1 Samuel 16:13;
Matthew 16:17-18; Isaiah 43:1**

Author of Faith

Fixing our eyes on Jesus, the author and perfecter of faith ...
HEBREWS 12:2

O God, You are the Author of Faith. Yes, Jesus, Son of God, One with God, You came to show us how to live. *Although You existed in the form of God, You did not regard equality with God a thing to be grasped, but You emptied Yourself, taking the form of a bond-servant, and were made in the likeness of men.* Thus, as a man, Your faith walk with Your Father began. You experienced hunger, fatigue, human weakness, and emotion, yet without sin. Your word says: *Therefore He had to be made like His brethren in all things, that he might become a merciful and faithful high priest in things pertaining to God, to make propitiation for the sins of the people. For since He Himself was tempted in that which He has suffered. He is able to come to the aid of those who are tempted.* Thank You, Jesus, for experiencing humanity so that You would know us completely, inside-out! And thank You for showing us how to be dependent on the Father when You experienced the different trials of each new day. You told Your disciples, *I do nothing on My own initiative, but I speak these things as the Father taught Me. And He who sent Me is with Me; He has not left Me alone, for I always do the things that are pleasing to Him.* Jesus, Your faith walk started with listening; then, You obeyed the voice of Your Father. And You did this through the power of the Holy Spirit. Ah, so this is how I, too, can live: You died in order that Your Spirit might live in me, and reign in me. Therefore, I can also choose to listen and obey when I hear Your word, be it through teaching, reading, or through *the Spirit who indwells me.* And I, too, can choose to *walk by faith, not by sight.* Indeed, I will fix my eyes on the Author of Faith so I can mimic the footsteps of my Savior.

**Philippians 2:6-7; Hebrews 2:17-18; John 8:28-29; 1 Corinthians 3:16;
2 Corinthians 5:7**

Perfecter of Faith

For it was fitting for Him, for whom are all things, and through whom are all things, in bringing many sons to glory, to perfect the author of their salvation through sufferings.
HEBREWS 2:10

O God, You are the Perfecter of Faith. Indeed, dear Jesus, Son of God, Son of Man, You came to show us how to live, start to finish. You walked by faith, completely dependent on the voice of Your Father, and You stepped into Your purpose with willing obedience. Your word says: *Therefore, since we have so great a cloud of witnesses surrounding us, let us also lay aside every encumbrance, and the sin which so easily entangles us, and let us run with endurance the race that is set before us, fixing our eyes on Jesus, the author and perfecter of faith, who for the joy set before Him endured the cross, despising the shame, and has sat down at the right hand of the throne of God. For consider Him who has endured such hostility by sinners against Himself, so that you may not grow weary and lose heart.* Yes, dear Jesus, You showed us, by example, how to live out our faith all the way to the finish line, no matter the circumstance, no matter the trial. And this is how You did it: while You stepped toward Your predetermined destiny, You fixed Your gaze on Your future glory. Jesus, thank You for Your steadfast resolve in completing Your faith walk, all the way to the cross. Your death and resurrection brought me hope and life forever. Help me, O God, to now live out my walk of faith to the end. And as I go forward each day, may I hear Your voice and obey You with each step, just as Jesus did. And may I, too, have a heavenly perspective, living by these challenging words: *If then you have been raised up with Christ, keep seeking the things above, where Christ is, seated at the right hand of God. Set your mind on the things above, not on the things that are on earth, for you have died and your life is hidden with Christ in God. When Christ, who is our life, is revealed, then you also will be revealed with Him in glory.* So with the hope of heaven in my heart, may I be able to say at the end of my days, *I have fought the good fight, I have finished the course, I have kept the faith.*

Hebrews 12:1-3; Colossians 3:1-3; 2 Timothy 4:7

One Who Prevails

So the word of the Lord was growing mightily and prevailing.
Acts 19:20

O God, You are the One Who Prevails. Your word says: *For as the rain and the snow come down from heaven, and do not return there without watering the earth, and making it bear and sprout, and furnishing seed to the sower and bread to the eater; so shall My word be which goes forth from My mouth; it shall not return to Me empty, without accomplishing what I desire, and without succeeding in the matter for which I sent it.* Yes, Lord, Your word prevailed through the prophets of old. Concerning Samuel, it says: *Thus Samuel grew and the Lord was with him and let none of his words fail. And all Israel from Dan even to Beersheba knew that Samuel was confirmed as a prophet of the Lord.* And You told Ezekiel: *Prophesy over these bones, and say to them, "O dry bones, hear the word of the Lord … breathe on these slain that they come to life."* Then Ezekiel reported, *So I prophesied as He commanded me, and the breath came into them, and they came to life, and stood on their feet, an exceedingly great army.* Your powerful word, O God, brings life! And You also prevailed through Your apostles as they spread the good news concerning Jesus, the resurrected Messiah: *and the word of God kept on spreading; And the number of the disciples continued to increase greatly in Jerusalem, and a great many of the priests were becoming obedient to the faith.* Dear Lord, these men of old inspire me, and I ask for the same blessing. Please, *fill me with Your Spirit so that I may speak Your word with boldness.* May I bring hope and truth and light to this world through the *God-breathed book* that I hold in my hands. I ask for understanding, I ask for opportunities, I ask for courage; yes please, O God, Prevail Your word through me.

Isaiah 55:10-11; 1 Samuel 3:19-20; Ezekiel 37:4,9-10;
Acts 6:7; 4:31; 2 Timothy 3:16

Instructional

The word of the LORD came to (Elijah) saying, "Go away from here and turn eastward, and hide yourself by the brook Cherith, which is east of the Jordan."

1 KINGS 17: 2–3

O God, You are Instructional. You spoke to Abraham, *Go forth from your country, and from your relatives and from your father's house, to the land which I will show you.* And You directed Samuel, *Fill your horn with oil, and go; I will send you to Jesse the Bethlehemite, for I have selected a king for Myself among his sons.* And You told King Jehoshaphat, *The battle is not yours but God's. Tomorrow go down against them. Behold, they will come up by the ascent of Ziz, and you will find them at the end of the valley in the front of the wilderness of Jeruel.* And You spoke to Joseph, *Arise and take the Child and His mother, and flee to Egypt, and remain there until I tell you; for Herod is going to search for the Child to destroy Him.* And You instructed Ananias, *Arise and go to the street called Straight, and inquire at the house of Judas for a man from Tarsus named Saul.* Dear Lord, thank You for being specific and purposeful in Your instruction concerning the progress of Your great name and Your people. Help my soul to be quiet enough to hear Your voice of guidance and truth; for Your word is full of wisdom and direction. Yes, dear Lord, I cling to this promise: *I will instruct you and teach you in the way which you should go; I will counsel you with My eye upon you.* Please allow me to hear, trust, and obey Your every Instruction.

**Genesis 12:1; 1 Samuel 16:1; 2 Chronicles 20:15-16; Matthew 2:13;
Acts 9:11; Psalm 32:8**

Avenger

But if you do what is evil, be afraid; for it does not bear the sword for nothing; for it is a minister of God, an avenger who brings wrath on the one who practices evil.

ROMANS 13:4

O God, You are the Avenger. You give us instruction: *Never take your own revenge, beloved, but leave room for the wrath of God, for it is written, "Vengeance is Mine, I will repay," says the Lord. But if your enemy is hungry, feed him, and if he is thirsty, give him a drink; for in so doing you will heap burning coals upon his head.* Yes, Lord, You are the One to avenge a wrong, because You are the only One who knows how to do it perfectly; in Your beautiful holiness, You are able to both stamp out evil as well as "woo" the evildoer at the same time, if he is willing. Thank You, Jesus, for absorbing the wrath that each one of us deserves. So Lord, help me not focus on others and their wrongs; but rather, let me consider my own walk with You. Help me take these words to heart concerning our relationship: *For this is the will of God, your sanctification, that is, that you abstain from sexual immorality; that each of you know how to possess his own vessel in sanctification and honor, not in lustful passion. ... and that no man transgress and defraud his brother in the matter because the Lord is the avenger in all these things. ... For God has not called us for the purpose of impurity, but in sanctification. Consequently, he who rejects this is not rejecting man but God who gives His Holy Spirit to you.* Convict my heart, O God, to leave all avenging to You. Instead of harboring ill will, help me to focus on walking with You uprightly, depending on Your Spirit to do so. Hear my prayer to You: *Acquit me of hidden faults. Also keep back Your servant from presumptuous sins; let them not rule over me; then I shall be blameless, and I shall be acquitted of great transgression.* I must thank You, Merciful Avenger, for walking the patient road of sanctification with me. Continue to convict and correct me as we walk forward together.

Romans 12:19-20; 1 Thessalonians 4:3-8; Psalm 19:12-13

Constant

The LORD will command His lovingkindness in the daytime; and His song will be with me in the night.

PSALM 42:8

O God, You are Constant. Thank You for Your continual care. You say to my heart, *I will never desert you, nor will I forsake you.* And You reassure me with these words: *Look at the birds of the air, that they do not sow, neither do they reap, nor gather into barns, and yet your heavenly Father feeds them. Are you not worth much more than they?* Yes, Lord, just as You tend to the birds of the air, You will also tend to me. You even tell me to pray in this way to You: *Give us this day our daily bread.* And You promise me You *will supply all my needs according to Your riches in glory in Christ Jesus.* So, forgive me Lord, when I feel as if You have taken a break from my issues. How foolish a thought. You are always present and always working, and You always have my best interest at heart! The psalmist says: *Evening and morning and noon, I will complain and murmur, and He will hear my voice.* Thank You for listening to me even when I don't make sense. Thank You for Your patience. Yes, dear Lord, thank You for *daily bearing my burdens.* Please realign my heart to trust You. Yes, I ask You to give me what is really necessary rather than what I think or feel is necessary. You groom and You grow; You guard and You guide. Indeed, O God, thank You for Your Constant care.

Hebrews 13:5; Matthew 6:26,11; Philippians 4:19; Psalms 55:17; 68:19

Innocent

You were not redeemed with perishable things like silver or gold from your futile way of life inherited from your forefathers, but with precious blood, as of a lamb unblemished and spotless, the blood of Christ.

1 PETER 1:18–19

O God, You are Innocent. Yes, Immanuel, You came to earth and lived blamelessly among us. And then, according to Your merciful plan, You chose to die a guilty man's death. Scripture says: *He made Him who knew no sin to be sin on our behalf, that we might become the righteousness of God.* Thank You, Jesus, for being *the Lamb of God that takes away the sin of the world.* I am humbled at the high price You paid; I am baffled by the love that was poured out. Allow my heart to take in all Your goodness as I meditate on this truth: *He is able to save forever those who draw near to God through Him, since He always lives to make intercession for them. For it was fitting that we should have such a high priest, holy, innocent, undefiled, separated from sinners and exalted above the heavens; who does not need daily, like those high priests, to offer up sacrifices, first for His own sins, and then for the sins of the people, because this He did once for all when He offered up Himself.* Again dear Lord Jesus, thank You for becoming the one and only perfect sacrifice! Your innocence has now been transferred to me because You defeated sin by Your death and resurrection. You promise: *There is now no condemnation for those who are in Christ Jesus. For the law of the Spirit of life in Christ Jesus has set you free from the law of sin and of death.* Hallelujah, Innocent One. I will eternally praise You for Your extreme love.

2 Corinthians 5:21; John 1:29; Hebrews 7:25-27; Romans 8:1-2

One Who Convicts

See to it that you do not refuse Him who is speaking. For if those did not escape when they refused Him who warned them on earth, much less will we escape who turn away from Him who warns from heaven.

HEBREWS 12:25

O God, You are the One Who Convicts. Dear Jesus, I am thankful for this promise that You made to your disciples: *But I tell you the truth, it is to your advantage that I go away; for if I do not go away, the Helper shall not come to you; but if I go, I will send Him to you. And He, when He comes, will convict the world concerning sin, and righteousness, and judgment.* And also, thank You for this promise: *If anyone loves Me, he will keep My word; and My Father will love him, and We will come to him, and make Our abode with him. ... But the Helper, the Holy Spirit, whom the Father will send in My name, He will teach you all things, and bring to your remembrance all that I said to you.* O God, I pray that I will not *quench the Spirit* that lives in me; for Your Spirit is full of power and grace. Rather, allow me to hear Your voice loud and clear; please give me a sincere desire to obey Your words even when they are contrary to what I would like to do or say in my flesh. Your word says: *To one who knows the right thing to do, and does not do it, to him it is sin.* So Lord, when Your Spirit convicts, may I be truly repentant, so that righteous actions follow suit. *You desire truth in the innermost being, and in the hidden part You will make me know wisdom.* Yes, Lord, my ultimate heart's desire is to obey Your guiding voice so that I will walk in *paths of righteousness for Your name's sake.*

John 16:7-8; 14:23,26; 1 Thessalonians 5:19; James 4:17; Psalms 51:6; 23:3

One Who Feeds

He said to me, "Son of man, feed your stomach, and fill your body with this scroll which I am giving you." Then I ate it, and it was sweet as honey in my mouth.

EZEKIEL 3:3

O God, You are the One Who Feeds. *Every day You provided manna for the Israelites in the dessert.* And also, You *gave nourishment both morning and evening to Elijah through the ravens that brought him bread and meat.* And on the grassy hillside, dear *Jesus, You fed the five thousand with only five loaves and two fish. And they all ate and were satisfied.* Dear God, thank You for Your beautiful physical provision that is portrayed throughout Your word. You are faithful. Likewise, I know You feed Your people spiritually. Of course, these miracles of physical nourishment point to how You provide complete fulfillment to our souls. Jesus, You said, *For the bread of God is that which comes down out of heaven, and gives life to the world. ... I am the bread of life; he who comes to Me shall not hunger, and he who believes in Me shall never thirst.* Each and every day, You promise to give me exactly what I need in Your word so that I can live confidently and completely. I ask for a holy hunger, O God. Make this my heart's cry: *The law of the Lord is perfect, restoring the soul; the testimony of the Lord is sure, making wise the simple; the precepts of the Lord are right, rejoicing the heart; the commandment of the Lord is pure, enlightening the eyes. ... They are sweeter also than honey and the drippings of the honeycomb.* Yes, O God, I want to feast on Your word.

**Exodus 16:14-15; 1 Kings 17:6; Mark 6:41-42;
John 6:33,35; Psalm 19:7-8,10**

Repairer

And you will be called the repairer of the breach.
ISAIAH 58:12

O God, You are the Repairer. You are the only One who knows how to make things right. You clearly see all things from all sides. God, at times I am just the opposite: inaccurate and misguided, agitated and perplexed, defensive and judgmental. I confess, I have made a mess once again. *I am like a broken vessel,* void of beauty and purpose. But with You, there is hope. You are the One who can put the pieces back together again. As a matter of fact, Your working, repairing hands can make my vessel even more appealing and productive than before. *Be pleased, O Lord, to deliver me; make haste, O Lord, to help me.* Yes, You say *a broken and contrite heart You will not despise.* I humbly ask, "Right my wrongs, O God, for Your name's sake." Yes, please come, *my Potter, for I am the work of Your hands.* I will completely submit to Your intricate design. Please place the fragments back together in Your divine way, piece by piece, so that I can be whole and filled and useful once again. I cling to this truth: *You will not withhold Your compassion from me; Your lovingkindess and Your truth will continually preserve me.* Do Your beautiful work, I pray. Indeed, only because of You, my Repairer, can I say one more time, *I give thanks to You, for I am fearfully and wonderfully made.*

Psalms 31:12; 40:13; 51:17; Isaiah 64:8; Psalms 40:11; 139:14

One Who Hears

Incline Your ear, O Lord and answer me; for I am afflicted and needy.
PSALM 86:1

O God, You are the One Who Hears. *Be gracious to me, O Lord ... my soul is greatly dismayed; but You, O Lord—how long? Return, O Lord, rescue my soul; save me because of Your lovingkindness. ... You know my frame; You are mindful that I am only dust.* Dear Abba, today, I am weary; today, I am weak; today, I am wandering. Sweet Savior, strengthen my faith, I pray. *Please God, hear my cry; give heed to my prayer. From the end of the earth I call to You when my heart is faint; lead me to the rock that is higher than I.* I pray, lift me up and *renew a steadfast spirit within me. ... Revive me, O Lord, according to Your word.* I need You; for You are my hope, my only living hope. Yes, I do know You will run to me, and I do know You will rescue me. So then, *I will wait for You, my soul does wait, and in Your word do I hope. My soul waits for the Lord more than the watchmen for the morning; indeed, more than the watchmen for the morning.* Yes, I know my Lord will come.

Psalms 6:2-4; 103:14; 61:1-2; 51:10; 119:107; 130:5-6

Impartial

For the LORD your God is the God of gods and the Lord of lords, the great, the mighty, and the awesome God who does not show partiality nor take a bribe.

DEUTERONOMY 10:17

O God, You are Impartial. You commanded through Moses, *You shall not show partiality in judgment; you shall hear the small and the great alike.* Also, Your word says: *With good will render service, as to the Lord, and not to men, knowing that whatever good thing each one does, this he will receive back from the Lord, whether slave or free. And masters, do the same things to them, and give up threatening, knowing that both their Master and yours is in heaven, and there is no partiality with Him.* With these words of instruction, I see that Your partiality has little to do with who is "small" and who is "great" or who is the "master" or who is the "slave"; the central issue is that You offer the same grace and love to all. You declare, *All have sinned and fallen short of the glory of God.* And at the same time, You *do not wish for any to perish but for all to come to repentance.* Yes, Lord, You offer every heart this message of eternal hope: *For God so loved the world, that He gave His only begotten Son that whoever believes in Him should not perish but have eternal life. For God did not send the Son into the world to judge the world, but that the world should be saved through Him. He who believes in Him is not judged; he who does not believe has been judged already, because he has not believed in the name of the only begotten Son of God.* Holy One, I thank You for the way of salvation! You have offered eternal life to all who are willing to receive Your gift by faith. You are beautifully sovereign, and *there is no partiality with You.*

Deuteronomy 1:17; Ephesians 6:7-9; Romans 3:23; 2 Peter 3:9; John 3:16-18; Romans 2:11

My Praise

He is your praise and He is your God, who has done these great and awesome things for you which your eyes have seen. Your fathers went down to Egypt seventy persons in all, and now the LORD your God has made you as numerous as the stars of heaven.

DEUTERONOMY 10:21–22

O God, You are my Praise. *For the Mighty One has done great things for me; and holy is His name.* Yes, Savior, *You brought me up out of the pit of destruction, out of the miry clay; and You set my feet upon a rock making my footsteps firm. You put a new song in my mouth, a song of praise to You.* I can now live with confidence. *You are the One who girds me with strength and makes my way blameless. You make my feet like hinds' feet, and set me upon my high places. You train my hands for battle, so that my arms can bend a bow of bronze. You have also given me the shield of Your salvation, and Your right hand upholds me; and Your gentleness makes me great. You enlarge my steps under me, and my feet have not slipped.* O Merciful God, my adoration continues: *I have beheld You in the sanctuary, and I have seen Your power and Your glory. Because Your lovingkindness is better than life, my lips will praise You. So I will bless You as long as I live; I will lift up my hands in Your name. My soul is satisfied as with marrow and fatness, and my mouth offers praises with joyful lips. When I remember You on my bed, I meditate on You in the night watches, for You have been my help. And in the shadow of Your wings I sing for joy. My soul clings to You; Your right hand upholds me.* O Lord God, day and night, forever and ever, You will be my Praise.

Luke 1:49; Psalms 40:2-3; 18:32-36; 63:2-8

Fortress

The LORD is my rock and my fortress and my deliverer, my God, my rock, in whom I take refuge; my shield and the horn of my salvation, my stronghold.

PSALM 18:2

O God, You are my Fortress. I love these words of truth: *Blessed be the Lord, my rock, who trains my hands for war, and my fingers for battle; my lovingkindness and my fortress, my stronghold and my deliverer; my shield and He in whom I take refuge, who subdues my people under me.* I may not have physical enemies coming up against me, but I am certain I have spiritual ones battling over my heart and mind; but Mighty One, I have nothing to fear because I am fortified with Your strength. Yes, *Your name is a strong tower, the righteous man runs into it and is safe.* With Your protection encompassing me, Satan's fiery darts are impenetrable; I can even laugh at his feeble attempts to *steal, kill, and destroy.* Thank You for Your promise: *Those who trust in the Lord are as Mount Zion, which cannot be moved, but abides forever. As the mountains surround Jerusalem, so the Lord surrounds His people forever.* Therefore, I will trust in You each and every day, each and every circumstance, no matter the arrows that are flying in my direction, nor the snares that are set for my feet. Indeed, *on God my salvation and my glory rest; the rock of my strength, my refuge is in God.* Most certainly, You are my Fortress forever.

Psalm 144:1-2; Proverbs 18:10; John 10:10; Psalms 125:1-2; 62:7

One Who Frustrates

The LORD nullifies the counsel of the nations; He frustrates the plans of the peoples.
PSALM 33:10

O God, You are the One Who Frustrates. Long ago, when all people spoke the same language, they decided together, *Come, let us build for ourselves a city, and a tower whose top will reach into heaven, and let us make for ourselves a name. ... And the Lord said, "Behold, they are one people, and they all have the same language. And this is what they began to do, and now nothing which they purpose to do will be impossible for them. Come, let Us go down and there confuse their language, that they may not understand one another's speech." So the Lord scattered them abroad from there over the face of the whole earth; and they stopped building the city.* O God, You frustrated the people's prideful plans. And then there's Jonah. You said to him, *Arise, go to Nineveh the great city, and cry against it, for their wickedness has come up before Me. But Jonah rose up to flee to Tarshish from the presence of the Lord. So he went down to Joppa, found a ship which was going to Tarshish, paid the fare, and went down into it to go with them to Tarshish from the presence of the Lord. And the Lord hurled a great wind on the sea and there was a great storm on the sea so that the ship was about to break up ... And they picked up Jonah, threw him into the sea. ... And the Lord appointed a great fish to swallow Jonah, and Jonah was in the stomach of the fish three days and three nights.* O God, You frustrated Jonah's disobedient plans. And then there's King Herod. He said to the magi, *Go and make careful search for the Child; and when you have found Him report to me, that I too may come and worship Him. ... But having been warned by God in a dream not to return to Herod, they departed for their own country by another way.* O God, You frustrated Herod's evil plans. Dear Lord, may I learn from these events of old. You frustrate the plans of wayward people so Your glory may prevail. I humbly ask You to do the same for me. Please, discontinue and redirect my ways if they are not in line with You. Yes, frustrate me right back into Your loving arms.

Genesis 11:4,6-8; Jonah 1:2-4,15,17; Matthew 2:8,12

Marvelous

Great and marvelous are Your works, O Lord God, the Almighty; righteous and true are Your ways, King of the nations!

REVELATION 15:3

O God, You are Marvelous. Dear Lord, please make me like Moses who saw a glimpse of Your glory on the mountain and said, *I must turn aside now, and see this marvelous sight, why the bush is not burned up.* At this encounter, his life was never the same. You called him, You challenged him, and You changed him. Yes, through Moses, You performed mighty wonders. Then and now, You continue to work in remarkable ways. *Great are Your works; they are studied by all who delight in them. Splendid and majestic is Your work; and Your righteousness endures forever. You have made Your wonders to be remembered.* O God, right now, I want to praise You for Your greatest work of all: The Messiah's entry into the world. Yes, Your work of salvation involved Your perfect Son. Truth speaks of it in this way: *The stone which the builders rejected has become the chief corner stone. This is the Lord's doing; it is marvelous in our eyes.* Yes, Jesus Christ, Cornerstone, You are the Marvelous One. I rejoice in Your wonderful work of forgiveness offered at the cross! Love came down, and love conquered all. Because of this truth I, too, have been called, challenged, and changed. Indeed, You promise and charge all Your people by saying: *But you are a chosen race, a royal priesthood, a holy nation, a people for God's own possession, that you may proclaim the excellencies of Him who has called you out of darkness into His marvelous light.*

Exodus 3:3; Psalms 111:2-4; 118:22-23; 1 Peter 2:9

Overwhelming

Then I said, "Woe is me, for I am ruined! Because I am a man of unclean lips, and I live among a people of unclean lips; for my eyes have seen the King, the LORD of hosts."

ISAIAH 6:5

O God, You are Overwhelming. *The voice of the Lord is upon the waters; the God of glory thunders, the Lord is over many waters. The voice of the Lord is powerful, the voice of the Lord is majestic. The voice of the Lord breaks the cedars; yes, the Lord breaks in pieces the cedars of Lebanon. And He makes Lebanon skip like the calf, and Sirion like a young wild ox. The voice of the Lord hews out flames of fire. The voice of the Lord shakes the wilderness; the Lord shakes the wilderness of Kadesh. The voice of the Lord makes the deer to calve, and strips the forests bare, and in His temple everything says, "Glory!"* Yes, dear Lord, *the heavens are telling of Your glory; and their expanse is declaring the work of Your hands. Day to day pours forth speech, and night to night reveals knowledge.* Awesome God, Your power and Your majesty overwhelm my heart and mind! But, at the same time, so does Your kind intention toward each one of us. I feel much like Peter and his friends when You, dear Jesus, stepped into their empty, fishless boat and said, *"Put out into the deep water and let down your nets for a catch."… And when they had done this, they enclosed a great quantity of fish; and their nets began to break and they signaled to their partners in the other boat, for them to come and help them. And they came, and filled both of the boats, so that they began to sink. But when Simon Peter saw that, he fell down at Jesus' feet, saying, "Depart from me, for I am a sinful man, O Lord!" For amazement had seized him and all his companions because of the catch of fish which they had taken.* Almighty One, thank you for also "stepping into my boat" with Your commanding care. Indeed, I am Overwhelmed by both Your vast power and Your personal presence.

Psalms 29:3-9; 19:1-2; Luke 5:4,6-9

My Trust

How blessed is the man who has made the LORD his trust, and has not turned to the proud, nor to those who lapse into falsehood.

PSALM 40:4

O God, You are my Trust. I can glean from these faith walkers of old: *Esther trusted in You as she approached the king's throne without invitation. … Daniel trusted in You as he went against King Darius' arrogant decree. … Hosea trusted in You when You gave him a questionable command.* Dear Lord, their trust in You was steadfast, resolved, and unwavering, even when the circumstances around them, as well as the outcome, were uncertain. Again I observe: *Joseph trusted in You as he unjustly sat in the prison cell. … David trusted in You as he hid in a cave from King Saul. … Stephen trusted in You as he was stoned to death by the rioting Jews.* O God, these men and women of faith convict my heart. I want my faith in You to resemble their faith in You! May I be able to say with absolute certainty, *When I am afraid, I will put my trust in You. In God, whose word I praise, in God I have put my trust; I shall not be afraid. What can mere man do to me? … For a day in Your courts is better than a thousand outside. I would rather stand at the threshold of the house of my God, than dwell in the tents of wickedness. For the Lord God is a sun and shield; the Lord gives grace and glory; no good thing does He withhold from those who walk uprightly. O Lord of hosts, how blessed is the man who trusts in You.* Indeed, because of Your great name, I will be steadfast, resolved, and unwavering.

Esther 4:16–5:1-2; Daniel 6:6-10; Hosea 1:2; Genesis 39:20; 1 Samuel 22:1; Acts 7:58-60; Psalms 56:3-4; 84:10-12

Generous

But if any of you lacks wisdom, let him ask of God, who gives to all generously and without reproach, and it will be given to him.

JAMES 1:5

O God, You are Generous. You are generous with Your time: You sit with me in the morning; You walk with me in the day; and You watch over me at night. You say to my heart, *I am with you always, even to the end of the age.* Also dear Lord, You are generous with Your touch: You reach out *and pull me from my pit;* You steady me by *holding my hand;* and You protect me *under Your wings.* And then, Heavenly Father, You are generous with Your treasure: You have given me a heartbeat; You have given me air to breathe; You have given me a life to live. Furthermore, You have given me *Your only begotten Son;* You have given me *Your invading Spirit;* and You have given me *Your inheritance* forever. So often, dear Lord, my finite, narrow mind forgets Your infinite, generous ways. The worries and woes of this world taint the truth of Your character. Please forgive my grumbling spirit and renew my perspective once again. Yes, Generous God, I want to daily live a life of gratitude. Therefore, please receive my praise offering: "I thank You for Your extended time; I thank You for Your redeeming touch; and I thank You for Your endless treasure."

Matthew 28:20; Psalm 40:2; Isaiah 41:10; Psalm 91:4; John 3:16; Ephesians 1:13; Colossians 1:12

Everywhere

"Can a man hide himself in hiding places, so I do not see him?" declares the LORD. "Do I not fill the heavens and the earth?" declares the LORD.

JEREMIAH 23:24

O God, You are Everywhere. You transcend time. You were there in the beginning, and You are here right now. *You are the same yesterday, today, and forever.* Also, You transcend space. *Where can I go from Your Spirit?* There is no place in the heavens or on this earth that is void of Your presence. *You have entered into the springs of the sea and have walked in the recesses of the deep. . . . You know the way to the dwelling of light, and darkness, where its place is.* How amazing and reassuring: You can be in all places at the same time. Indeed, God of the universe, You are everywhere! To think, You can be intricately involved with operating the galaxies, as well as intimately involved with each one of us, no matter where we are, north, south, east, or west. *For in You, we live and move and exist.* And You ask each of our hearts, *Am I a God who is near and not a God far off?* The answer to this rhetorical question is a resounding, "Yes, *Immanuel,* You are near!" So I praise You, Heavenly Father, that You are in every place; and I thank You, sweet Savior, that You are right here with me.

Hebrews 13:8; Psalm 139:7; Job 38:16,19; Acts 17:28;
Jeremiah 23:23; Matthew 1:23

Esteemed

But the LORD, who brought you up from the land of Egypt with great power and with an outstretched arm, Him you shall fear, and to Him you shall bow yourselves down, and to Him you shall sacrifice.

2 KINGS 17:36

O God, You are Esteemed. You declare, *"For from the rising of the sun, even to its setting, My name will be great among the nations, and in every place incense is going to be offered to My name, and a grain offering that is pure; for My name will be great among the nations,"* says the Lord of hosts. ... *There is none like You; You are great, and great is Your name in might. Who would not fear You, O King of the nations? Indeed it is Your due! For among all the wise men of the nations, and in all their kingdoms, there is none like You.* Sovereign Lord, someday all kings and kingdoms will humbly bend their knee and esteem You as the Almighty One. You are powerful and holy and majestic. You are beautiful and grand and perfect. You are radiant and mighty and pure. Indeed, You are the One I will worship now. You are the One I will praise today: Yes, I will lift Your name on high: *I will extol You, my God, O King; and I will bless Your name forever and ever. Every day I will bless You, and I will praise Your name forever and ever. Great is the Lord, and highly to be praised. And His greatness is unsearchable. One generation shall praise Your works to another, and shall declare Your mighty acts.* Most certainly, *with my mouth I will give thanks abundantly to the Lord; and in the midst of many I will praise Him.* For You are highly Esteemed.

Malachi 1:11; Jeremiah 10:6-7; Psalms 145:1-4; 109:30

One Who Revives

You who seek God, let your heart revive.

PSALM 69:32

O God, You are the One Who Revives. *As the deer pants for the water brooks, so my soul pants for You. My soul thirsts for God, for the living God; when shall I come and appear before God?* Yes, Lord, I need You. *For the sake of Your name, O Lord, revive me. In Your righteousness bring my soul out of trouble.* Only You can bring me peace. Only You can bring me strength. Only You can bring me joy. I will cling to Your promise that says: *I will allure her, bring her into the wilderness, and speak kindly to her. Then I will give her vineyards from there, and the valley of Achor as a door of hope.* Dear Lord, how I need Your kind words right now. Please give me ears to hear. Please give me a heart to receive. Please, O God, I earnestly pray, *Drip down, O heavens, from above, and let the clouds pour down righteousness; let the earth open up and salvation bear fruit, and righteousness spring up with it.* Yes, as I seek You, I will wait for You to come in righteousness and in hope. For You promise, *I will open rivers on the bare heights, and springs in the midst of the valleys; I will make the wilderness a pool of water, and the dry land fountains of water.* I am confident that You will come. Yes, You, O God, *who has shown me many troubles and distresses, will revive me again, and will bring me up again from the depths of the earth. May You increase my greatness, and turn to comfort me.*

Psalms 42:1; 143:11; Hosea 2:14-15; Isaiah 45:8; 41:18; Psalm 71:20-21

My Sanctuary

Cry aloud and shout for joy, O inhabitant of Zion, for great in your midst is the Holy One of Israel.

ISAIAH 12:6

O God, You are my Sanctuary. *Give ear to my prayer, O God; and do not hide Yourself from my supplication. Give heed to me, and answer me; I am restless in my complaint and am surely distracted. … I said, "Oh, that I had wings like a dove! I would fly away and be at rest. Behold, I would wander far away, I would lodge in the wilderness. I would hasten to my place of refuge from the stormy wind and tempest."* And then, I recall this to mind, *How lovely are Your dwelling places, O Lord of hosts! My soul longed and even yearned for the courts of the Lord; my heart and my flesh sing for joy to the living God. The bird also has found a house, and the swallow a nest for herself, where she may lay her young, even Your altars, O Lord of hosts, my King and my God. How blessed are those who dwell in Your house! They are ever praising You.* Yes, O Lord, You are my resting place, my rejoicing place. *For a day in Your courts is better than a thousand outside.* Therefore, I will proclaim this truth with a whole heart: *One thing I have asked from the Lord, that I shall seek: that I may dwell in the house of the Lord all the days of my life, to behold the beauty of the Lord, and to meditate in His temple. For in the day of trouble He will conceal me in His tabernacle; in the secret place of His tent He will hide me. He will lift me up on a rock.* Indeed, O God, You are my resting place, You are my rejoicing place, You are my Sanctuary.

Psalms 55:1-2,6-8; 84:1-4,10; 27:4-5

Splendid

I remember the days of old; I meditate on all Your doings; I muse on the work of Your hands.

PSALM 143:5

O God, You are Splendid. *Bless the Lord, O my soul! O Lord my God, You are very great; You are clothed with splendor and majesty, covering Yourself with light as a cloak, stretching out heaven like a tent curtain. You lay the beam of Your upper chambers in the waters; You make the clouds Your chariot; You walk upon the wings of the wind; Your make the winds Your messengers, flaming fire Your ministers. ... I saw the Lord sitting on a throne, lofty and exalted, with the train of His robe filling the temple. Seraphim stood above Him each having six wings; with two he covered his face, and with two he covered his feet, and with two he flew. And one called out to another and said, "Holy, Holy, Holy, is the Lord of hosts, the whole earth is full of His glory."* Awesome God, *You reign, You are clothed with majesty; You have clothed and girded Yourself with strength; indeed, the world is firmly established, it will not be moved. Your throne is established from of old; You are from everlasting. ... Let the glory of the Lord endure forever; let the Lord be glad in His works; He looks at the earth and it trembles; He touches the mountains, and they smoke. I will sing to the Lord as long as I live; I will sing praise to my God while I have my being. Let my meditation be pleasing to Him; as for me, I shall be glad in the Lord.* What more can I add to Your word, O God? Most certainly, Almighty One, You are more than Splendid!

Psalm 104:1-4; Isaiah 6:1-3; Psalms 93:1-2; 104:31-34

God of the Morning

The Lord GOD has given Me the tongue of disciples, that I may know how to sustain the weary one with a word. He awakens me morning by morning, He awakens my ear to listen as a disciple.

ISAIAH 50:4

O God, You are God of the Morning. Yes, dear Lord, wake me up to You, O God, wake me up to You. I do not want to start my day without You. *Let me hear Your lovingkindness in the morning; for I trust in You. Teach me the way in which I should walk; for to You I lift up my soul.* For You are the One who whispers in my ear as I turn the pages of Your holy book. I know and believe that *Your word is a lamp unto my feet and light unto my path.* I do not want to take one step without You from the beginning of this day to the end. Therefore, please give me a determined mindset to not miss You in the morning moments! Help me to realize that rest for my soul is just as important, and more so, than sleep for my body. For You are the One who gives me strength. Make me determined to rise up, dear God. Yes, I will claim these words of truth: *My heart is steadfast, O God, my heart is steadfast; I will sing, yes, I will sing praises! Awake, my glory; awake, harp and lyre, I will awaken the dawn! I will give thanks to You, O Lord, among the peoples; I will sing praises to You among the nations. For Your lovingkindness is great to the heavens, and Your truth to the clouds. Be exalted above the heavens, O God; let Your glory be above all the earth.* Ah, yes, I recognize this: when I sit with You in the morning, my perspective of the day changes. No longer are my problems too big, and no longer are You too small. Indeed, *in the morning, O Lord, You will hear my voice; in the morning I will order my prayer to You and eagerly watch.* Thank You; I can now rise up with hope and joy and peace.

Psalms 143:8; 119:105; 57:7-11; 5:3

God of the Daytime

This is the day which the LORD has made; let us rejoice and be glad in it.
PSALM 118:24

O God, You are God of the Daytime. Please Lord Jesus, I ask You to *make Your face shine upon Your servant, and teach me Your statutes.* Yes, dear Lord, *establish my footsteps in Your word, and do not let any iniquity have dominion over me.* I want this day to be Your day, with You living both in and through me. I ask that I would recall to mind the things I have learned in Your word and then have the courage to live them out. *Lead me in Your truth and teach me, for You are the God of my salvation.* And Holy Spirit, I ask You to speak to me all day long. Yes, I want to *walk by the Spirit so that I do not carry out the deeds of the flesh.* I ask You to fill me with Your love so that I can give it away to those who cross my path. Indeed, I want to operate from Your wellspring that overflows, not from my own vessel that is so inadequate. So today, from dawn to dusk, *O Lord, I will seek Your face.* I will *trust in You with all my heart, and I will not lean on my own understanding. In all my ways I will acknowledge You, and You will make my paths straight.* Yes, God of the Daytime, please be Master over my every waking moment.

Psalms 119:135,133; 25:5; Galatians 5:16; Psalm 27:8; Proverbs 3:5-6

God of the Night

My eyes anticipate the night watches, that I may meditate on Your word.
PSALM 119:148

O God, You are God of the Night. *You neither slumber nor sleep. … You will protect me from all evil; You will keep my soul.* Therefore, I will *meditate in my heart upon my bed, and I will be still. I will offer the sacrifices of righteousness, and I will trust in You.* Yes, Lord, help me to *take every thought captive* so that I might dwell on things that are pleasing to You. As yet another day comes to a close, remind me of Your words of direction and truth as I rest my weary head: *Be anxious for nothing, but in everything by prayer and supplication with thanksgiving let your requests be made known to Me. And My peace, which surpasses all comprehension, shall guard your hearts and your minds. … Whatever is true, whatever is honorable, whatever is right, whatever is pure, whatever is lovely, whatever is of good repute, if there is any excellence and if anything worthy of praise, let your mind dwell on these things.* Yes, Lord, I will dwell on You and Your wonders. Again You promise, *The steadfast of mind I will keep in perfect peace, because he trusts in Me.* As I learn to completely rest in You, I will breathe in, and I will breathe out, and I will let go. And *Your song will be with me in the night, a prayer to the God of my life.*

Psalms 121:4,7; 4:4-5; 2 Corinthians 10:5; Philippians 4:6-8; Isaiah 26:3; Psalm 42:8

God of the Needy

For He stands at the right hand of the needy, to save him from those who judge his soul.
PSALM 109:31

O God, You are God of the Needy. Dear Jesus, You entered the world of the afflicted and responded with hope. You *healed the blind beggar Bartimeaus. ... You healed the woman suffering from years of bleeding. ... You healed the paralytic who was let down through the roof.* Just as You touched these in their physical affliction, You will also touch my troubled soul. Most certainly, *my soul weeps because of grief; strengthen me according to Your word. ... Incline Your ear, O Lord, and answer me; for I am afflicted and needy.* Yes, Lord, I am calling out to You from a desperate place. I ask for hope; I ask for peace; I ask for wisdom; I ask for strength. I ask for a strong faith like these people of old. For You delight to work powerfully on behalf of those who believe in You. So touch me with Your healing hand, I pray. Through this hardship, I will claim Your promise and cling to its truth: *For He will deliver the needy when he cries for help, the afflicted also, and him who has no helper. He will have compassion on the poor and needy, and the lives of the needy he will save.* I thank You, my Savior, for coming to me Yourself.

Mark 10:46-52; 5:25-34; 2:3-12; Psalms 119:28; 86:1; 72:12-13

Lord of the Sabbath

Jesus said to them, "The Sabbath was made for man, and not man for the Sabbath. So the Son of Man is Lord even of the Sabbath."

MARK 2:27–28

O God, You are Lord of the Sabbath. After *the heavens and the earth were completed, and all their hosts ... You rested on the seventh day.* Almighty One, You have given me an example to follow. You know that rest is for my own good concerning my mind, body, and soul. I love Your promise: *If because of the Sabbath, you turn your foot from doing your own pleasure on My holy day, and call the Sabbath a delight, the holy day of the Lord honorable, and shall honor it, desisting from your own ways, from seeking your own pleasure, and speaking your own word, then you will take delight in the Lord, and I will make you ride on the heights of the earth; and I will feed you with the heritage of Jacob your father, for the mouth of the Lord has spoken.* Dear Lord, help me to take Your command to heart. Again, rest is a necessary thing that You have designed for my benefit. Rest draws me back to You. Yes, Your word says: *Those who wait for the Lord will gain new strength; they will mount up with wings like the eagles.* So dear Lord, I pray that I will regard Your command to *remember the Sabbath day and keep it holy;* for it is bountiful blessing to me, not a burdensome boundary. Yes, I will remember these words: *There remains therefore a Sabbath rest for the people of God. For the one who has entered His rest has himself also rested from his works, as God did from His. Let us therefore be diligent to enter that rest.* Yes, Lord, I must choose to set aside time to rest in You. For You are Lord of the Sabbath.

Genesis 2:1-2; Isaiah 58:13-14; 40:31; Exodus 20:8; Hebrews 4:9-11

God of Clarity

Then He opened their minds to understand the Scriptures.

LUKE 24:45

O God, You are the God of Clarity. I love this picture of old after Nehemiah read Your word to the Israelites: *And all the people went away to eat, to drink, to send portions and to celebrate a great festival, because they understood the words which had been made known to them.* And dear Jesus, I also love this story concerning You and Your disciples: *Two of them were going that very day to a village named Emmaus, which was about seven miles from Jerusalem. And they were conversing with each other about all these things which had taken place. And it came about that while they were conversing and discussing, Jesus Himself approached, and began traveling with them. But their eyes were prevented from recognizing Him. ... And He said to them, "Was it not necessary for the Christ to suffer these things and to enter into His glory?" And beginning with Moses and with all the prophets, He explained to them the things concerning Himself in all the Scriptures ... And their eyes were opened and they recognized Him. ... And they said, "Were not our hearts burning within us while He was speaking to us on the road, while He was explaining the Scriptures to us?"* God, I too, am Your disciple, so I ask for this same kind of experience today! As I consider the truths found in Your word, I pray that I will walk with You, and listen to You, and talk with You; I pray that I will ask You questions, and meditate on Your answers. And then, I pray that You will bless me with clarity and wisdom and discernment. Make my heart also burn within me as I discover new and life-altering revelations. Yes, God of Clarity, please *give me understanding that I may learn Your commandments.* And then may I say with gladness, *I have inherited Your testimonies forever, for they are the joy of my heart.*

Nehemiah 8:12; Luke 24:13-16,26-27,31-32; Psalm 119:73,111

God of Growth

You therefore, beloved, knowing this beforehand, be on your guard so that you are not being carried away by the error of unprincipled men and fall from your own steadfast-ness, but grow in the grace and knowledge of our Lord and Savior Jesus Christ.

2 Peter 3:17–18

O God, You are the God of Growth. *How blessed is the man that does not walk in the counsel of the wicked, nor stand in the path of sinners, nor sit in the seat of scoffers! But his delight is in the law of the Lord, and in His law he meditates day and night. And he will be like a tree firmly planted by streams of water, which yields its fruit in its season, and its leaf does not wither; and in whatever he does, he prospers.* Remind me, dear Lord, that my growth is directly related to my heart's meditation and response to Your word. Just like a plant wilts and dries up without water, so will my soul without the *washing of water with the word.* So through the working of Your Spirit in me, I ask that Your holy Scriptures become my maturing lifeline. I want to *grow up in all aspects into You,* dear Jesus. And Lord, help me to not simply read Your word, but by Your strength, give me the ability to obey it; because obedience is where growth takes place. For You promise: *But one who looks intently at the perfect law, the law of liberty, and abides by it, not having become a forgetful hearer but an effectual doer, this man shall be blessed in what he does.* Yes, God of Growth, pour Your living word over me, in me, and through me. It's time for me to grow up.

Psalm 1:1-3; Ephesians 5:26; 4:15; James 1:25

One Who Renews

Create in me a clean heart, O God, and renew a steadfast spirit within me.
PSALM 51:10

O God, You are the One Who Renews. Yes, O Lord, *Your lovingkindnesses indeed never cease, for Your compassions never fail; they are new every morning; great is Your faithfulness.* When I think I have nothing left, You come. Over and over again, I have cried out to You in times of fear and dismay. *I called on Your name, O Lord, out of the lowest pit. You have heard my voice, "Do not hide Your ear from my prayer for relief, from my cry for help." O Lord, You pleaded my soul's cause; You have redeemed my life.* Thank You for coming to my aid one more time. Yes, *You saved me, not on the basis of deeds which I have done in righteousness, but according to Your mercy, by the washing of regeneration and renewing by the Holy Spirit, whom You poured out upon me richly through Jesus Christ my Savior.* Again thank You, Faithful One, for breathing Your mighty power into my soul. I am back on my feet, standing steady in Your strength. And once again, I am a living testimony to Your promise: *Those who wait for the Lord will gain new strength; they will mount up with wings like eagles, they will run and not get tired, they will walk and not become weary.* O how I love the One Who Renews my spirit!

Lamentations 3:22-23,55-58; Titus 3:5-6; Isaiah 40:31

One Who Lifts My Head

For in the day of trouble He will conceal me in His tabernacle; in the secret place of His tent He will hide me; He will lift me up on a rock. And now my head will be lifted up above my enemies around me, and I will offer in His tent sacrifices with shouts of joy; I will sing, yes, I will sing praises to the LORD.

PSALM 27:5–6

O God, You are the One Who Lifts my Head. Dear Lord, I am surrounded by my enemies! Fear grips me; dismay engulfs me; dread steals my breath. I don't know if I'm going to make it through this day, this hour, this moment. Please, *be gracious to me, O Lord; behold my affliction from those who hate me, You who lifts me up from the gates of death.* Indeed, I am oppressed; I am exhausted; I am overwhelmed. *O Lord, how my adversaries have increased! Many are rising up against me. Many are saying of my soul, "There is no deliverance for him in God." But You, O Lord, are a shield about me, my glory, and the One who lifts my head. I was crying to the Lord with my voice, and He answered me from His holy mountain. I lay down and slept; I awoke, for the Lord sustains me.* O God, You are present, You are faithful, You are real. I can rest, I can trust, I can breathe once again. O Lord, I will continue to cry out to You through this ongoing trial. I will not stop grasping for You as I face the unknown; for You are my only hope. I know You will see me through—day and night, and night and day, and day and night, and night and day—*The Lord has heard my supplication, the Lord receives my prayer. All my enemies will be ashamed and greatly dismayed; they will turn back, they will suddenly be ashamed.* Indeed, when I am bent to despair and my heart is broken, You, sweet Savior, will always be the One Who Lifts my Head.

Psalms 9:13; 3:1-5; 6:9-10

One Who Speaks

For He spoke, and it was done; He commanded, and it stood fast.
PSALM 33:9

O God, You are the One Who Speaks. *You said, "Let there be light"; and there was light. ... And You said, "Let there be an expanse in the midst of the waters"* and it happened. And *You said, "Let dry land appear"; and it was so.* And the creation story unfolds. Yes, by Your powerful words, O God, You *created the heavens and the earth. ... Praise Him, highest heavens, and the waters that are above the heavens! Let them praise the name of the Lord, for He commanded and they were created. He has also established them forever and ever; He has made a decree which will not pass away. Praise the Lord from the earth, sea monsters and all deeps; fire and hail, snow and clouds; stormy wind, fulfilling His word.* Awesome God, Your powerful voice overwhelms me! Your majestic voice humbles me. To think, You also speak to Your people! You can choose to speak in a tumultuous *whirlwind*, but You can also speak in a *gentle blowing.* In whatever from or fashion, Your words are delivered with fortified strength. So let my ears hear Your promises that are spoken through a voice filled with determined love. Yes, Awesome God, in the same way in which You spoke the stars into the universe, impress these unwavering words of Yours, and many more like them, deep within my heart: *"For the mountains may be removed and the hills may shake, but My lovingkindness will not be removed from you, and My covenant of peace will not be shaken," says the Lord who has compassion on you.* Ah, Your resounding voice has penetrated, and I will embrace Your truth with joy!

Genesis 1:3,6,9,11,1; Psalm 148:4-8; Job 38:1; 1 Kings 19:12; Isaiah 54:10

One Who Gives Hearing

For the time will come when they will not endure sound doctrine; but wanting to have their ears tickled, they will accumulate for themselves teachers in accordance to their own desires; and will turn away their ears from the truth and will turn aside to myths.

2 TIMOTHY 4:3–4

O God, You are the One Who Gives Hearing. Dear Jesus, when You walked the earth things like this happened: *And they brought to Him one who was deaf and spoke with difficulty, and they entreated Him to lay His hand upon him. And He took him aside from the multitude by himself, and put His fingers into his ears, and after spitting, He touched his tongue with the saliva; and looking up to heaven with a deep sigh, He said to him, "Ephphatha!" that is, "Be opened!" And his ears were opened, and the impediment of his tongue was removed, and he began speaking plainly. ... And they were utterly astonished, saying, "He has done all things well; He makes even the deaf to hear, and the dumb to speak."* Jesus, You are the Miracle Worker! I praise You for Your wonderful acts of mercy. I ask for yet one more miracle today. Please, Convicting One, open the ears of my unbelieving friends. Please do amazing things with Your holy touch of grace. Let them hear Your truth with absolute clarity; and then, let it sear deep into their hearts, transforming them forever. Remove all abstract clamor so they can hear You. You say in earnest, *Behold, I stand at the door and knock; if anyone hears My voice and opens the door, I will come in to him, and dine with him, and he with Me.* Will You work one more wonder today, I pray? Open their ears so they can hear Your persistent knocking and Your gracious calling. Yes, Lord, this is my heart's desire. I want the ones I love to hear You, and respond to You, and dine with You. Your voice is beautifully alluring: *Listen carefully to Me, and eat what is good, and delight yourself in abundance. Incline your ear and come to Me. Listen, that you may live.* Indeed, Miracle Worker, You have the words of Life. Please give them ears to hear.

Mark 7:32-35,37; Revelation 3:20; Isaiah 55:2-3

God Who Gives Sight

For with You is the fountain of life; in Your light we see light.
PSALM 36:9

O God, You are the One Who Gives Sight. Dear Jesus, when You walked the earth things this like this happened: *And as He was going out from Jericho with His disciples and a great multitude, a blind beggar named Bartimaeus, the son of Timaeus, was sitting by the road. And when he heard that it was Jesus the Nazarene, he began to cry out and say, "Jesus, Son of David, have mercy on me!" ... And answering him, Jesus said, "What do you want Me to do for you?" And the blind man said to Him, "Rabboni, I want to regain my sight!" And Jesus said to him. "Go your way; your faith has made you well." And immediately he regained his sight and began following Him on the road.* Jesus, You are the Miracle Worker! I praise You for Your healing touch. Gracious One, I ask for yet one more miracle today. Will You please touch the eyes of my unbelieving friends? Allow Your truth to become crystal clear, and awaken them to Your radiant glory. Make the glitter of this world lose its sparkle, and the glamour to lose its appeal. Yes, *I pray that the eyes of their heart may be enlightened, so that they may know what is the hope of Your calling, what are the riches of the glory of Your inheritance in the saints, and what is the surpassing greatness of Your power to those who believe.* Will You work one more wonder today? For this is my heart's desire. I want those I love, who don't know You, to see You through new eyes of faith, and to embrace You as their lifelong Savior, and then to live with You forever. Yes, Giver of Sight, touch their eyes so they will miraculously proclaim, *I was blind, but now I see!*

Mark 10:46-47,51-52; Ephesians 1:18-19; John 9:25

One Who Heals the Lame

With a leap, he stood upright and began to walk; and he entered the temple with them, walking and leaping and praising God.

ACTS 3:8

O God, You are the One Who Heals the Lame. Dear Jesus, when You walked the earth, things like this happened: *And they came, bringing to Him a paralytic, carried by four men. And being unable to get to Him because of the crowd, they removed the roof above Him; and when they had dug an opening, they let down the pallet on which the paralytic was lying. And Jesus seeing their faith said to the paralytic, "My son, your sins are forgiven."* And to the questioning Jews, He said, *"Which is easier to say to the paralytic, 'Your sins are forgiven': or to say, 'Arise, and take up your pallet and walk'? But in order that you may know that the Son of Man has authority on earth to forgive sins"*—He said to the paralytic—*"I say to you, rise, take up your pallet and go home." And he rose and immediately took up the pallet and went out in the sight of all; so that they were all amazed and were glorifying God, saying, "We have never seen anything like this."* Jesus, You indeed are the Miracle Worker. You can make a lame man walk! I praise You for Your wonderful works. Healing One, I ask for yet one more miracle today. Will you touch the hearts of my friends who don't know You? They are wandering through this world, crippled by this culture, and they don't even know it. Show them a different way; show them Your way that is abundant and rich and full. *Bring them up out of the pit of destruction, out of the miry clay; set their feet upon a rock and make their footsteps firm.* Will You work one more wonder today? Yes, dear Lord, this is my heart's desire. I want them to take Your hand, and I want them to be lifted up, and I want them to dance with You for the rest of their days. May the ones I love proclaim from a faith-filled heart, *I will exult in the Lord, I will rejoice in the God of my salvation. The Lord God is my strength, and He has made my feet like hinds' feet, and makes me walk on my high places.*

Mark 2:3-5,9-12; Psalm 40:2; Habakkuk 3:18-19

One Who Loosens Tongues

And He was casting out a demon, and it was mute; when the demon had gone out, the mute man spoke; and the crowds were amazed.

LUKE 11:14

O God, You are the One Who Loosens Tongues. Dear Jesus, while You walked the earth things like this happened: *And He was going about in all Galilee, teaching in the their synagogues, and proclaiming the gospel of the kingdom, and healing every kind of disease and every kind of sickness among the people. And the news about Him went out into all Syria; and they brought to Him all who were ill, taken with various diseases and pains, demoniacs, epileptics, paralytics; and He healed them.* Indeed, Jesus, You are the Miracle Worker. I love Your compassionate touch. O God, I ask You for one more miracle today. Would You please loosen my tongue so that I can give praise to Your name? Yes, I want to accurately and boldly tell the world of Your good news. Is it true that I can *speak the very utterances of God?* And is it true that *I am Your ambassador for Christ, as though You are entreating through me?* O dear Lord, help me not to take this calling lightly. Instead, as Paul asked, so do I: *that utterance may be given to me in the opening of my mouth, to make known with boldness the mystery of the gospel;* and also, *that I would make it clear in the way I ought to speak.* So Mighty One, will You do one more miracle today? I can identify with Isaiah who humbly cried in Your majestic presence, *I am a man of unclean lips, and I live among a people of unclean lips.* But this is my heart's desire—that You would touch my mouth with Your holiness, and that You would instill in my voice a boldness; and that I would become Your faithful messenger. Yes, I want to shout to the world with truth and joy, *O give thanks to the Lord, for He is good; for His lovingkindness is everlasting.*

Matthew 4:23-24; 1 Peter 4:11; 2 Corinthians 5:20; Ephesians 6:19; Colossians 4:4; Isaiah 6:5; 1 Chronicles 16:34

My Master

Masters, grant to your slaves justice and fairness, knowing that you too have a Master in heaven.

COLOSSIANS 4:1

O God, You are my Master. You teach us with warning, *No one can serve two masters; for either he will hate the one and love the other, or he will hold to one and despise the other. You cannot serve God and wealth.* O God, how I want my heart to belong completely to You—nothing else, no one else. Yes, I want to proclaim this truth honestly: *Your lovingkindness is before my eyes and I have walked in Your truth. I do not sit with deceitful men, nor will I go with pretenders. I hate the assembly of evildoers, and I will not sit with the wicked. I shall wash my hands in innocence, and I will go about Your altar, O Lord, that I may proclaim with the voice of thanksgiving, and declare all Your wonders.* Yes, Lord, my deep longing is to hear Your voice and obey it, not out of duty, but out of delight. For Your ways are altogether righteous and good. Again, may I be able to truthfully say, *With all my heart I have sought You; do not let me wander from Your commandments. Your word I have treasured in my heart, that I may not sin against You.* Indeed, Master Jesus, I will bend my knee to You, and I will listen to Your voice, and I will walk obediently; for I am Your willing *bond-servant, ... set apart for the sake of the gospel.* And as I live out my days with You in command, I will keep attentive to Your kind and rewarding whisper, *Well done, good and faithful servant; you were faithful with a few things, I will put you in charge of many things; enter into the joy of your Master.*

Matthew 6:24; Psalms 26:3-7; 119:10-11; Romans 1:1; Matthew 25:23

Door

You shall make a window for the ark...and set the door...in the side of it...So they went into the ark to Noah, by twos of all flesh in which was the breath of life. Those that entered, male and female of all flesh, entered as God had commanded him; and the LORD closed it behind him.

GENESIS 6:16; 7:15–16

O God, You are the Door. Yes, Jesus, Your words are so clear: *Truly, truly, I say to you, I am the door of the sheep. All who came before Me are thieves and robbers, but the sheep did not hear them. I am the door; if anyone enters through Me, he shall be saved, and shall go in and out, and find pasture. The thief comes only to steal, and kill, and destroy; I came that they might have life, and might have it abundantly.* Dear Lord, I want to hear and follow Your voice and live life in abundance! I don't want to be out-side of Your care or misled by the enemy. But I must choose, by faith, to enter into Your plentiful provision through Your specified way, not only for my salvation, but also for my safety and sanctification. Jesus, You said to Your disciples long ago, *I am the way, and the truth, and the life; no one comes to the Father but through Me.* Indeed, only You Jesus, can bring true hope, peace, joy, and forgiveness. And only through faith in You can we receive these things. Yes, *through You we have our access in one Spirit to the Father. ... So we are no longer strangers and aliens, but we are fellow citizens with the saints, and are of God's household.* Dear Jesus, thank You for providing the way! Thank You for being the Door that has swung open wide to me so that I may enter in! I will rejoice over this promise as I walk across Your threshold: *But as many as received Him to them He gave the right to become children of God, even to those who believe in His name.* Ah, through the Door, I have found kindness, I have found beauty, I have found protection, I have found *green pastures,* I have found *quiet waters.*

John 10:7-10; 14:6; Ephesians 2:18-19; John 1:12; Psalm 23:2

Amen

For as many as are the promises of God, in Him they are yes; therefore also through Him is our Amen to the glory of God through us.

2 CORINTHIANS 1:20

O God, You are the Amen. *Forever, O Lord, Your word is settled in heaven.* Indeed, Jesus, You are the Absolute Yes; You are the "let it be so"; You are the Final Word. If You say it, You mean it. If You promise it, You keep it. If You command it, it will come to pass. So if You say, *I am with you always, even to the end of the age,* then that's Your absolute yes. And if You say, *Peace I leave with you, my peace I give to you; not as the world gives, do I give to you,* then this is Your "let it be so." And if You say, *I will come again, and receive you to Myself; that where I am, there you may be also,* then this is Your final word. Therefore, from these three promises and so many more, I can conclude with certainty that Your peaceful presence is with me, both now and forever. Amen and amen! To think, Your promises are limitless! O God, from start to finish, Your word never wavers, and Your foundation never cracks. What You say happens, and nothing or no one can change it. *The sum of Your word is truth, and every one of Your righteous ordinances is everlasting.* So I will dive deep into Your promises and live with strength, freedom, and delight. Because of You, my Jesus, I have no fear. I am gracefully surrounded by Your absolute yes, Your "let it be so," and Your final word. Most certainly, Righteous One, You are *the Amen.*

Psalm 119:89; Matthew 28:20; John 14:27,3; Psalm 119:160; Revelation 3:14

My Lifeline

For to me, to live is Christ.

PHILIPPIANS 1:21

O God, You are my Lifeline. I cannot and do not want to draw one breath without You. I cannot and do not want one beat of my heart to be absent from You. *You are my strength and my song. ... You are the portion of my inheritance and my cup. ... You are my shield and the horn of my salvation, my stronghold.* You are my Comforter and my Friend. I cannot and will not live without You. Thank You for meeting my every need; thank You for hearing me when I cry; thank You for Your tender loving care; thank You for Your words of instruction. Because of Your lovingkindness, this truth has become my battle cry, *Whom have I in heaven but You? And besides You, I desire nothing on earth. My flesh and my heart may fail, but You are the strength of my heart and my portion forever. ... The nearness of God is my good; I have made the Lord God my refuge, that I may tell of all Your works.* Indeed, O God, You are my Lifeline, every breath, every heartbeat, every day and every night. Always and forever, *You are the help of my countenance and my God.*

Psalms 118:14; 16:5; 18:2; 73:25-26,28; 43:5

Mindful

You understand my thought from afar.

PSALM 139:2

O God, You are Mindful. *You know the thoughts of man, that they are a mere breath.* And *You know our frame; You are mindful that we are only dust.* Thank You God, for being patient with me. You know my limits, and You are not bothered by them. You allowed them in order to make me more dependent on You. But Lord, sometimes I get frustrated with my weaknesses and inabilities, both mentally and physically. Instead of this reaction, help me learn to rest in You. Yes, You made me a particular way for a particular purpose. Let me hear You say, *My grace is sufficient for you, for power is perfected in weakness.* Lord, You know me better than I know myself. You understand my heart, and You mercifully give me the grace to grow. Thank You for being *greater than my heart.* So when I am weak or bewildered or disappointed or exasperated, I will hear Your voice calling, *Come to Me, all who are weary and heavy-laden, and I will give you rest. Take My yoke upon you, and learn from Me, for I am gentle and humble in heart, and You shall find rest for your souls.* Yes, I will come to You. And, I will rest by bringing You all my weaknesses and woes, all my questions and concerns. *Your understanding is inscrutable. You give strength to the weary, and to the one who lacks might, You increase power.* Indeed, I will rest my body and soul in the One who is mercifully Mindful of me.

Psalms 94:11; 103:14; 2 Corinthians 12:9; 1 John 3:20;
Matthew 11:28-29; Isaiah 40:28-29

Upright One

The way of the righteous is smooth; O Upright One, make the path of the righteous level.
ISAIAH 26:7

O God, You are the Upright One. Yes, *righteousness belongs to You, O Lord, but to us open shame.* Truly, *there is none righteous, not even one; there is no one who understands, there is none who seeks for God; we all have turned aside, together we have become useless; there is none who does good, not even one.* And still, *we have not sought Your favor because we have not turned from our iniquity and have not given attention to Your truth.* Our plight seems helpless; our predicament seems hopeless. Who can save us from this wayward path? The only answer is this truth: *Thanks be to God through Jesus Christ our Lord.* Jesus Messiah, You have given me a new heart, a heart that seeks You, a heart that now longs for You. Yes, I rejoice in Your fulfilled promise: *I will give you a new heart and put a new spirit within you; I will remove the heart of stone from your flesh and give you a heart of flesh. And I will put My Spirit within you and cause you to walk in My statutes.* By Your powerful Spirit in me, I can now overcome my tendency to turn away from You. I am overwhelmed, for I have done nothing to earn Your holy touch. Because of You, I will now sing with gladness, *Good and upright is the Lord; therefore He instructs sinners in the way. He leads the humble in justice, and He teaches the humble His way. All paths of the Lord are lovingkindness and truth to those who keep His covenant and His testimonies.* Yes, Upright One, You have pulled me from a pit, You have set me on my feet, and You have caused me to walk in Your ways. And I am eternally grateful.

Daniel 9:7; Romans 3:10-12; Daniel 9:13; Romans 7:25;
Ezekiel 36:26-27; Psalm 25:8-10

One Who Works

For I proclaim the name of the LORD; Ascribe greatness to our God! The Rock! His work is perfect, for all His ways are just; a God of faithfulness and without injustice, righteous and upright is He.

DEUTERONOMY 32:3-4

O God, You are the One Who Works. You cause the sun to shine and the earth to turn. You make the waves to roll and the rivers to flow. You send down the rain, and You bring up its produce. *Shout joyfully to God, all the earth; Sing the glory of His name; make His praise glorious. Say to God, "How awesome are Your works!"* Yes, *come and see the works of God, Who is awesome in His deeds toward the sons of men. He turned the sea into dry land; they passed through the river on foot; there let us rejoice in Him! He rules by His might forever; His eyes keep watch on the nations.* Dear Lord, I thank You for sustaining all of nature as well as tending to mankind. You indeed are an awesome and mighty God, a kind and gracious God. For *You pardon all our iniquities; You heal all our diseases; You redeem our lives from the pit; You crown us with lovingkindness and compassion; You satisfy our years with good things, so that our youth is renewed like the eagle. You perform righteous deeds, and judgments for all who are oppressed.* Again, thank You. I love how You love Your people, working wonders in hearts and minds! And I will cling to this promise as You continue to faithfully mold Your glory into me: *He who began a good work in you will perfect it until the day of Christ Jesus.* One more time, thank You Faithful God, how awesome are Your Works!

Psalm 66:1-3,5-7; 103:3-6; Philippians 1:6

One Who Rebuilds

Then they will rebuild the ancient ruins, they will raise up the former devastations, and they will repair the ruined cities, the desolations of many generations.

ISAIAH 61:4

O God, You are the One Who Rebuilds. Long ago, Your temple in Jerusalem had been destroyed; however, You worked through the heart of king Cyrus of Persia who said, *The Lord, the God of heaven, has given me all the kingdoms of the earth, and He has appointed me to build Him a house in Jerusalem, which is in Judah. Whoever there is among you, all His people, may his God be with him! Let him go up to Jerusalem which is in Judah, and rebuild the house of the Lord, the God of Israel; He is the God who is in Jerusalem.* Likewise, Jerusalem's protective walls had been destroyed, but You used Nehemiah to lead the people. He said, *You see the bad situation we are in, that Jerusalem is desolate and its gates burned by fire. Come let us rebuild the wall of Jerusalem that we may no longer be a reproach.* O God, just as the temple and walls of Jerusalem were torn, so too, our hearts are broken. We have *acted very corruptly against You and have not kept the commandments, nor the statues, nor the ordinances which You commanded.* But here is the good news to those who confess their sins before You: You forgive, You restore, and You redeem. You speak these promised words both to Your city and to our hearts: *On the day that I cleanse you from all your iniquities, I will cause the cities to be inhabited, and the waste places will be rebuilt. ... Then the nations that are left round about you will know that I, the Lord, have rebuilt the ruined places and planted that which was desolate; I, the Lord, have spoken and will do it.* Yes, Lord, if You can rebuild a devastated city and its surrounding wall, You can certainly rebuild our fragmented, yet humbled hearts. Please, come Lord Jesus, do Your mighty work.

Ezra 1:2-3; Nehemiah 2:17; 1:7; Ezekiel 36:33,36

One Who Transforms

But we all, with unveiled face, beholding as in a mirror the glory of the Lord, are being transformed into the same image from glory to glory, just as from the Lord, the Spirit.

2 CORINTHIANS 3:18

O God, You are the One Who Transforms. I hear You say to my heart, *Behold, like the clay in the potter's hand, so are you in My hand.* God please make me, mold me, and move me into a vessel of Your pleasing. Keep my heart soft and workable within Your trustworthy hands. Pull out anything that is conflicting, and change anything that is distorted. I want to be a *vessel of honor, sanctified and useful to You, my Master, prepared for every good work.* I know You know what is best for me. Use every circumstance and every relationship to groom and transform me into a purer reflection of Your glory. Thank You for Your living word that reshapes my thinking. I again hear You speak to my heart, *Do not be conformed to this world, but be transformed by the renewing of your mind, that you may prove what My will is, that which is good and acceptable and perfect.* Indeed, God, Your word changes me. The more I meditate on it, the more I understand Your transforming work of grace on my behalf. *You give me a garland instead of ashes, the oil of gladness instead of mourning, the mantle of praise instead of a spirit of fainting.* Thank You! Continue Your good work in and through me. Yes, Potter of my moldable heart and *Perfecter of my faith,* I want to be more and more and more like You, so that I may say with beautiful boldness, *I have been crucified with Christ; and it is no longer I who live but Christ who lives in me; and the life which I now live in the flesh I live by faith in the Son of God, who loved me, and delivered Himself up for me.*

**Jeremiah 18:6; 2 Timothy 2:21; Romans 12:2; Isaiah 61:3;
Hebrews 12:2; Galatians 2:20**

Owner

The earth is the LORD's and all it contains, the world, and those who dwell in it.
PSALM 24:1

O God, You are the Owner. I hear You say, *For every beast of the forest is Mine, the cattle on a thousand hills. I know every bird of the mountains, and everything that moves in the field is Mine.* Indeed, *O Lord, how many are Your works! In wisdom You have made them all; the earth is full of Your possessions. There is the sea, great and broad, in which are swarms without number, animals both small and great.* All people groups belong to You as well. *For it is You who possesses all the nations.* And some day, the beautiful promise will be fulfilled that *all nations will fear Your name, and all the kings of the earth Your glory.* For You are deserving of all our praise, both far and wide, both now and forever! Come, loving Lord, take ownership of my heart and mind, my body and soul. Yes, I want to say these words with sincere conviction, *Behold, the bondslave of the Lord; be it done to me according to your word.* Invade me and involve me in Your ways, kind Master. Thank You for Your faithfulness to me as Your cherished possession. It warms my heart to hear the Owner of all things whisper to me in adoration, *You are mine.*

Psalms 50:10-11; 104:24-25; 82:8; 102:15; Luke 1:38; Isaiah 43:1

Omniscient

But You know me, O LORD; You see me; and You examine my heart's attitude toward You.

JEREMIAH 12:3

O God, You are Omniscient. You know all things and You see all things, everywhere, all the time. How is this possible? Yes, *great is our Lord, and abundant in strength; Your understanding is infinite.* Dear God, my temporal mind cannot grasp Your endless abilities. *You count the number of the stars, and You give names to all of them. ... You know when a sparrow falls. ... You know the time the mountain goats give birth, and You observe the calving of the deer. ...* Again, *Your understanding is inscrutable!* How amazing to think that You know me in this way as well! *You know when I sit down and when I rise up; You understand my thoughts from afar; You scrutinize my path and my lying down, and are intimately acquainted with all my ways. Even before there is a word on my tongue, behold, O Lord, You know it all.* Yes, Lord, *You know the secrets of my heart.* O God, here is my secret that I will shout to the world: "Your love is true, Your love is constant, Your love is unchanging!" Yes, God, Your all-encompassing love is my moment-by-moment strength. I will say one more time, "I love You, Omniscient One; for Your uninhibited ways are remarkable to me."

**Psalms 147:5,4; Matthew 10:29; Job 39:1; Isaiah 40:28;
Psalms 139:2-4; 44:21**

Servant

And Jesus stopped and called them, and said, "What do you want Me to do for you?"
MATTHEW 20:32

O God, You are the Servant. I hear Your words concerning Your Son: *Behold, My Servant, whom I uphold; My chosen one in whom My soul delights. I have put My Spirit upon Him; He will bring forth justice to the nations.* Yes, *Christ Jesus who although existed in the form of God, did not regard equality with God a thing to be grasped, but emptied Himself, taking the form of a bond-servant.* The King of kings became a bond-servant? The Lord of lords became a helper? Indeed, Jesus, You came and spoke these redeeming words to all humanity, *The Son of Man did not come to be served, but to serve, and to give His life as a ransom for many.* So Gracious One, not only did You serve Your people, but You also died for them. I will be forever awed at Your unfathomable sacrifice! Thank You. Savior, I know You have called me to be like You; this is Your heart's desire. Help me to follow Your example of serving the downtrodden, the lonely, the weary, the sick, and the weak. Impress this picture upon my heart and mind: *Jesus rose from supper ... and taking a towel, He girded Himself about. Then He poured water into the basin, and began to wash the disciples' feet.* Great King and loving Servant, show me today whom I need to serve. I want to be like You.

Isaiah 42:1; Philippians 2:6-7; Matthew 20:28; John 13:4-5

God Who Celebrates

So they ate and drank that day before the LORD with great gladness.
1 CHRONICLES 29:22

O God, You are the God Who Celebrates. In the days of old, *You appointed specific times for different feasts for the Israelite nation. Each one was full of rest, remembering, and rejoicing because of Your goodness and Your provision.* Also, You celebrated with Your people when Your temple, made by Solomon, was complete: *When all the Levitical singers came ... clothed in fine linen, with cymbals, harps, and lyres, they stood east of the altar; and with them one hundred and twenty priests blowing trumpets in unison when the trumpeters and the singers were to make themselves heard with one voice to praise and to glorify the Lord, and when they lifted up their voice accompanied by trumpets and cymbals and instruments of music, and when they praised the Lord saying, "He indeed is good for His lovingkindness is everlasting," then the house, the house of the Lord, was filled with a cloud, so that the priests could not stand to minister because of the cloud, for the glory of the Lord filled the house of God.* Yes, God, You love to celebrate with Your people! For You know, and You want us to know, that *Your joy is our strength!* So let us feast on Your goodness, and let us dance with Your delight. Let our hearts both hear You applaud and see You smile. Encourage us to rejoice in Your lovingkindness and to be glad in Your good news, because others need to hear the salvation song! For Your greatest celebration comes when one who was once lost has been found. Indeed, *there is joy in the presence of the angels of God over one sinner who repents.* O Lord of Celebration, I want to rejoice with You!

Leviticus 23: 1-44; 2 Chronicles 5:12-14; Nehemiah 8:10; Luke 15:10

Full of Glory

Be exalted above the heavens, O God; let Your glory be above all the earth.
PSALM 57:11

O God, You are Full of Glory. Long ago, Isaiah saw and heard the angels singing in Your throne room, *Holy, Holy, Holy, is the Lord of hosts, the whole earth is full of His glory.* And still, today, the angels are singing praises to You. Yes, the brilliant holiness that surrounds You is eternal and unchanging. Indeed, Your name and Your honor are timeless, in heaven and on earth. On the other hand, O God, we *all have sinned and fall short of Your glory.* Our wrongs keep us away from Your rights. Our evil is diametrically opposed to Your good. And our darkness is as dark as Your light is light. But there is good news! Scripture proclaims: *And the Word became flesh, and dwelt among us, and we have beheld His glory, glory as of the only begotten from the Father, full of grace and truth.* Yes, through Your Son, You provided a way for sinners to enter and remain in Your radiant presence. Jesus, the perfect sacrifice, paid the penalty so we may now have *the hope of glory living in our hearts.* What a marvelous mystery! So therefore, I will stand as Moses did, my fellow heir long ago, and shout to You in worship, "O God of mercy, *show me Your glory."* Yes, every day, I ask You to fill me with Your radiant presence so I can bear Your light in this dark world.

Isaiah 6:3; Romans 3:23; John 1:14; Colossians 1:27; Exodus 33:18

Passionate

"I will vindicate the holiness of My great name which has been profaned among the nations, which you have profaned in their midst. Then the nations will know that I am the LORD," declares the Lord GOD, "when I prove Myself holy among you in their sight."
EZEKIEL 36:23

O God, You are Passionate. Nothing You do is halfhearted or halfway. When You created the earth and all that is in it, You did it with eagerness and perfection. After each day, You looked with satisfaction and *saw that it was good.* Your creation, in all its beauty, sings to You. And also, You love Your children with fervor. This is evident as I see how You saved the Israelites from the Egyptians; with Your mighty power, You *swept the sea back by a strong east wind all night, and turned the sea into dry land, so the waters were divided. And the sons of Israel went through the midst of the sea on the dry land, and the waters were like a wall to them on their right hand and on their left.* Your people went through and then rejoiced. And God, I see Your passion displayed toward each of Your desperate children: *My cry for help before Him came into His ears. Then the earth shook and quaked; and the foundations of the mountains were trembling and were shaken, because He was angry. Smoke went up out of His nostrils, and fire from His mouth devoured; coals were kindled by it. He bowed the heavens also, and came down with thick darkness under His feet. And He rode upon a cherub and flew; and He sped upon the wings of the wind. ... He sent from on high, he took me; he drew me out of many waters. He delivered me from my strong enemy.* O God, thank You for passionately pursuing and rescuing Your people! Your ardent love went to the extreme of *sending Your Son to be a propitiation for our sins.* Yes, the cross is Your ultimate passion on display for all mankind to see and receive. Therefore, I will join with the chorus of both Your creation and Your children, "Thank You Passionate God, for doing nothing halfhearted or halfway!"

Genesis 1:25; Exodus 14:21-22; Psalm 18:6-10,16-17; 1 John 4:10

Approachable

Draw near to God and He will draw near to you.

JAMES 4:8

O God, You are Approachable. You lured Moses into Your presence: *When the Lord saw that he turned aside to look, God called to him from the midst of the bush, and said, "Moses, Moses!" And he said, "Here I am."* And You also called out to a young boy who was ministering in the temple: *Then the Lord came and stood and called as at other times, "Samuel! Samuel!" and Samuel said, "Speak, for Your servant is listening."* And Jesus, when You came to earth as the God-Man, You also drew individuals toward Yourself. I see Your kind intention toward the blind beggar who was crying out to You in the streets: *And Jesus stopped and said, "Call him here." And they called the blind man, saying to him, "Take courage, arise! He is calling for you." And casting aside his cloak, he jumped up and came to Jesus.* And also, I hear the compassion in Your request toward Mary when her brother Lazarus had died. With hopeful words, she was told, *The teacher is here, and is calling for you.* Jesus, Your loving presence today is now more than just momentary; it is eternal. You made it possible that we can come to You anytime, anywhere. *We have confidence to enter the holy place by Your blood, by a new and living way which You inaugurated for us through the veil, that is, Your flesh.* Yes, *the veil of the temple was torn in two*, and we can enter in! Yes, because of You, *I can now draw near to the throne of grace, that I may receive mercy and may find grace to help in time of need.* Thank You for luring me; thank You for calling me; thank You for caring for me; thank You for sacrificing Yourself on my behalf. Your Approachability is my salvation.

Exodus 3:4; 1 Samuel 3:10; Mark 10:49-50; John 11:28; Hebrews 10:19-20; Matthew 27:51; Hebrews 4:16

One Who Calms

And He got up and rebuked the wind and said to the sea, "Hush, be still."
MARK 4:39

O God, You are the One Who Calms. I confess to You right now that my thoughts and emotions are in a whirlwind. I cannot rest. I want to manage and control each and every situation and make it "right." I know this is impossible in and of my own strength, but it doesn't keep me from worrying and trying! So I come to You, and *I pour out my complaint before You and tell You all my trouble;* for You are my safe place. Thank You for Your patience as You listen; thank You for Your lovingkindness as You work. As I pour out my issues, O God, I pray that I will be attentive enough to the peace-filled words that You long to pour in. Allow me to learn from the disciples of long ago: *Jesus came and stood in their midst, and said to them, "Peace be with you." And when He had said this, He showed them both His hands and His side. The disciples therefore rejoiced when they saw the Lord. Jesus therefore said to them again, "Peace be with you; as the Father has sent Me, I also send you." And when He had said this, He breathed on them, and said to them, "Receive the Holy Spirit."* Dear Jesus, sweet Savior of mine, hallelujah! You are in my midst! Please breathe Your peace into me once again so that my troubled heart will be quieted. And then Lord, help me to focus on You, the One Who Calms, instead of my present circumstances that only stir up unproductive strife within my soul. For You promise in Your word: *You keep him in perfect peace whose mind is stayed on You, because he trusts You.* Therefore, I will *trust in You with all my heart and not lean on my own understanding*, and I will also choose to meditate on who You are: You are all-knowing, You are able, You are strong, You are good, You are sovereign, You are at work. Ah, in remembering who You are, I can rest. Yes, I can now hear You gently whisper these words of promise into my quieted soul, *Cease striving and know that I am God.* Indeed, You are the One Who Calms.

Psalm 142:2; John 20:19-22; Isaiah 26:3; Proverbs 3:5; Psalm 46:10

Patient

The Lord is not slow about His promise, as some count slowness, but is patient toward you, not wishing for any to perish but for all to come to repentance.

2 PETER 3:9

O God, You are Patient. *You know my frame.* Yes, You know my limits. You help me take one step at a time. Thank You. I have so much to learn. Your heart's desire is for me to *grow in the grace and knowledge of my Lord and Savior Jesus Christ.* Ah, grow in the grace and knowledge of Jesus. Why? Because the more I understand about Your amazing grace, the more grace I will then give; and the more knowledge I gain about Your divine character, the wiser I will live in relation to others. As a result, I will become more like You. Yes, I will then affect the world around me for Your kingdom purposes. I confess that sometimes I feel as if I am taking one step forward and two steps back in my walk with You; indeed, there are times I know I am not *walking in a manner worthy of the calling of which I have been called, with all humility and gentleness, with patience, showing forbearance to others in love.* Instead, I stumble and fall, and I am harsh and unkind. I'm sorry, dear Jesus. Forgive me once again; *seventy time seven times,* I ask You to forgive. Pick me up, and take hold of my hand so I can get back in holy step with You once more. *You are compassionate and gracious, slow to anger and abounding in lovingkindness.* Indeed, dear Lord, *Your love is patient*; and *Your patience is my salvation.*

Psalm 103:14; 2 Peter 3:18; Ephesians 4:1-2; Matthew 18:22; Psalm 103:8; 1 Corinthians 13:4; 2 Peter 3:15

Eternal Life

For God so loved the world, that He gave His only begotten Son, that whoever believes in Him should not perish, but have eternal life.

JOHN 3:16

O God, You are Eternal Life. This is another concept that my feeble mind can hardly grasp: a future home, full of a beautiful, perfect, painless life forever and ever and ever. So much of this earthly life is just the opposite. It can be ugly, full of messes and sadness and hurts. O God, thank You for *setting eternity in our hearts.* Deep down, we all know there has to be something more than what this temporal life can give. During our present and sometimes harsh circumstances, You have promised beautiful futuristic things: *Things which eye has not seen and ear has not heard, and which have not entered the heart of man, all that God has prepared for those who love Him.* Therefore, I will cling to Your promise today and hope for Your glory that is coming. You say *that You have given us eternal life, and this life is in Your Son. He who has the Son has the life; he who does not have the Son does not have the life.* And also Jesus, You tell us, *I am the way, and the truth, and the life; no man comes to the Father, but through Me.* So it is plain to see that in order to receive this eternal life with You in heaven, I must receive the One who gives it. Saving One, I hear You proclaim to each one of us with longing, *I am the resurrection and the life; he who believes in Me shall live even if he dies, and everyone who lives and believes in Me shall never die. Do you believe this?* Yes, Jesus, I believe this with all my heart, and I know I will live with You forever.

Ecclesiastes 3:11; 1 Corinthians 2:9; 1 John 5:11-12; John 14:6; 11:25-26

Supernatural

The LORD will fight for you while you keep silent.

EXODUS 14:14

O God, You are Supernatural. It is the eleventh hour, so I am asking for Your abundant grace and Your mighty power to intervene this very minute. I am pleading for something heavenly to happen in this human situation. I cling to this story of old, and ask for the same supernatural power today: *So Peter was kept in the prison, but prayer for him was being made fervently by the church to God. On the very night when Herod was about to bring him forward, Peter was sleeping between two soldiers, bound with two chains; and guards in front of the door were watching over the prison. And behold, an angel of the Lord suddenly appeared, and a light shone in the cell; and he struck Peter's side and roused him saying, "Get up quickly." And his chains fell off his hands. And the angel said to him, "Gird yourself and put on your sandals." And he did so. And he said to him, "Wrap your cloak around you and follow me." ... And when they passed through the first and second guard, they came to the iron gate that leads into the city, which opened for them by itself; and they went out along one street; and immediately the angel departed from him.* O Lord, I ask You to do this very same work today. There are so many hearts that are locked in a prison of lies and deceit. Come into their darkness and shed Your light. Awaken their souls to Your freeing truth. Cause Your wonder-working power to strike hardened hearts with Your tender mercy and Your gentle love. Remove chains of deception and addiction that bind them to this world; by Your grace, help each one of them to get dressed with *Your garments of salvation and Your robes of righteousness.* Open the gates to the one way that brings complete freedom, which is Jesus, only Jesus. O God, I ask for You to show up in this mighty way right now. I believe in You, Father, I believe in Your Son, I believe in Your Spirit. I am tired, I am weary, and I have no fight left in me. Yet because of You, I am not without hope. So I will continue my rock solid stance; and in this place, I will lift up my fervent and faith-filled *prayers to You, without ceasing.* Please do Your supernatural work in the hearts and in the lives of the ones I love. For I cling to the promise that You have come to *proclaim liberty to captives, and to set prisoners free.*

Acts 12:5-8,10; Isaiah 61:10; 1 Thessalonians 5:17; Isaiah 61:1

My Song

Miriam the prophetess, Aaron's sister, took the timbrel in her hand, and all the women went out after her with timbrels and with dancing. Miriam answered them, "Sing to the LORD, for He is highly exalted; the horse and his rider He has hurled into the sea."

EXODUS 15:20–21

O God, You are my Song. Indeed, *the Lord is my strength and my song, and He has become my salvation; this is my God, and I will praise Him; my father's God, and I will extol Him.* I once was empty, void of purpose, but then You came. *You brought me up out of the pit of destruction, out of the miry clay; You set my feet upon a rock making my footsteps firm. And You put a new song in my mouth, a song of praise to You, O God.* Therefore, I will join the chorus of old and agree with these ancient words: *Sing for joy in the Lord, O righteous ones; praise is becoming to the upright. Give thanks to the Lord with the lyre; sing praises to Him with a harp of ten strings. Sing to Him a new song; play skillfully with a shout of joy. For the word of the Lord is upright; and all His work is done in faithfulness.* I will sing of Your goodness, and I will sing of Your love. I will sing of Your presence, and I will sing of Your power. I will sing of Your comfort, and I will sing of Your grace. You are the music inside my soul; You are the rhythm that I keep. Yes, *I will go out with joy, and be led forth with peace; the mountains and the hills will break forth into shouts of joy before me, and all the trees of the field will clap their hands.* May I, and all those who call You Savior, always be about Your good news, *filled with Your Spirit … singing and making melody with our hearts to You.* For this lost world needs to hear Your salvation Song.

Exodus 15:2; Psalms 40:2-3; 33:1-4; Isaiah 55:12; Ephesians 5:18-19

My Safe Place

You have enclosed me behind and before, and laid Your hand upon me.

PSALM 139:5

O God, You are my Safe Place. *You cover me with Your pinions, and under Your wings I seek refuge; Your faithfulness is a shield and bulwark.* Yes, God, thank You for this promise in Your word: *He who dwells in the shelter of the Most High will abide in the shadow of the Almighty. I will say to You, "My refuge and my fortress, my God, in whom I trust!"* Thank You for being my Safe Place, O God. I must confess to You that all too often I wander from Your care. I then begin to hear the enemy's deceitful lies of pride or shame, confusing them for truth. And I also feel the evil one's fiery darts of pressure and worry, misinterpreting them as from You. Forgive me Lord. I will once again run to You for rest and protection, for realignment and strength. For *You are my keeper. ... You will protect me from all evil; You will keep my soul.* Yes, please remind me one more time of Your words, *In repentance and rest you shall be saved, in quietness and trust is your strength.* Indeed, O God, I am safe with You. I am now settled, knowing that You are by my side; and as a result, *in the shadow of Your wings I will sing for joy.*

Psalms 91:4,1-2; 121:5,7; Isaiah 30:15; Psalm 63:7

One Who is for Us

From my distress I called upon the LORD; the LORD answered me and set me in a large place. The LORD is for me; I will not fear; what can man do to me?

PSALM 118:5–6

O God, You are the One Who is for Us. I repeat the words of the victorious psalmist; *Had it not been the Lord who was on our side, when men rose up against us; then they would have swallowed us alive, when their anger was kindled against us; then the waters would have engulfed us, the stream would have swept over our soul; then the raging water would have swept over our soul. Blessed be the Lord, who has not given us to be torn by their teeth. Our soul has escaped as a bird out of the snare of the trapper; the snare is broken and we have escaped. Our help is in the name of the Lord, who made heaven and earth.* Thank You, God, for standing beside us; thank You, Savior, for fighting for us. Indeed, You are the Victorious Warrior! All of your children can confidently shout, *If God is for us, who is against us?* So continue on, I pray, *gird your sword on Your thigh, Mighty One, in Your splendor and Your majesty! And in Your majesty ride on victoriously, for the cause of truth and meekness and righteousness.* Defeat the enemy, trample the foe, and *deliver us from evil.* Yes, Lord, I will forever praise You as the God Who is for Us, His people whom He loves.

Psalm 124:2-8; Romans 8:31; Psalm 45:3-4; Matthew 6:13

One Who Looks

"For My hand made all these things, thus all these things came into being," declares the LORD. *"But to this one I will look, to him who is humble and contrite of spirit, and who trembles at My word."*

ISAIAH 66:2

O God, You are the One Who Looks. *The Lord looks from heaven; He sees all the sons of men; from His dwelling place He looks out on all the inhabitants of the earth, He who fashions the hearts of them all, He who understands all their works. ... Behold, the eye of the Lord is on those who fear Him, on those who hope for His lovingkindness.* Dear Lord, look at me, I pray. I hope for Your lovingkindness all the day long, and You most certainly provide! Yes, I take courage in the fact that *Your eyes search to and fro throughout all the earth to strongly support those whose hearts are completely Yours.* My heart belongs to You, O God! I ask You to look my way! For in Your look, there is mercy and forgiveness, there is grace and compassion, there is strength and joy. I have done nothing to gain Your gaze; for You are the One who gave me a heart that fears You and a soul that longs for You. I am merely the prodigal who has come home. I deserved nothing, but You turned Your head and looked my way: *But while he was still a long way off, his father saw him, and felt compassion for him, and ran and embraced him and kissed him.* Oh Father, I will praise You for Your lovingkindness, and I will rejoice in Your strength. Oh, how I thank You for Looking at me.

Psalm 33:13-15,18; 2 Chronicles 16:9; Luke 15:20

Initiator

We love, because He first loved us.

1 JOHN 4:19

O God, You are the Initiator. Forgive me when I confuse this issue! So often I think I am the one who started this relationship. On the contrary, You are the One who *chose me in Him before the foundation of the world.* And You are the One who *made me alive together with Christ.* And You are the One who *filled me with Your Spirit.* Indeed, You are the Initiator of all these things! And also, You are the One who said, *Follow Me.* And You are the One who *began a good work in me.* And You are the One who *will perfect it.* Again and again, O God, I see that these words of Yours are truth: *You did not choose Me, I chose you.* And You initiated this love that I hold in my heart: *In this is love, not that we loved God but that He loved us and sent His Son to be a propitiation for our sin.* Thank You for Your gracious pursuit and Your intentional capture. As a result, I want to pursue others in this same way. Yes, please grow Your love inside of me so I can reach out to others. And remind me that going forward without Your love would be in vain. So, daily I ask You to *create in me a clean heart, O God, and renew a steadfast spirit in me.* Be the Initiator of my thoughts, my words, and my deeds. Yes, may the relationship I initiate with others be a beautiful overflow from the relationship that You initiated with me. Because ultimately, I want them to have You.

Ephesians 1:4; 2:5; Romans 5:5; Matthew 4:19; Philippians 1:6; John 15:16; 1 John 4:10; Psalm 51:10

Righteous

For the LORD is righteous; He loves righteousness; the upright will behold His face.

PSALM 11:7

O God, You are Righteous. Yes, God, You are *righteous with respect to all Your deeds which You have done.* You can do no wrong. Your sovereign hand is both good and blameless. You are completely accurate in Your wisdom and *all of Your commandments are truth.* Again I praise You, *Righteous are You, O Lord, and upright are Your judgments. You have commanded Your testimonies in righteousness and exceeding faithfulness.* On the other hand, Your people are a mess. We are not worthy to stand before You. As a matter of fact, we deserve only Your wrath because of our sin. But there is good news: Jesus the Righteous came into our mess, died for our mess, and conquered our mess! *He made Him who knew no sin to be sin on our behalf, that we might become the righteousness of God in Him.* Now I hold onto this beautiful promise: *And if Christ is in you, though the body is dead because of sin, yet the spirit is alive because of righteousness.* Hallelujah for this good news both today and forever! O Righteous One, I thank You for making me Your righteous one!

Daniel 9:14; Psalm 119:151,137-138; 2 Corinthians 5:21; Romans 8:10

God of Blessings

The LORD bless you, and keep you; the LORD make His face shine on you, and be gracious to you; the LORD lift up His countenance on you, and give you peace.

NUMBERS 6:24–26

O God, You are the God of Blessings. Indeed, dear God, You *have blessed us with every spiritual blessing in the heavenly places in Christ: You chose us in Him before the foundation of the world, that we should be holy and blameless before Him. In love You predestined us to adoption as sons through Jesus Christ. … You freely bestowed Your grace on us. … You redeemed us through Your blood, and forgave us of our trespasses, according to the riches of Your grace, which You lavished upon us.* On and on, You bless and bless! To think *You have sealed us in Christ with the Holy Spirit of promise* and You have given us a life with You forever! O God, forgive me when I complain about my current situation, or when I shake my fist at You saying, "Not enough!" Forgive my short-sightedness in the midst of diverse circumstances, thinking I have been cheated of deserved happiness. Help me count my blessings from above. I ask You to recall them to my mind and allow them to reenergize my heart. Indeed, Your extravagant generosity and Your abundant grace flows, and I am a filled vessel once again. And now, O God, it's my turn: *Bless the Lord, O my soul; and all that is within me, bless His holy name. Bless the Lord, O my soul, and forget none of His benefits; Who pardons all our iniquities; Who heals all our diseases; Who redeems our life from the pit; Who crowns us with lovingkindness and compassion.* Most certainly, O God, on and on, You Bless and Bless.

Ephesians 1:3-8,13; Psalm 103:1-4

My Cup

The LORD is the portion of my inheritance and my cup.

PSALM 16:5

O God, You are my Cup. Your word explains the Lord's Supper: *The Lord Jesus in the night in which He was betrayed took bread; and when He had given thanks, he broke it, and said, "This is My body, which is for you; do this in remembrance of Me." In the same way He took the cup also, after supper, saying, "This cup is the new covenant in My blood; do this, as often as you drink it, in remembrance of me." For as often as you eat this bread and drink the cup, you proclaim the Lord's death until He comes.* Dear Jesus, thank You for this visual reminder of who You are: the Messiah, the perfect sacrifice for imperfect mankind. It took Your holy blood to redeem my tarnished soul. I humbly hold Your cup and drink. And as I sip in forgiveness, I then identify with You. For Your word also says: *Is not the cup of blessing which we bless a sharing in the blood of Christ? Is not the bread which we break a sharing in the body of Christ?* Yes, Lord, let Your ways be my ways; cause me to think Your divine thoughts, to see the broken and the lost, and to have Your compassionate hands and Your purposeful feet. Give me a heart that beats for You, whether I am drinking from the *river of delights* or from *a sponge of sour wine*. Yes, Lord, either way, *whether in having abundance or suffering need,* I want You to be my portion. Because with You, *my cup overflows.*

1 Corinthians 11:23-26; 10:16; Psalm 36:8; John 19:29;
Philippians 4:12; Psalm 23:5

Trustworthy

It is better to take refuge in the Lord than to trust in man. It is better to take refuge in the Lord than to trust in princes.

PSALM 118:8-9

O God, You are Trustworthy. I hear You earnestly say to my heart, *Trust in Me, and do good; dwell in the land and cultivate faithfulness. Delight yourself in Me; and I will give you the desires of your heart. Commit your way to Me, trust also in Me, and I will do it.* O God, I do trust You, because I know *it is impossible for You to lie.* Even when I can't seem to make sense of what is happening around me, I know that You are up to something, and I know the end result will be positive and transforming, making me more like You. Just help me in the meantime to trust You still. I need Your peace, I need Your strength, I need Your word. Yes, in times of question and uncertainty, I will recall Your word and cling to it: *My soul, wait in silence of God only, for my hope is from Him. He only is my rock and my salvation, my stronghold; I shall not be shaken. On God my salvation and my glory rest; the rock of my strength, my refuge is in God. Trust in Him at all times, O people; pour our your heart before Him; God is a refuge for us.* Yes, Lord at all times, I will trust in You. Thank You, God, for being one hundred percent reliable; thank You for being my safe place; thank You for understanding me; thank You for Your plan for me. Indeed, You are altogether Trustworthy; therefore, *I will run the way of Your commandments, for You will enlarge my heart.* Today, in this minute, and then in the next, and the next, I will *trust in the Lord.*

Psalm 37:3-5; Hebrews 6:18; Psalms 62:5-8; 119:32; 4:5

One Who Preserves

You, O LORD, will keep them; You will preserve him from this generation forever.
PSALM 12:7

O God, You are the One Who Preserves. Yes, Lord, *preserve me, for I take refuge in You. I said to the Lord, "You are my Lord; I have no good besides You."* I ask You to uphold all of Your goodness that is promised in Your word. So often I feel under attack from the enemy who comes only *to steal, and kill, and destroy.* I need Your covering, and You are gracious and faithful to give it. Yes, remind me that *You have clothed me with strength.* With You, the enemy has no power over me. Indeed, *You preserve the simple; I was brought low, and You saved me.* I can say to myself with assurance, *Return to your rest, O my soul, for the Lord has dealt bountifully with you.* So again and again, I thank You for Your protection and Your care. *Now may the God of peace Himself sanctify me entirely; and may my spirit and soul and body be preserved complete, without blame at the coming of our Lord Jesus Christ.* Thank You, O God. The One Who Preserves is the One I love.

Psalm 16:1; John 10:10; Isaiah 52:1; Psalm 116:6,7; 1 Thessalonians 5:22

One Who Guards

The LORD will guard your going out and your coming in from this time forth and forever.
PSALM 121:8

O God, You are the One Who Guards. Dear Jesus, You proclaimed, *I am the good shepherd; the good shepherd lays down His life for the sheep. He who is a hireling, and not a shepherd, who is not the owner of the sheep, beholds the wolf coming, and leaves the sheep, and flees, and the wolf snatches them and scatters them. He flees because he is a hireling, and is not concerned about the sheep. I am the good shepherd; and I know My own, and My own know Me, even as the Father knows Me and I know the Father; and I lay down My life for the sheep.* Good Shepherd, I thank You for guarding Your flock even to the point of death. What intense love You have for Your people! Forgive me when I wander away from this love and into the "care" of another. These "hirelings"— be it money, or power, or pleasure—are both fragile and fallible; You, however, are mighty and wise. So protect me from myself, I pray, as well as from all the temptations on the other side of the fence. Please *gather me in Your arms and carry me.* I want to learn to trust You at all times, both when the pastures are green as well as when I enter *the valley of the shadow of death.* Even in this place, help me to know You have Your watchful eye on me; therefore, I can declare with confidence, *I will fear no evil because Your rod and Your staff will comfort me.* Yes, I must choose to stay close to my Guardian, for He is the only true and *great Shepherd of the sheep.*

John 10:11-15; Isaiah 40:11; Psalm 23:4; Hebrews 13:20

King of Heaven

To You I lift up my eyes, O You who are enthroned in the heavens!
PSALM 123:1

O God, You are the King of Heaven. Yes, *hallowed be Your name.* I catch an awe-filled glimpse of my future and eternal home: *And behold, a throne was standing in heaven, and One sitting on the throne. And He who was sitting was like a jasper stone and a sardius in appearance; and there was a rainbow around the throne, like an emerald in appearance. And around the throne were twenty-four thrones; and upon the thrones I saw twenty-four elders sitting, clothed in white garments, and golden crowns on their heads. And from the throne proceed flashes of lightning and sounds and peals of thunder. And there were seven lamps of fire burning before the throne, which are the seven Spirits of God; and there was a sea of glass like crystal. ... And the twenty-four elders will fall down and worship Him who sits on the throne, and will worship Him who lives forever and ever, and will cast their crowns before the throne, saying, "Worthy are You, our Lord and our God, to receive glory and honor and power; for You created all things, and because of Your will they existed, and were created."* Majestic King of Heaven, how can I stand before You? All that is in me cries out, *Unclean!* Forgive me when I belittle You in my heart and mind! You are way beyond what I can imagine—in power, in majesty, and in creativity. Indeed, *when I consider the heavens, the work of Your fingers, the moon and the stars, which You have ordained; what is man, that You take thought of him? And the son of man, that You care for him?* Your mercy astounds me; Your grace envelopes me; Your love compels me. So with my small voice I will sing along with the grandiose worship that my ears will someday fully hear: *Praise the Lord from the heavens; Praise Him in the heights! Praise Him, all His angels; Praise Him all His hosts! Praise Him sun and moon; Praise Him, all stars of light! Praise Him, highest heavens, and the waters that are above the heavens! Let them praise the name of the Lord.*

Matthew 6:9; Revelation 4:2-6,10-11; Isaiah 6:5; Psalms 8:3-4; 148:1-5

King of Earth

For a child will be born to us, a son will be given to us; and the government will rest on His shoulders; and His name will be called Wonderful Counselor, Mighty God, Eternal Father, Prince of Peace.

ISAIAH 9:6

O God, You are King of the Earth. As Creator, *You gave birth to the earth and to the world.* And as King, You rule over all You have made in wisdom. But God, You are not so far away from any of us. No, You are the God who is with us. I thank You for sending Your Son from heaven to earth to rule over us in power and in love. *He glorified You here, having accomplished the work which You sent Him to do.* He lived perfectly, died mercifully, and was raised eternally. *You have put all things in subjection under His feet, and gave Him as head over all things.* And You have also proclaimed that *at the name of Jesus every knee should bow, of those who are in heaven, and of earth, and under the earth, and that every tongue should confess that Jesus Christ is Lord, to the glory of God the Father.* Dear Jesus, Righteous Ruler, I do bend my knee and I do confess You as Lord of my heart. I am thankful that *righteousness and justice are the foundation of Your throne, and lovingkindness and truth go before You. How blessed are the people who know the joyful sound! O Lord, they walk in the light of Your countenance.* I thank You for the peace that You have brought to each of us that call you Savior. May generation after generation honor and praise You as King of all the Earth.

Psalm 90:2; John 17:4; Ephesians 1:22; Philippians 2:10-11; Psalm 89:14-15

Stronger One

And the great dragon was thrown down, the serpent of old who is called the devil and Satan, who deceives the whole world; he was thrown down to the earth, and his angels were thrown down with him.

REVELATION 12:9

O God, You are the Stronger One. I know for sure there is an *adversary, the devil, who prowls about like a roaring lion seeking someone to devour*; but I am also confident in the truth that You are more powerful than this enemy. Indeed, You are *the Lord strong and mighty, the Lord mighty in battle.* In the beginning, You let the cunning serpent know who would ultimately win the ongoing battle between life and death, light and darkness, good and evil. You prophesied, *I will put enmity between you and the woman, and between your seed and her seed; He shall bruise you on the head, and you shall bruise him on the heel.* Yes, Jesus, I know this fulfilling truth about You: *The Son of God appeared for this purpose, that He might destroy the works of the devil.* Appointed One, at the cross and the empty grave, You indeed conquered both sin and death. Thank You, my Savior. And now, because of grace from You and faith in You, I can live by this truth: *You are from God, little children, and have overcome them; because greater is He who is in you than he who is in the world.* Therefore, *when I am afraid, I will trust in You. In God whose word I praise, in God I have put my trust.* Yes, I will stand firm and fight, placing my confidence in the Lord Almighty; because He always has been and forever will be the Stronger One.

1 Peter 5:8; Psalm 24:8; Genesis 3:15; 1 John 3:8; 4:4; Psalm 56:3-4

My Heartbeat

I will give them a heart to know Me, for I am the LORD; and they will be My people, and I will be their God, for they will return to Me with their whole heart.

JEREMIAH 24:7

O God, You are my Heartbeat. I agree with these words of truth: *The heart is more deceitful than all else and is desperately sick. Who can understand it?* Lord, we are a fallen and faithless people who only deserve Your wrath. But I rejoice in Your mercy in spite of our waywardness. You promised salvation to us by intervening with Your grace. You said, *I will give you a new heart and put a new spirit within you; and I will remove the heart of stone from your flesh and give you a heart of flesh. And I will put My Spirit within you and cause you to walk in My statutes.* Wonderful God, You fulfilled Your promise by sending us Your Son! Your lovingkindness has prevailed over me. You have won my heart and now it beats for You! I believe and long to live by this truth: *I have been crucified with Christ, and it is no longer I who lives but Christ lives in me; and the life which I now live in the flesh I live by faith in the Son of God, who loved me, and delivered Himself up for me.* Yes, *whatever things were gain to me, those things I have counted loss for the sake of Christ. More than that, I count all things to be loss in view of the surpassing value of knowing Christ Jesus my Lord, for whom I have suffered the loss of all things, and count them but rubbish in order that I may gain Christ.* Most certainly, *for to me, to live is Christ, and to die is gain.* Yes, God, my utmost desire on this earth is that You would become my every Heartbeat.

Jeremiah 17:9; Ezekiel, 36:26-27; Galatians 2:20; Philippians 3:7-8; 1:21

Gracious

Therefore the LORD longs to be gracious to you.
ISAIAH 30:18

O God, You are Gracious. Your grace has saved me, Your compassion has embraced me, forever. I am overwhelmed with Your tenderness, I am overtaken by Your love. Thank You *for teaching me;* thank You for *bringing me to Your banquet table;* thank You for mercifully *drawing a line in the sand.* Indeed, Your blessings toward me are abundant. You extend Your gracious hand over and over again even when I was in the pit of destruction or the pigsty of sin. I thank You for pursuing me, even though You know *all the things I have done.* And thank You for choosing me even though You knew I would *deny you* time and time again. And thank You for dying for me even though You heard my heart cry out, *Let Him be crucified!* I am astounded by Your mercy, I am humbled by Your forgiveness. Again, Your blessings multiply within my thankful heart; they are more numerous than I can count. Indeed Lord God, You are more Gracious to me than I could ever imagine or deserve. Thank You.

**Luke 12:12; Song of Solomon 2:4; John 8:6-11; 4:29; 13:38;
Matthew 27:23**

Compassionate

And therefore He waits on high to have compassion on you.

Isaiah 30:18

O God, You are Compassionate. Thank You for looking my way with a tender gaze when I cry out to You. Indeed, _You are near to the brokenhearted and You save those who are crushed in spirit._ You know we need You, O God; I am thankful You come to the aid of humbled hearts. _You are gracious and compassionate, slow to anger and abounding in lovingkindness. You will not always strive with us; nor will You keep Your anger forever. You have not dealt with us according to our sins, nor rewarded us according to our iniquities._ Thank You, dear Lord. Now, please hear the prayer of Your repentant people: _For Your sake, O Lord, let Your face shine on Your desolate sanctuary, O my God, incline Your ear and hear! Open Your eyes and see our desolations and the city which is called by Your name; for we are not presenting our supplications before You according to any merits of our own, but on account of Your great compassion. O Lord, hear! O Lord, forgive! O Lord, listen and take action! For Your own sake, O my God, do not delay; because Your city and Your people are called by Your name._ Thank You, O God, that You do hear, You do forgive, and You do act! Most assuredly _Your compassions never fail._

Psalms 34:18; 103:8-10; Daniel 9:17-19; Lamentations 3:22

Independent

In the beginning God created the heavens and the earth. The earth was formless and void, and darkness was over the deep, and the Spirit of God was moving over the surface of the waters.

GENESIS 1:1–2

O God, You are Independent. The apostle Paul described You with these words: *The God who made the world and all things in it, since He is Lord of heaven and earth, does not dwell in temples made with hands; neither is He served by human hands, as though He needed anything, since He Himself gives to all life and breath and all things. … For in Him we live and move and exist.* Yes, Lord, You are the Sovereign God, who can exist independently of everyone and everything. But we, on the other hand, *can do nothing apart from You.* Forgive me Lord, when I think I can! Yes, forgive me when I think I am the independent one, making my own plans without regard to You. Remind me again of Your redirecting words, *"To whom then will you liken Me that I should be his equal?" says the Holy One. Lift up your eyes on high and see who has created these stars, the One who leads forth their host by number, He calls them all by name; because of the greatness of His might and the strength of His power not one of them is missing. … Do you not know: Have you not heard? The Everlasting God, the Lord, the Creator of the ends of the earth does not become weary or tired. His understanding is inscrutable.* Also, I hear You plead, *There is no other God besides Me, a righteous God and a Savior; there is none except Me. Turn to Me, and be saved, all the ends of the earth; for I am God, and there is no other.* Once again, forgive me, Independent One, for taking the reins from Your hands and acting as my own little god; this dependent child has humbly returned to You.

Acts 17:24-25,28; John 15:5; Isaiah 40:25-26,28; Isaiah 45:21-22

My Purpose

For woe is me if I do not preach the gospel.
1 CORINTHIANS 9:16

O God, You are my Purpose. When I waver in the doubtful question of, "Why am I here? Does my life really matter?", remind me of Your commanding words: *Go therefore and make disciples of all the nations, baptizing them in the name of the Father, and the Son and the Holy Spirit.* Indeed, those of us who call You Savior are now *set apart for the gospel of God.* I pray You will grow me in this area of sharing Your good news. I want to be able to truthfully say these words from my heart, *But I do not consider my life of any account as dear to myself, in order that I may finish my course, and the ministry which I received from the Lord Jesus, to testify solemnly of the gospel of the grace of God.* Yes, dear Lord, may *Your love control me, having concluded this, that one died for all, therefore all died; and He died for all, that though we who live should no longer live for ourselves, but for Him who died and rose again on our behalf.* Lord, I do want to die to myself and live for You! And I do want to be an *ambassador for Christ, as though You were entreating through me.* And I do want to proclaim Your good news to the world. Most certainly, O God, I am here for a reason, and my life does matter. You have commanded me to know You and to make You known. Indeed, You are my Purpose.

Matthew 28:19; Romans 1:1; Acts 20:24; 2 Corinthians 5:14-15,20

One Who Establishes

He has made you and established you.

DEUTERONOMY 32:6

O God, You are the One Who Establishes. You say to Your children, *Commit your way to Me, trust also in Me, and I will do it.* Lord God, I want to commit my way to You, and I want to fully trust in You. Please remove any plans of mine that are not in line with Your will; establish me in Your truth. May I glean from this particular teaching of Yours, dear Jesus: *Everyone who comes to Me, and hears My words, and acts upon them, I will show you whom he is like: he is like a man building a house, who dug deep and laid a foundation upon the rock; and when a flood rose, the torrent burst against that house and could not shake it, because it had been well built. But the one who has heard, and has not acted accordingly, is like a man who built a house upon the ground without any foundation; and the torrent burst against it and immediately it collapsed, and the ruin of that house was great.* Your words, O Lord, are indeed my foundation, and You, dear Jesus, are my *Cornerstone. . . . Because You are at my right hand, I will not be shaken* by the torrents of trial or the attacks of the enemy. Yes, Your fortifying strength surrounds me. So during this tumultuous time, I will cling to Your promise with expectant hope: *After you have suffered a little while, the God of all grace, who called you to His eternal glory in Christ, will Himself perfect, confirm, strengthen and establish You.* Yes, dear Establisher, no matter the circumstance, I will commit my way fully to You.

Psalm 37:5; Luke 6:48-49; Acts 4:11; Psalm 16:8; 1 Peter 5:10

One Who Reveals

Call to Me and I will answer you, and I will tell you great and mighty things, which you do not know.

JEREMIAH 33:3

O God, You are the One Who Reveals. *Let Your name, O God, be blessed forever and ever, for wisdom and power belong to You. And it is You who changes the times and the epochs; You remove kings and establish kings; You give wisdom to wise men, and knowledge to men of understanding. It is You who reveals the profound and hidden things; You know what is in the darkness, and the light dwells with You.* Yes, Lord, thank You for this reassuring truth that *darkness and light are alike to You.* Help me to trust that You are sovereign and in control even when I do not see or know what You are doing. *Your ways are higher than my ways, and Your thoughts are higher than my thoughts.* However, You also *hide things from the wise and intelligent and reveal them to babes.* Therefore, I ask for a childlike faith, one that leans into Your wisdom and rests in Your timing. Show me what I need to know in order to stay on Your path day in and day out. As I dig deep into Your word, I ask for a *spirit of wisdom and revelation in the knowledge of You. ... That the eyes of my heart would be enlightened, so I may know the hope of Your calling, what are the glorious riches in the inheritance of the saints.* Yes, Lord, reveal to me each morning something new and glorious about Yourself, and I will cherish it all the day long.

Daniel 2:20-22; Psalm 139:12; Isaiah 55:9; Luke 10:21; Ephesians 1:17-18

All-Wise

For the LORD gives wisdom; from His mouth come knowledge and understanding.
PROVERBS 2:6

O God, You are All-Wise. I hear You implore each of your children, *My son, if you receive my sayings, and treasure my commandments within you, make your ear attentive to wisdom, and incline your heart to understanding; for if you cry for discernment, lift your voice for understanding, if you seek her as silver, and search for her as for hidden treasures; then you will discern the fear of Me, and discover the knowledge of Me.* Lord, I ask for a heart that receives You, treasures You, listens to You, and obeys You. I know that veering off Your protective path and onto any other tempting route only leads to a destructive dead end. Yes, in You alone, dear Jesus, *are hidden all the treasures of wisdom and knowledge.* And Your name is *Wonderful Counselor!* Indeed, my heart wants Your treasures, and my soul longs for Your wonders. Therefore, *I will give attention to Your words; and I will incline my ear to Your sayings. I will not let them depart from my sight; and I will keep them in the midst of my heart. For they are life to me when I find them, and health to my whole body. And I will watch over my heart with all diligence, for from it flows the springs of life.* Yes, I will trust and obey the words of my All-Wise God.

Proverbs 2:1-5; Colossians 2:3; Isaiah 9:6; Proverbs 4:20-23

Disciplining God

Foolishness is bound up in the heart of a child; the rod of discipline will remove it far from him.

PROVERBS 22:15

O God, You are the Disciplining God. *I know, O Lord, that Your judgments are righteous, and that in faithfulness You have afflicted me.* But I also know that *You will not always strive with me; nor will You keep Your anger forever. You have not dealt with me according to my sins, nor rewarded me according to my iniquities.* Somewhere between Your intentional affliction and Your greater grace comes Your necessary discipline. I know You correct me because You love me. Your Word says: *He who spares his rod hates his son, but he who loves him disciplines him diligently.* Help me not to resist You, flailing about in protest; but instead, help me to humbly yield to the truth that *You discipline me for my good, so that I may share in Your holiness.* Help me to know *all discipline for the moment seems not to be joyful, but sorrowful; yet if I am trained by it, afterwards it yields the peaceful fruit of righteousness.* Yes, I need Your directional hand to bring me back when I wander foolishly or ignorantly from Your care. So dear Lord, I will submit to Your loving correction, because ultimately, *Your rod and Your staff, they comfort me.*

Psalm 119:75; 103:9-10; Proverbs 13:24; Hebrews 12:10-11; Psalm 23:4

One Who Purchases

Is not He your Father who has bought you? He has made you and established you.
DEUTERONOMY 32:6

O God, You are the One Who Purchases. For we were once enslaved to sin, but then You came. You saw our ongoing captivity, and You knew that without Your intervention there was no way to freedom. Savior, You did come, and You did purchase our freedom; however, it was at a magnificent price. *We were not redeemed with perishable things like silver or gold from our futile way of life inherited from our forefathers, but with precious blood, as of a lamb unblemished and spotless, the blood of Christ.* Most certainly, *what the Law could not do, weak as it was through the flesh, God did: sending His own Son in the likeness of sinful flesh and as an offering for sin, He condemned sin in the flesh, in order that the requirement of the Law might be fulfilled in us.* Thank You, God of Grace, for this undeserved favor! I am now *freed from sin and enslaved to You, and I derive my benefit, resulting in sanctification, and the outcome, eternal life.* Incredible, this amazing grace has fallen on me forever! Again, thank You for coming, and thank You for purchasing, and thank You for pardoning. Thank You for eternal life! O God, cause me to daily live with Your holy challenge in mind as You speak these words to my heart: *Do you not know that your body is a temple of the Holy Spirit who is in you, whom you have from Me, and that you are not your own? For you have been bought with a price; therefore glorify Me in your body.* Yes, I will live for the One Who Purchased me.

1 Peter 1:18-19; Romans 8:3-4; 6:22; 1 Corinthians 6:19-20

God Who Multiplies

But the word of the Lord continued to grow and to be multiplied.
ACTS 12:24

O God, You are the One Who Multiplies. You exhibited this power when You, through *Elijah, caused the widow's jars to be filled with oil*, over and over and over. You proved this as well, when You, *Jesus, took the five loaves and two fish from the small boy, and caused the meager portion to feed five thousand.* And You showed Your expanding power again when *You commanded the empty nets of the fisherman to suddenly be overcome with masses of fish, so much so their nets began to break.* Indeed, You are the multiplying God. I pray that I would be like the poor widow, and the small boy, and the obedient fishermen; in faith, I want to bring my meager gifts to You and then watch You work wonders for Your glory. For You promise that *You are able to do exceedingly abundantly above all that we can ask or think according to the power that works within us.* Do Your work, O God, in and through me. Hear me proclaim, *Many, O Lord my God, are the wonders which You have done, and Your thoughts toward us; there is none to compare with You; if I would declare and speak of them, they would be too numerous to count.*

**1 Kings 17:12-16; Matthew 14:13-21; Luke 5:4-6;
Ephesians 3:20; Psalm 40:5**

Satisfied

As a result of the anguish of His soul, He will see it and be satisfied; By His knowledge the Righteous One, My Servant, will justify the many, as He will bear their iniquities.

ISAIAH 53:11

O God, You are Satisfied. Because of Your holiness, sin must be dealt with; for Your word says: *The wages of sin is death.* Yes, I have sinned against You and I deserve death, nothing else. I cannot earn my way to You with good deeds because even *my righteous deeds are like a filthy garment.* So ultimately, death is the only satisfying answer that You will accept for my sin. How hopeless this sounds … until the full story is revealed: *The wages of sin is death, but the free gift of God is eternal life in Christ Jesus our Lord.* Jesus, You took my place, You paid my wage, *You laid down Your life.* Yes, *when the kindness of God our Savior and His love for mankind appeared, He saved us, not on the basis of deeds which we have done in righteousness, but according to His mercy.* Yes, O God, *You demonstrated Your own love toward us, in that while we were yet sinners, Christ died for us. Much more then, having now been justified by His blood, we shall be saved from Your wrath through Him.* Almighty God, You looked at the death of Your perfect Son and You were Satisfied. I am humbled by Your absolute holiness, and I am awed by Your inviting love.

**Romans 6:23; Isaiah 64:6; Romans 6:23; John 10:15;
Titus 3:4-5; Romans 5:8-9**

Captivating

They said to one another, "Were not our hearts burning within us while He was speaking to us on the road, while He was explaining the Scriptures to us?"

LUKE 24:32

O God, You are Captivating. Yes, Jesus, everywhere You went You drew a crowd. Your wonders were mind-boggling: *healing the paralytic ... giving the blind man his sight ... raising the synagogue official's daughter from the dead.* And Your words were life-giving: *All were speaking well of Him, and were wondering at the gracious words which were falling from His lips; and they were saying, "Is this not Joseph's son?"* And also: *The Jews were marveling, saying, "How has this man become learned, having never been educated?"* If these men only realized that the One who was speaking was the Author of knowledge. Captivate me, O God, completely—not with a mere turning of my head in temporary curiosity, but a turning of my heart in eternal truth. Yes, please take over my whole heart; I want to be mesmerized by Your healing hand of mercy and Your gracious words of life. Let words such as these resonate within me like the air I breathe: *Peace I give to you. ... Your sins are forgiven. ... Your faith has made you well. ... I go to prepare a place for you.* Yes, Lord Jesus, Captivate my whole heart both today and forever.

Mark 2:1-12; 8:22-25; 5:35-43; Luke 4:22; John 7:15; 14:27;
Mark 2:5; 5:34; John 14:2

One Who Awakens

Awake, sleeper, and arise from the dead, and Christ will shine on you.
EPHESIANS 5:14

O God, You are the One Who Awakens. I hear Your words to Your people: *Awake, awake, clothe yourself in your strength, O Zion; clothe yourself in your beautiful garments, O Jerusalem, the holy city. ... Shake yourself from the dust, rise up, O captive Jerusalem; loose yourself from the chains around your neck, O captive daughter of Zion.* Yes, dear Lord, Your heart's desire is that all men everywhere would respond to Your gracious alarm that was sounded from heaven to earth 2,000 years ago: *I bring you good news of a great joy which shall be for all the people; for today in the city of David there has been born for you a Savior, who is Christ the Lord.* Again You implore: *Arise, shine for your light has come, and the glory of the Lord has risen upon you. For behold, darkness will cover the earth, and deep darkness the peoples; but the Lord will rise upon you, and His glory will appear upon you.* Please, dear Lord, awaken lost souls to Your eternal glory. I beg You to touch hearts with Your saving grace. My heart's desire is Your heart's desire: I want all people to know You as their Lord and Savior, *not wishing for any to perish but for all to come to repentance.* Yes, I want each one to *be made alive together with Christ.* O God of the dawning Light, please Awaken the souls of the ones I love.

Isaiah 52:1-2; Luke 2:10-11; Isaiah 60:1-2; 2 Peter 3:9; Ephesians 2:5

Same

Jesus Christ is the same yesterday and today and forever.
HEBREWS 13:8

O God, You are the Same. *In the beginning was the Word, and the Word was with God and the Word was God. He was in the beginning with God. All things came into being by Him, and apart from Him nothing came into being that has come into being. In Him was life, and the life was the light of men.* This light of life that was in the beginning has never been extinguished and will never be snuffed out. Indeed, O God, You are the *Alpha and the Omega, who is and was and is to come;* and during all of time, You have remained the same. Yes, the *One who was in the midst of the fire with Shadrach, Meshach and Abed-nego* is also standing right beside me. And the *One who ran with David to the battle line* is also the One who runs with me. And the *One who was in the storm-tossed boat of the disciples* is also the One who stays with me. Yes, Your character is unchanging. You are always the Protector, You are always the Warrior, You are always the Comforter. Indeed, *Your lovingkindness, O Lord, is from everlasting to everlasting on those who fear You, and Your righteousness to children's children.* Thank You for the consistency of Your character and the stability of Your truth. Your "Sameness," O God, is my security today, tomorrow, and forever.

John 1:1-4; Revelation 1:8; Daniel 3:25; 1 Samuel 17:48;
Mark 4:39; Psalm 103:17

God of Might

Behold, the Lord GOD will come with might, with His arm ruling for Him. Behold, His reward is with Him and His recompense before Him.

ISAIAH 40:10

O God, You are the God of Might. Yes, Lord, *You are strong and mighty, You are mighty in battle.* I have read of Your wonders: *The walls of water falling on the Egyptian army so Your people can escape to freedom. … the walls of Jericho falling to the ground so Your people can conquer a city. … the dividing wall of enmity falling so that all people can be saved forever.* Yes, I will cling to these words of truth: *The Lord your God is in your midst, a victorious warrior. He will exult over you with joy, He will be quiet in His love, He will rejoice over you with shouts of joy.* God of Might, I will rest in Your strong tower of safety, security, and salvation; and there, I will proclaim Your goodness with psalms of old such as this: *Who is this who comes from Edom, with garments of glowing colors from Bozrah, this One who is majestic in His apparel, marching in the greatness of His strength? "It is I who speak in righteousness, mighty to save."* Yes, indeed, *there is none like You. O Lord; You are great, and great is Your name in might.*

Psalm 24:8; Exodus 14:27; Joshua 6:20; Ephesians 2:14; Zephaniah 3:17; Isaiah 63:1; Jeremiah 10:6

Bondage Breaker

And suddenly there came a great earthquake, so that the foundations of the prison house were shaken; and immediately all the doors were opened and everyone's chains were unfastened.

ACTS 16:26

O God, You are the Bondage Breaker. I agree with the words of Paul: *For we know that the Law is spiritual; but I am of flesh, sold into bondage to sin. For that which I am doing, I do not understand; for I am not practicing what I would like to do, but I am doing the very thing I hate.* Dear Lord, please help me in this wretched place that I once again find myself. I am reminded of these words: *The cords of death encompassed me, and the torrents of ungodliness terrified me. The cords of Sheol surrounded me; the snares of death confronted me.* Likewise, O Lord, worry twists around me, dismay straps me down, and fear paralyzes me. Come Lord Jesus and break these bonds one more time. I do not want these sins to overtake my heart. Only You can set me free from them, and all other strongholds. You alone are the Bondage Breaker. Say to my soul the same words You spoke to Lazarus and the surrounding people when You raised him from the dead: *Lazarus, come forth. … Unbind him and let him go.* And then remind me over and over that *it was for freedom that Christ set me free.* Yes, dear Jesus, continually break my bonds so that I can serve You with joy and abandon.

Romans 7:14-15; Psalm 18:4-5; John 11:43-44; Galatians 5:1

Inexhaustible

The Everlasting God, the LORD, the Creator of the ends of the earth does not become weary or tired.

ISAIAH 40:28

O God, You are Inexhaustible. To think, You never run out of energy, Your strength is limitless, and Your power continues on and on. I can't imagine this concept in my own flesh, but I can trust and be thankful it is a certain truth concerning You. Because of who You are, I can claim promises such as this: *I will lift up my eyes to the mountains; from where will my help come? My help comes from the Lord, who made heaven and earth. He will not allow your foot to slip; He who keeps you will not slumber. Behold, He who keeps Israel will neither slumber nor sleep. The Lord is your keeper; the Lord is your shade on your right hand. The sun will not smite you by day, nor the moon by night. The Lord will protect you from all evil; He will keep your soul. The Lord will guard your going out and your coming in from this time forth and forever.* Yes, Lord, I will praise You for Your inexplicable and immeasurable strength. *You heal the brokenhearted, and bind up their wounds. You count the number of the stars; You give names to all of them. Great are You Lord, and abundant in strength; Your understanding is infinite, You support the afflicted; and Your bring down the wicked to the ground.* On and on and on and on, You give, You care, You keep, You provide, You bind up, You count, You understand, You support, You bring down. Indeed, O God, You are Inexhaustible!

Psalms 121:1-8; 147:3-6

Victor

He is not here, but He has risen.

LUKE 24:6

O God, You are the Victor. Help me remember the battle is already won! So often in my days I feel defeated; I feel as if the enemy has triumphed over me. Make my heart understand this is a lie. Remind me my adversary's goal is to make me ineffective for Your kingdom, and he will go to great lengths to kick me while I am down. But You, O God, are for me, and You are the true Victor. Yes, I know that I know that I know You hold the victory! Help me to remember the big picture in the midst of my small battles: *You have fought for me*, and at the cross *You redeemed me with Your precious blood*; and because of the empty tomb, my *death has been swallowed up in victory*. Yes, You are triumphantly alive. You are the sovereign King, and *Your banner over me is love*. Remind me that Your victorious spirit lives in me! Because of this truth, I can and will defeat any tactic of my enemy. Yes, as I fight my current battles, I will cling to these words of truth: *You are from God, little children, and have overcome them; because greater is He who is in you than he who is in the world*. Most certainly, *Your divine power has granted to me everything I need pertaining to life and godliness*. Therefore, with a renewed spirit I will boast about my righteous Victor. With both confidence and joy my soul will proclaim, "Indeed, the battle is already won!"

**Exodus 14:14; 1 Peter 1:19; 1 Corinthians 15:54; Song of Solomon 2:4;
1 John 4:4; 2 Peter 1:3**

Exalted One

I will sing to the LORD, for He is highly exalted.
EXODUS 15:1

O God, You are the Exalted One. *Who is like You among the gods, O Lord? Who is like You, majestic in holiness, awesome in praises, working wonders?* I hear You declare with both hope and certainty, *Cease striving and know that I am God; I will be exalted among the nations, I will be exalted in the earth.* Yes, please make my soul be still enough to remember who You are: You are good, You are great, You are grand; You are patient, You are peace, You are power. You are light, You are love, You are Lord. Indeed, I will meditate on You, Mighty One. You are the *way, the truth, and the life,* and *Your kingdom is righteousness, and peace, and joy.* No one can compare to Your holiness, Your mercy, or Your strength. So I will lift my hands high in praise, as I bow my head low in adoration. Most certainly, *the Lord lives and blessed be my rock; and exalted be God, the rock of my salvation.* Thank You for reminding me that meditating on You brings me back to a place of praise to You. Therefore, I will declare these words with all my heart: *I will bless the Lord at all times; His praise shall continually be in my mouth. My soul shall make its boast in the Lord; the humble shall hear it and rejoice. O magnify the Lord with me and let us exalt His name together.*

Exodus 15:11; Psalm 46:10; John 14:6; Romans 14:17;
2 Samuel 22:47; Psalm 34:1-3

God of the Weary

Come to Me, all who are weary and heavy-laden, and I will give you rest.
MATTHEW 11:28

O God, You are God of the Weary. Your word promises, *a bruised reed You will not break, and a dimly burning wick You will not extinguish.* I confess, dear Lord, I am depleted—physically, emotionally, and spiritually. I feel as if I have nothing left to give. I'm empty. Please come into my current situation and fill me with Your peace. Breathe these words of hope into my worn out body and soul: *Do you not know? Have you not heard? The Everlasting God, the Lord, the Creator of the ends of the earth does not become weary or tired. His understanding is inscrutable. He gives strength to the weary, and to him who lacks might He increases power. Though youths grow weary and tired, and vigorous young men stumble badly, yet those who wait for the Lord will gain new strength; they will mount up with wings like eagles, they will run and not get tired, they will walk and not become weary.* O God, these words are like music to me. I hear the reassuring melody, and You are the resonating cord. Help me to choose to sing. You are my strength when I am weak; You are my peace when I am confused; You are my hope when I am void of it. Yes, *by faith not by sight,* I will begin to sing, and I will begin to trust, and I will begin to walk forward. And I will hear You say, *My presence will go with you and I will give you rest.*

Isaiah 42:3; 40:28-31; 2 Corinthians 5:7; Exodus 33:14

Excellent

Be exalted above the heavens, O God; let Your glory be above all the earth.
PSALM 57:5

O God, You are Excellent. You are excellent in Your wonders; You are excellent in Your word; You are excellent in Your loyalty; You are excellent in Your love. *My heart is steadfast, O God, my heart is steadfast; I will sing, yes, I will sing praises! Awake, my glory; awake, harp and lyre, I will awaken the dawn! I will give thanks to You, O Lord, among the peoples; I will sing praises to You among the nations. For Your lovingkindness is great to the heavens, and Your truth to the clouds. Be exalted above the heavens, O God; let Your glory be above all the earth.* You are excellent in Your faithfulness; You are excellent in Your forgiveness; You are excellent in Your kindness; You are excellent in Your kingship. *Praise the Lord! Praise, O servants of the Lord. Praise the name of the Lord. Blessed be the name of the Lord from this time forth and forever. From the rising of the sun to its setting the name of the Lord is to be praised.* I will praise You for Your excellent creation; I will praise You for Your excellent authority; I will praise You for Your excellent salvation; I will praise You for Your excellent redemption. Yes, indeed, O Lord, *how excellent is Your name in all the earth!*

Psalms 57:7-11; 113:1-3; 8:1

Ruler of the Nations

For the kingdom is the LORD's and He rules over the nations.

PSALM 22:28

O God, You are Ruler of the Nations. *O clap your hands, shout to God with the voice of joy. For the Lord Most High is to be feared, a great King over all the earth. He subdues peoples under us, and nations under our feet. He chooses our inheritance for us, the glory of Jacob whom He loves. God has ascended with a shout, the Lord, with the shout of a trumpet. Sing praises to God, sing praises; sing praises to our King, sing praises. For God is the King of all the earth; sing praises with a skillful psalm. God reigns over the nations, God sits on His holy throne. The princes of the people have assembled themselves as the people of the God of Abraham; for the shields of the earth belong to God; He is highly exalted.* Most certainly, Almighty One, I will worship You as Sovereign Ruler over all mankind, past, present, and future. *There is none like You, O Lord; You are great, and great is Your name in might. Who would not fear You, O King of the nations? Indeed it is Your due! For among all the wise men of the nations, and in all their kingdoms, there is none like You.* Therefore, *ascribe to the Lord the glory due His name; bring an offering, and come before Him; worship the Lord in holy array. Tremble before Him all the earth; indeed, the world is firmly established, it will not be moved. Let the heavens be glad, and let the earth rejoice; and let them say among the nations, "The Lord reigns."*

Psalm 47:1-9; Jeremiah 10:6-7; 1 Chronicles 16:28-31

God of the Afflicted

The Spirit of the Lord GOD is upon me, because the LORD has anointed me to bring good news to the afflicted.

ISAIAH 61:1

O God, You are the God of the Afflicted. I hold onto to this beautiful promise: *The afflicted and needy are seeking water, but there is none, and their tongue is parched with thirst; I, the Lord, will answer them Myself, as the God of Israel I will not forsake them. I will open rivers on the bare heights, and springs in the midst of the valleys; I will make the wilderness a pool of water, and the dry land fountains of water.* Thank You, O God, for personally coming to my rescue. You are the Intimate One who runs to my aid. There, You will either change my circumstance or change my perspective, for You know which is best for me. These ancient words give me present-day hope: *O people in Zion, inhabitant in Jerusalem, you will weep no longer. I will surely be gracious to you at the sound of your cry; when I hear it, I will answer you.* Again, thank You for hearing me; thank You for answering me; thank You for being gracious to me in times of trouble. *You put my tears in a bottle;* they are neither unseen nor unfelt by You. Indeed, You give me hope by saying, *O afflicted one, storm-tossed, and not comforted, behold, I will set your stones in antimony, and your foundations I will lay in sapphires. Moreover, I will make your battlements of rubies, and your gates of crystal, and your entire wall of precious stones. ... In righteousness you will be established.* Thank You my Savior, Redeemer, and Friend.

Isaiah 41:17-18; 30:19; Psalm 56:8; Isaiah 54:11-12,14

Gift Giver

For God so loved the world, that He gave His only begotten Son, that whoever believes in Him shall not perish, but have eternal life.

JOHN 3:16

O God, You are the Gift Giver. I love these words of truth: *The wages of sin is death but the free gift of God is eternal life in Christ Jesus our Lord.* To think, You have given me eternal life! Yes, when I placed my trust in You, dear Jesus—Your life, Your death, and Your resurrection—I received incomprehensible blessing of life forever. My soul shouts with awe and gratitude, *Thanks be to God for Your indescribable gift!* And the good news is, I don't have to wait until my last breath here on this earth to receive this lavish life. No, newness of life begins with You right now. Your word says, *the love of God has been poured out within our hearts through the Holy Spirit who was given to us.* Yes, dear Lord, through Your Spirit I have been given *love, joy, peace, patience, kindness, goodness, faithfulness, gentleness, and self-control.* O Gift Giver, Your grace abounds! I embrace Your words of promise: *I came that you might have life and have it abundantly.* So today and tomorrow, and the next day, and the next, and for all eternity, I will praise You for Your overwhelming generosity. Indeed, *every good thing bestowed and every perfect gift is from above, coming down from the Father of lights, with whom there is no variation or shifting of shadow.* Oh yes, how good the Gift Giver is to me!

**Romans 6:23; 2 Corinthians 9:15; Romans 5:5; Galatians 5:22-23;
John 10:10; James 1:17**

One Who Questions

Do you not know? Have you not heard?

ISAIAH 40:28

O God, You are the One Who Questions. Yes, Lord, *You called to Adam in the garden, saying, "Where are you?"* May this simple question resonate within me, causing me to consider, "Where is my heart in relation to You?" And You spoke to Job in reproof from a whirlwind saying, *Where were you when I laid the foundations of the earth?* God, may this question to Job remind me of Your almighty power and my humble insignificance in relation to creating and sustaining the universe. And You asked Jonah, *Do you have good reason to be angry?* Again, dear Lord, may these words cause me to rethink my motives when I see things from a selfish perspective. And to the disciples, You questioned, *Why are you timid, you men of little faith?* Dear Lord, in times of trouble, I hear You ask me about my own wavering faith as well. And to Saul, You asked, *Why are You persecuting me?* Lord, this question hurts my heart; may I never intentionally slander or be ashamed of Your name! Cause me to listen to the questions You have presented before these men of old, and then help me to carefully evaluate my own relationship with You. Yes, I want to be a follower who walks with You as Friend, reveres You as Creator, submits to You as Sovereign Lord, believes in You as the All-Powerful One, and proclaims You as the Savior of the world. You extended Your loving mercy to each one of these biblical men; I thank You that You will do the same for me. May Your holy questions continually bring about divine answers from my heart.

Genesis 3:9; Job 38:4; Jonah 4:4; Matthew 8:26; Acts 9:4

One Who Answers

"Sirs, what must I do to be saved?" They said, "Believe in the Lord Jesus, and you shall be saved."

ACTS 16:30–31

O God, You are the One Who Answers. Yes, dear Lord Jesus, You respond to people's questions with the truth of Yourself. I will glean from these characters of old: *Now when John in prison heard the works of Christ, he sent word by his disciples, and said to Him, "Are you the Expected One, or shall we look for someone else?" And Jesus answered and said to them, "Go and report to John what you hear and see: the blind receive sight and the lame walk, the lepers are cleansed and the deaf hear, and the dead are raised up and the poor have the gospel preached to them. And blessed is he who keeps from stumbling over Me."* Also, there was Nicodemus who *said to Him, "How can a man be born when he is old? He cannot enter a second time into his mother's womb and be born, can he?" Jesus answered, "Truly, truly, I say to you, unless one is born of water and the Spirit, he cannot enter into the kingdom of God."* And also, *Pilate therefore said to Him, "So You are a king?" Jesus answered, "You say correctly that I am a king. For this I have been born, and for this I have come into the world, to bear witness to truth. Everyone who is of the truth hears My voice."* And You answered Your own question through Your angels as they spoke the greatest message to the women outside the empty tomb: *Why do you seek the living One among the dead? He is not here, but He has risen.* Yes, Lord Jesus, You have risen indeed! Now I will join the company and say with gladness, *On the day I called, You answered me; You have made me bold with strength in my soul.* I thank You, O Lord, for offering to all mankind the perfect Answer, Jesus Christ.

Matthew 11:3-6; John 3:4-5; 18:37; Luke 24:5-6; Psalm 138:3

One Who Opens

He who is holy, who is true, who has the key of David, who opens and no one will shut.
REVELATION 3:7

O God, You are the One Who Opens. Yes, O Lord, You opened the floodgates of heaven and caused *the rain to fall upon the earth for forty days and forty nights.* And later, You opened up the sky again and sent *bread from heaven* for forty years in the desert land. And then even later, You promised to all Your people, *I, the Lord, will answer them Myself, as the God of Israel I will not forsake them, I will open rivers on the bare heights, and springs in the midst of the valleys; I will make the wilderness a pool of water, and the dry land fountains of water.* And then, Lord Jesus, on multiple occasions, *You opened the eyes of the blind so that each one could see clearly.* Dear Lord, help me understand the purpose of these supernatural events is to open the eyes of my own heart to who You are: a righteous, benevolent, powerful, and compassionate Savior. You long for me to know You in these ways. You desire to abide in me through Your Spirit, yet You will not forcefully invade. You say to each one of us with longing, *Ask, and it shall be given to you; seek, and you shall find; knock, and it shall be opened to you. For everyone who asks receives, and he who seeks finds, and to him who knocks it shall be opened.* Yes, O Lord, I thank You for the work of gracefully Opening my heart to You. Please come in and abide forever.

Genesis 7:12; Exodus 16:4; Isaiah 41:17-18; John 9:25; Matthew 7:7-8

One Who Closes

*He who is holy, who is true, who has the key of David, who opens and no one will shut,
and who shuts and no one opens …*

REVELATION 3:7

O God, You are the One Who Closes. Yes, Lord, once sin entered, You closed Adam and Eve *out of the garden of Eden.* You then sent them forward with the promise of redemption. And later, *You closed the door of the ark behind Noah and all those who entered it.* You then sent them forward with the promise of protection. And still later, *You sent Your angel to shut the lions' mouths when Daniel was cast into their den.* You then sent him forward as a man of power. And *when Elijah fervently prayed, You closed the heavens and stopped the rain for three years and six months.* You then sent this message forward to teach us to pray. O God, You closed gates, doors, mouths, and the heavens to exhibit Your holiness, protection, care, and purpose. Cause me to be satisfied when You choose to close a door in my life today. Remind me that You know best, and You have best, even when it doesn't feel best. Your plan is always to send me forward, in my growth and knowledge of You. Help me to trust You and Your ways. Yes, I will choose to rest in this reassuring promise: *You have enclosed me behind and before, and laid Your hand upon me.* Dear Lord, as You Close in on me, I will walk forward with You.

Genesis 3:24; 7:16; Daniel 6:22; James 5:17; Psalm 139:5

Magnified

Let all who seek You rejoice and be glad in You; and let those who love Your salvation say continually, "Let God be magnified."

PSALM 70:4

O God, You are Magnified. *Give ear, O heavens, and let me speak; and let the earth hear the words of my mouth. Let my teaching drop as the rain, my speech distill as the dew, as the droplets on the fresh grass and as the showers on the herb. For I proclaim the name of the Lord; ascribe greatness to our God! The Rock! His work is perfect for all His ways are just; a God of faithfulness and without injustice, righteous and upright is He.* In addition, *Your lovingkindness, O Lord, extends to the heavens, Your faithfulness reaches to the skies. Your righteousness is like the mountains of the deep. Your judgments are like a great deep. You preserve man and beast.* Again and again, *I will praise the name of God with song, and I shall magnify Him with thanksgiving.* Yes, Lord, *as for me I will hope continually. And I will praise You yet more and more. My mouth shall tell of Your righteousness, and of Your salvation all day long; for I do not know the sum of them. I will come with the mighty deeds of the Lord God; I will make mention of Your righteousness, Yours alone.* Dear God, all my desire is in You; may it be said concerning my thoughts, words, and deeds that *the name of the Lord Jesus was magnified* in my life. Yes, with loving conviction and hopeful influence, I will stay the course. *I will bless the Lord at all times; His praise shall continually be in my mouth. My soul shall make its boast in the Lord and the humble will hear it and rejoice.*

Deuteronomy 32:1-4; Psalm 36:5-6; Psalm 69:30; Psalm 71:14-16; Acts 19:17; Psalm 34:1-2

One Who Humbles

"I, Nebuchadnezzar, was at ease in my house and flourishing in my palace."

DANIEL 4:4

O God, You are the One Who Humbles. Your word says: *There are six things which You hate, yes, seven which are an abomination to You: haughty eyes, a lying tongue, and hands that shed innocent blood, a heart that devises wicked plans, feet that run rapidly to evil, a false witness who utters lies, and one who spreads strife among brothers.* Dear Lord, because of Your holiness, You must deal with each one of these sins, not only for our good, but for Your glory. I see how You humbled *Pharaoh because he would not let Your people go.* And I see how you humbled *Moses when he disobeyed You by striking the rock.* And I see how You humbled *Your servant Eli because he was negligent in his priestly duties.* And I see how You humbled *Haman when he tried to destroy Your nation Israel.* Yes, Lord, You say that *You will not give Your glory to another.* Indeed, *Your works are true and Your ways are just, and You are able to humble those who walk in pride.* Please, Lord, forgive me for trying to make my own plans, or for trying to get my own way in spite of how it might affect my relationship with You and those around me. I hear Your words: *Return to Me, for I am gracious and compassionate, slow to anger, abounding in lovingkindness, and relenting of evil.* Thank You, O God, for mercifully putting me in my proper place. For *You are opposed to the proud, but You give grace to the humble.*

Proverbs 6:16-19; Exodus 10:7; Numbers 20:7-12; 1 Samuel 3:11-13; Esther 7:9-10;Isaiah 42:8; Daniel 4:37; Joel 2:13; James 4:6

One Who Exalts

Humble yourselves in the presence of the Lord, and He will exalt you.
JAMES 4:10

O God, You are the One Who Exalts. Your word says: *Blessed are the poor in spirit, for theirs is the kingdom of heaven. Blessed are those who mourn, for they shall be comforted. Blessed are the gentle, for they shall inherit the earth.* Yes, dear Lord, You favor those whose hearts are bent toward You in humble adoration. I see how You exalted the young boy *Samuel to be a great prophet in Israel.* And I see how You chose t*he shepherd boy David and made him a mighty king.* And I see how You found favor with lowly *Mary and called her to be the mother of the long awaited Messiah.* And I see how You, dear Jesus, exalted *the poor widow who gave all that she had into the treasury.* Dear Lord, I love how You love the simple, the humble, and the meek. Help me to take heed and abide by these words of truth: *He has done mighty deeds with His arm; He has scattered those who were proud in the thoughts of their hearts. He has brought down rulers from their thrones, and has exalted those who were humble.* Trusting You, O God, is the best way, the only way. Yes, just King, I will bend my knee to the One Who Exalts.

**Matthew 5:3-5; 1 Samuel 3:19-20; 16:12-13;
Luke 1:30-32; 21:1-4; 1:51-52**

One Who Washes

Purify me with hyssop, and I shall be clean; wash me, and I will be whiter than snow.
PSALM 51:7

O God, You are the One Who Washes. Yes, Lord, I am reminded of the story of Naaman who had leprosy: *Elisha sent a messenger to him saying, "Go and wash in the Jordan seven times, and your flesh shall be restored to you and you shall be clean". … So he went down and dipped himself seven times in the Jordan, according to the word of the man of God; and his flesh was restored like the flesh of a little child, and he was clean.* And another time much later, dear Jesus, *a leper came to You, and bowed down to You and said, "Lord, if You are willing, You can make me clean. And You stretched out Your hand and touched him and said, "I am willing; be cleansed."* And immediately, the *leprosy was cleansed.* God, indeed, You are always willing! I know both of these true stories point to the greater truth of the cleansing of my soul. I hear You say to me and all the world, *Do you want to be made well?* And You offer salvation: *Come now, let us reason together, though your sins are as scarlet, they will be as white as snow; though they are red like crimson, they will be like wool.* Through Your perfect blood that You willingly shed at the cross, dear Jesus, we have perfect healing, perfect forgiveness. Yes, dear Messiah, I want to be made well. Thank You for *washing me thoroughly from my iniquity, and cleansing me from my sin.*

2 Kings 5:10,14; Matthew 8:2-3; John 5:6; Isaiah 1:18; Psalm 51:2

september 25

Friend of Sinners

When Jesus came to the place, He looked up and said to him, "Zacchaeus, hurry and come down, for today I must stay at your house."

LUKE 19:5

O God, You are a Friend of Sinners. I love how this passage speaks clearly about Your heart: *Now all the tax-gatherers and the sinners were coming near Him to listen to Him. And both the Pharisees and the scribes began to grumble, saying, "This man receives sinners and eats with them." And He told them this parable, saying, "What man among you, if he has a hundred sheep and has lost one of them does not leave the ninety-nine in the open pasture, and go after the one which is lost, until he finds it? And when he has found it, he lays it on his shoulders, rejoicing. And when he comes home, he calls together his friends and his neighbors, saying to them, 'Rejoice with me, for I have found my sheep which was lost!' I tell you that in the same way, there will be more joy in heaven over one sinner who repents, than over ninety-nine righteous persons who need no repentance."* O God, thank You for Your pursuit; thank You for Your mercy; thank You for Your great love. You say in truth, *It is not those who are well who need a physician, but those who are sick. I have not come to call the righteous but sinners to repentance.* Indeed, *You touched the leper. . . . You forgave the adulteress. . . . You dined with sinners.* You listened; You understood; You cared. You spoke truth; You explained; You influenced. You gave grace and mercy, wisdom and instruction. And Your *kindness led to repentance.* Dear Savior, I want to thank You for sitting with me.

Luke 15:1-7; 5:31-32,12-13; John 8:10-11; Matthew 9:11; Romans 2:4

Unhindered

And (Paul) stayed two full years in his own rented quarters and was welcoming all who came to him, preaching the kingdom of God and teaching concerning the Lord Jesus Christ with all openness, unhindered.

ACTS 28:30–31

O God, You are Unhindered. Indeed, nothing prohibits Your will from being done. Your word through the apostle Paul says, *We have this treasure in earthen vessels, that the surpassing greatness of the power may be of God and not from ourselves; we are afflicted in every way, but not crushed; perplexed, but not despairing; persecuted, but not forsaken; struck down, but not destroyed; always carrying about in the body the dying of Jesus, that the life of Jesus also may be manifested in our body.* Yes, dear Lord, Paul and his companions, *as servants of God, ... suffered afflictions, hardships, distresses, beatings, imprisonment, tumults, labors,* all for the sake of the gospel, and Your good news prevailed mightily through them! The ultimate enemy could not inhibit the persistent progression of the truth about Jesus being Savior of the world. Paul again attests to this as he urges his fellow believers, *Remember Jesus Christ, risen from the dead, descendant of David, according to my gospel, for which I suffer hardship even to imprisonment as a criminal; but the word of God is not imprisoned.* So dear Lord, help me to take courage as I continue my walk of faith day to day. When obstacles come, help me to know that You are at work through them. Help me to trust You more. You know what You are doing, even when I don't. I will remember Your ancient words today as I move faithfully forward: *Be steadfast immovable, always abounding in the work of the Lord, knowing that your toil is not in vain in the Lord.* Yes, dear Lord, may Your gospel be Unhindered through me.

2 Corinthians 4:7-11; 6:4-5; 2 Timothy 2:8-9; 1 Corinthians 15:58

One Who Separates

He who is not with Me is against Me; and he who does not gather with Me scatters.
MATTHEW 12:30

O God, You are the One Who Separates. First of all, in love, *You have given us eternal life, and this life is in Your Son.* Thank You for this gift. I know I will never lose my salvation, even when I mess up, again and again. But You also say this: *For faith, if it has no works, is dead, being by itself.* So I understand that salvation is not a mindless box that I check, but a heartfelt life that I live, following Jesus as my Lord and Master. For You say to each of us, *Come, follow Me.* I will never live my faith out perfectly, but I can learn and grow each day. Jesus, You know every heart, and see true faith. You explain it this way: *But when the Son of Man comes in His glory, and all the angels with Him, then He will sit on His glorious throne. And all the nations will be gathered before Him; and He will separate them from one another, as the shepherd separates the sheep from the goats; and He will put the sheep on His right, and the goats on the left. Then the King will say to those on His right, "Come, you who are blessed of My Father, inherit the kingdom prepared for you from the foundation of the world. For I was hungry, and you gave Me something to eat; I was thirsty, and you gave Me drink; I was a stranger, and you invited Me in; naked, and you clothed Me; I was sick and you visited Me; I was in prison, and you came to Me. ... Truly I say to you, to the extent that you did it to one of these brothers of Mine, even the least of them, you did it to Me." Then He will also say to those on His left, "Depart from Me, accursed ones, into the eternal fire which has been prepared for the devil and his angels; for I was hungry, and you gave Me nothing to eat; I was thirsty, and you gave Me nothing to drink; I was a stranger, and you did not invite Me in; naked, and you did not clothe Me; sick, and in prison, and you did not visit Me. ... Truly I say to you, to the extent that you did not do it to one of the least of these, you did not do it to Me." And these will go away into eternal punishment, but the righteous into eternal life.* O God, Your words are truth. You will separate those who truly believe with their hearts from those who do not. Dear Lord, I truly believe! I ask You to make my faith come alive; *separate me unto the gospel.* I want to follow You more and more each day. Continue to help me; for I am Your sheep in Your fold.

1 John 5:11; James 2:17;Matthew 4:19; Matthew 25:31-36, 41-46; Romans 1:1

One Who Hates Evil

Seek good and not evil, that you may live; and thus may the LORD God of hosts be with you, just as you have said! Hate evil, and love good, and establish justice in the gate!
AMOS 5:14-15

O God, You are the One Who Hates Evil. Wickedness brings such calamity on the people You love. And God, You so loved the world! Help me always remember, Satan is the evil one, not You. He is the one who deceives and *holds people captive to do his will.* Yes, he is called *the god of this world who has blinded the minds of the unbelieving, that they might not see the light of the gospel of the glory of Christ, who is the image of God.* But, You, O God hold the ultimate answer and the end of the story. First, You tell us to *put on Your full armor so that we will be able to stand firm against the schemes of the devil.* Second, You, dear Jesus, pray for each of us saying, *I do not ask You to take them out of the world, but to keep and protect them from the evil one.* And third, You fight for us concerning evil: *Gird You sword on Your thigh, O mighty One, in Your splendor and majesty! And in Your majesty ride on victoriously. ... Your arrows are in the heart of the King's enemies. Your throne, O God, is forever and ever; a scepter of uprightness is the scepter of Your kingdom. You have loved righteousness, and hated wickedness.* Almighty One, Your word promises that on some great day You will finally destroy all the evil in this world: *And the devil who deceived them was thrown into the lake of fire and brimstone, where the beast and the false prophet are also; and they will be tormented day and night forever and ever. ... And there will be a new heaven and a new earth. ... He will wipe away every tear from their eyes; and there shall no longer be any death; there shall no longer be any mourning, or crying, or pain,* because the God Who Hates Evil will have destroyed it completely.

**2 Timothy 2:26; 2 Corinthians 4:4; Ephesians 6:11; John 17:15;
Psalm 45:3-7; Revelation 20:10; 21:1,4**

Better Master

For the mind set on the flesh is death, but the mind set on the Spirit is life and peace.
ROMANS 8:6

O God, You are the Better Master. Jesus, You say so clearly, *No man can serve two masters.* God, I ask for Your help. So quickly my heart becomes divided and I am swayed to serve things other than You; and these false gods only leave me anxious, dissatisfied, and guilt-ridden. Help me to take Your life-giving words to heart: *Do you not know that when you present yourselves to someone as slaves of obedience, you are slaves of the one whom you obey, either of sin resulting in death, or of obedience resulting in righteousness? But thanks be to God that though you were slaves of sin, you became obedient from the heart to that form of teaching to which you were committed, and having been freed from sin, you became slaves of righteousness.* You make it clear to me by saying: *For if you are living according to the flesh, you must die; but if by the Spirit you are putting to death the deeds of the body, you will live.* Yes, dear Lord, I want to live! I know and believe that bondage to You is really freedom in You. Your ways are good and kind and merciful. Dear Jesus, let me remember Your heartfelt plea: *It was for freedom that I set you free; therefore keep standing firm and do not be subject again to a yoke of slavery.* Indeed, my God, You are the Better Master.

Matthew 6:24; Romans 6:16-18; 8:13; Galatians 5:1

One Who Upholds

For I am the LORD your God, who upholds your right hand.

Isaiah 41:13

O God, You are the One Who Upholds. Indeed, You uphold me with Your promising word. You say, *Do not fear, for I am with you; do not look about you, for I am your God. I will strengthen you, surely I will help you, surely I will uphold you with My righteous right hand.* Also, You uphold me with Your awesome power: *For You have a strong arm; Your hand is mighty, Your right hand is exalted.* And, You uphold me by Your Spirit: *I will put My Spirit within you and you will come to life.* Furthermore, You uphold me with Your people: *So it came about when Moses held his hand up, that Israel prevailed, and when he let his hand down, Amalek prevailed. But Moses' hands were heavy. Then they took a stone and put it under him, and he sat on it; and Aaron and Hur supported his hands, one on one side and one on the other. Thus his hands were steady until the sun set.* O God, thank You for the ways in which You fortify me! Yes, because of You, *when I am weak, then I am strong.* I pray, through Your strength, that I, too, can help uphold a struggling friend or stranger. Yes, through *Your power that mightily works within me,* cause me to *strengthen the hands that are weak and the knees that are feeble, and make straight paths for the feet, so that the limb which is lame may not be put out of joint, but rather be healed.* Indeed, O God, I praise You for the way You work. For You are the One Who Upholds through Your word, Your power, Your Spirit, and Your people.

**Isaiah 41:10; Psalm 89:13; Ezekiel 37:14; Exodus 17:11-12;
2 Corinthians 12:10; Colossians 1:29; Hebrews 12:12-13**

Music Lover

Righteousness and justice are the foundation of Your throne; lovingkindness and truth go before You. How blessed are the people who know the joyful sound! O LORD, they walk in the light of Your countenance.

PSALM 89:14-15

O God, You are the Music Lover. You created rhythm and rhyme, melody and movement. Yes, there is music beautifully blaring from on high: *Praise the Lord! Praise the Lord from the heavens; praise Him in the heights! Praise Him all His angels; praise Him, all His hosts!* I can only imagine the holy voices and heavenly motions of the myriads of angels, singing and dancing with joy. And then on earth, You handed this same command down to Your people, and Your response was powerful: *And all the Levitical singers, Asaph, Heman, Jeduthun, and their sons and kinsmen, clothed in fine linen, with cymbals, harps, and lyres, standing east of the altar, and with them one hundred and twenty priests blowing trumpets in unison when the trumpeters and the singers were to make themselves heard with one voice to praise and to glorify the Lord, and when they lifted up their voice accompanied by trumpets and cymbals and instruments of music, and when they praised the Lord saying, "He indeed is good for His lovingkindness is everlasting," then the house, the house of the Lord, was filled with a cloud, so that the priests could not stand to minister because of the cloud, for the glory of the Lord filled the house of God.* Dear Music Lover, I, too, want to *sing praises to Your name, O Most High.* Yes, I will join the chorus in both heaven and on earth! *Praise Him with trumpet sound; praise Him with harp and lyre. Praise Him with timbrel and dancing; praise Him with stringed instruments and pipe. Praise Him with loud cymbals; praise Him with resounding cymbals. Let everything that has breath praise the Lord. Praise the Lord!*

Psalm 148:1-2; 2 Chronicles 5:12-14; Psalms 9:2; 150:3-6

One Who Exists

The fool has said in his heart, "There is no God."
PSALM 14:1

O God, You are the One Who Exists. I cannot walk outside without knowing Your existence is an absolute truth. *The heavens are telling of Your glory; and their expanse is declaring the work of Your hands. Day to day pours forth speech, and night to night reveals knowledge.* Your word says to each one of us: *For since the creation of the world His invisible attributes, His eternal power and divine nature, have been clearly seen, being understood through what has been made, so that we are without excuse.* Ah yes, so all people of all nations of all history have been given clear evidence to discern that there is a Creator God who makes Himself known through His magnificent creation. Dear Merciful One, I ask You to take our blinders off so we can see You through eyes of faith! May each one of us declare from our hearts these truths about You: *You are the God who made the world and all things in it. You are the Lord of heaven and earth, who does not dwell in temples made with hands; neither are You served by human hands, as though You needed anything, since You Yourself give to all life and breath and all things. You made from one, every nation of mankind to live on all the face of the earth, having determined their appointed times, and boundaries of their habitation, that we should seek You, if perhaps we might grope for You and find You, though You are not far from each one of us; for in You we live and move and exist.* Yes, God, I believe in You. And I know for sure, *in Your hand is the life of every living thing, and the breath of all mankind.* Indeed, if You did not exist, then neither would I.

Psalm 19:1-2; Romans 1:20; Acts 17:24-28; Job 12:10

God of Free Will

Behold, I stand at the door and knock; if anyone hears My voice and opens the door, I will come in to him and will dine with him, and he with Me.

REVELATION 3:20

O God, You are the God of Free Will. In Your sovereignty, You knock at the door of our hearts, waiting for a response. Because of Your love, You do not force Your way in and take over. But God, You do know Your way is most certainly the way of truth. And You also know all other paths only lead to our demise. You said to Your people of old as they graciously entered the promised land: *See, I am setting before you today a blessing and a curse: the blessing, if you listen to the commandments of the Lord your God, which I am commanding you today; and the curse, if you do not listen to the commandments of the Lord your God, but turn aside from the way which I am commanding you today, by following other gods which you have not known.* Again, You do not force us to believe in You and to obey You, but You do give us fair warning of the consequences if we don't. And how it grieves Your heart when we freely choose to walk away from Your protective love! You continue Your plea with Your people through Moses, *For this commandment which I command you today is not too difficult for you, nor is it out of reach … but the word is very near you, in your mouth and in your heart, that you may observe it. See, I have set before you today life and prosperity, and death and adversity … So choose life in order that you may live, you and your descendants, by loving the Lord your God, by obeying His voice, and by holding fast to Him.* Dear Jesus, I hear You knocking! Please come in and take over because I am so prone to chase after other gods. Fortify my free will in Your protective one. I will rely on Your promise: *And I shall give them one heart, and shall put a new spirit within them. And I shall take the heart of stone out of their flesh and give them a heart of flesh, that they may walk in My statutes and keep My ordinances, and do them. Then they will be My people, and I shall be their God.* Yes, Lord, please be Commander of my Free Will.

Deuteronomy 11:26-29; 30:11,14-15,19-20; Ezekiel 11:19-20

Treasure

Guard, through the Holy Spirit who dwells in us, the treasure which has been entrusted to you.

2 TIMOTHY 1:14

O God, You are the Treasure. Dear Jesus, You say to Your followers, *Do not lay up for yourselves treasures upon earth, where moths and rust destroy, and where thieves break in and steal. But lay up for yourselves treasures in heaven, where neither moths nor rust destroys, and where thieves do not break in or steal; for where your treasure is, there will your heart be also.* You also explain, *The kingdom of heaven is like a treasure hidden in the field, which a man found and hid; and from joy over it he goes and sells all that he has, and buys the field. Again, the kingdom of heaven is like a merchant seeking fine pearls, and upon finding one pearl of great value, he went and sold all that he had, and bought it.* Dear Jesus, King of heaven, You are the great Treasure of my soul! Nothing on earth compares to You. You have filled me with Yourself and now I have hope. *And this hope does not disappoint, because the love of God has been poured out within my heart through the Holy Spirit who was given to me.* In You, I am rich; in You, I am content; in You, I am overflowing with joy. Indeed, I can declare with the psalmist, *The Lord is my Shepherd, I shall not want!* So dear Lord, as I live out my days, with the earthly temptations coming my way, help me to hold tightly to the satisfying truths in Your word. May I daily dwell on the eternal jewels that I have hidden in my heart. Yes, each day, humble me with this remarkable truth: *We have this treasure in earthen vessels, that the surpassing greatness of the power may be of God and not from ourselves.* Indeed, I will hold fast to Your abundance.

Matthew 6:19-21; 13:44-46; Romans 5:5; Psalm 23:1; 2 Corinthians 4:7

Greater One

Surely You are not greater than our father Abraham, who died? The prophets died too; whom do You make Yourself out to be?

JOHN 8:53

O God, You are the Greater One. Dear Jesus, all of your prophets spoke of You, and their lifestyles even portrayed glimpses of You. And then, You fulfilled all these prophecies when You entered the world as the God-Man. You stood in the midst of the unbelieving Jews and said, *"Your father Abraham rejoiced to see My day, and he saw it and was glad."* The Jews therefore said to Him, *"You are not yet fifty years old, and have You seen Abraham?"* Jesus said to them, *"Truly, truly, before Abraham was born, I am."* And also, You sat with the woman at the well and answered her question, *"You are not greater than our father Jacob, are You, who gave us the well, and drank of it himself, and his sons, and his cattle?"* Jesus answered and said to her, *"Everyone who drinks of this water shall thirst again; but whoever drinks of the water that I shall give him shall never thirst; but the water that I shall give him shall become in him a well of water springing up to eternal life."* Indeed, Anointed Messiah, You are greater than all prophets and kings. Even though You were called *the Son of David,* King David himself, knowing his proper place, *in the Spirit called You "Lord."* And Jesus, You say again, concerning Yourself, *Something greater than Jonah is here* and *Something greater than Solomon is here.* Therefore I will worship You and You alone with all my heart. For You, O God, have always been and forever will be the Greater One.

John 8:56-58; 4:12-14; Matthew 22:42-43; 12:41-42

God of Good Works

For we are His workmanship, created in Christ Jesus for good works, which God pre-pared beforehand, that we would walk in them.

EPHESIANS 2:10

O God, You are the God of Good Works. Your word makes the salvation message very clear: *For by grace you have been saved through faith, and that it is not of yourselves, it is a gift of God; not as a result of works, that no one should boast.* May I never be deceived that I have to climb a merit ladder to reach heaven; for this is impossible. However, You do call each of us to be Your hands and feet on this earth. So prod me, dear Lord, to move away from my comfortable lifestyle and step into whatever You have planned. Renew my vision concerning these instructional words, *You are the light of the world. A city on a hill cannot be hidden. Nor do men light a lamp, and put it under the peck-measure, but on the lampstand; and it gives light to all who are in the house. Let your light shine before men in such a way that they may see your good works, and glorify your Father who is in heaven.* Yes, Lord, fill me with Your light and send me out into this dark world. As I go, help me to obey Your words and hold onto Your promises: *Love your enemies, and do good, and lend, expecting nothing in return; and your reward will be great, and you will be sons of the Most High; for He Himself is kind to ungrateful and evil men. Be merciful, just as your Father is merciful. And do not judge and you will not be judged; and do not condemn, and you will not be condemned; pardon, and you will be pardoned. Give, and it will be given to you; good measure, pressed down, shaken together, running over, they will pour into your lap. For by your standard of measure it will be measured to you in return.* Lord, I confess, I need Your Spirit to do these good works! As I walk forward in faith, I will cling to You promising words, *I am able to make all grace abound to you, that always having all sufficiency in everything, you may have an abundance for every good deed.* Yes, Lord, shine Your light through me and be glorified through each one of my Good Works.

Ephesians 2:8-9; Matthew 5:14-16; Luke 6:35-38; 2 Corinthians 9:8

One Who Sows

Listen to this! Behold, the sower went out to sow.
MARK 4:3

O God, You are the One Who Sows. Dear Jesus, You taught this concept in this parable: *It came about when he was sowing, some seed fell beside the road, and the birds came and ate it up. And other seed fell on the rocky ground where it did not have much soil; and immediately it sprang up because it had no depth of soil. And after the sun had risen, it was scorched; and because it had no root, it withered away. And other seed fell among the thorns, and thorns came up and choked it, and it yielded no crop. And other seeds fell into the good soil and as they grew up and increased, they yielded a crop and produced thirty, sixty, and a hundredfold.* And then You explained Your story: *The sower sows the word. And these are the ones who are beside the road where the word is sown; and when they hear, immediately Satan comes and takes away the word which has been sown in them. And in a similar way these are the ones on whom seed was sown on the rocky places, who, when they hear the word, immediately receive it with joy; and they have no firm root in themselves, but are only temporary; then, when affliction or persecution arises because of the word, immediately they fall away. And others are the ones on whom seed was sown among the thorns; these are the ones who have heard the word, and the worries of the world, and the deceitfulness of riches, and the desires for other things enter in and choke the word, and it becomes unfruitful. And those are the ones on whom seed was sown on the good soil; and they hear the word and accept it, and bear fruit, thirty, sixty, and a hundredfold.* O God, sow Your word into me, I pray. Make my heart resemble the good soil. Remove rocks of unbelief and thorns of worry, deceit, and worldly desire. I ask for deep roots of rich faith in Your love so that I may bear fruit that brings glory to Your name. Yes, Sower of the word, sow Your beautiful seed in me.

Mark 4:4-8,14-20

One Who Reaps

Many are the sorrows of the wicked, but he who trusts in the LORD, lovingkindness shall surround him. Be glad in the LORD and rejoice, you righteous ones; and shout for joy, all you who are upright in heart.

PSALM 32:10–11

O God, You are the One Who Reaps. Your word warns: *Do not be deceived, God is not mocked; for whatever a man sows, this he will also reap. For the one who sows to his own flesh shall from the flesh reap corruption, but the one who sows to the Spirit shall from the Spirit reap eternal life.* So Lord, I see and understand that a lot (not all) of the things that happen to me, good or bad, are the direct result of the good or bad choices I make. Forgive me when I blame You for my own foolishness. But Your word also gives hope: *For just as you presented your members as slaves to impurity and to lawlessness, resulting in further lawlessness, so now present your members as slaves to righteousness, resulting in sanctification. For when you were slaves of sin, you were free in regard to righteousness. Therefore what benefit were you then deriving from the things of which you are now ashamed? For the outcome of these things is death. But now having been freed from sin and enslaved to God, you derive your benefit, resulting in sanctification, and the outcome, eternal life. For the wages of sin is death, but the free gift of God is eternal life in Christ Jesus our Lord.* O God, You came to sow Your truth into our hearts so that I could reap everlasting life! Indeed, through Jesus' death You say, *If He would render Himself as a guilt offering, He will see His offspring.* And also, *Unless a grain of wheat falls into the earth and dies, it remains by itself alone; but if it dies, it bears much fruit.* Thank You, dear Jesus, for dying that I might live. I pray now that I can be like You. Help me sow with sacrificial living and Spirit-led loving. And help me not to *sow sparingly because then I will reap sparingly;* instead, help me to *sow bountifully so that I can reap bountifully.* Yes, Lord, as I walk through my days, I will adhere to this encouraging promise: *And let us not lose heart in doing good, for in due time we shall reap if we do not grow weary.* Thank You for Your example, thank You for Your strength, and thank You for Your endurance. With You in me, I will keep sowing, and reaping, and sowing, and reaping, and sowing...

**Galatians 6:7-8; Romans 6:19-23; Isaiah 53:10; John 12:24;
2 Corinthians 9:6; Galatians 6:9**

Forerunner

This hope we have as an anchor of the soul, a hope both sure and steadfast and one which enters within the veil, where Jesus has entered as a forerunner for us.

HEBREWS 6:19–20

O God, You are the Forerunner. Indeed, Jesus, You came to earth to show us how to live both fully and flawlessly. Of course, You, being the God-Man did this without sin. But this is also true: *Although You were a Son, You learned obedience from the things which You suffered.* So dear Jesus, living a sinless life on this earth was not done "with ease" as a result of Your divine power; on the contrary, Your life was full of blood, sweat, and tears due to Your human nature. Scripture attests to this: *Although You existed in the form of God, You did not regard equality with God a thing to be grasped, but You emptied Yourself, taking the form of a bond-servant, and being made in the likeness of men. And being found in appearance as a man, You humbled Yourself by becoming obedient to the point of death, even death on a cross.* So I see and understand that You, dear Jesus, were fully dependent on Your Father's voice as well as fully submissive to His direction. And by the Spirit in You, You listened and You obeyed. Dear Forerunner, again, You showed us how to live! *You Yourself were tempted in that which You suffered, therefore You are able to come to the aid of those who are tempted.* Indeed, You have run this race; You know every twist and turn, every hill and valley, every rough place and smooth. Therefore, I will come to You for direction, inspiration, and strength. Yes, Lord, I ask You to *fill me with Your Spirit*, so that I too may *hear and know Your voice,* and then *keep Your word.* Forerunner, I want to trace Your steps.

Hebrews 5:8; Philippians 2:6-8; Hebrews 2:18; Ephesians 5:18; John 10:27; John 14:23

God of Work and Rest

A lazy man does not roast his prey, but the precious possession of a man is diligence.
PROVERBS 12:27

O God, You are the God of Work and Rest. This is evident in Your command, *You shall work six days, but on the seventh day you shall rest.* God, I pray that I will heed both instructions, working diligently, then resting peacefully; for You know this routine is for my greater good. Indeed, rest renews my strength. So I pray against both working too much and working too little. Yes, help me diligently *multiply the talents You have given to me instead of burying them,* whether it's due to fear, or laziness, or procrastination. I pray that I will do nothing more or nothing less than exactly what You have called me to do. Your word teaches this thought-provoking truth: *According to the grace of God which was given to me, as a wise master builder I laid a foundation, and another is building upon it. But let each man be careful how he builds upon it. For no man can lay a foundation other than the one which is laid, which is Jesus Christ. Now if any man builds upon the foundation with gold, silver, precious stones, wood, hay, straw, each man's work will become evident; for the day will show it, because it is to be revealed with fire; and the fire itself will test the quality of each man's work. If any man's work which he has built upon it remains, he shall receive a reward. If any man's work is burned up, he shall suffer loss; but he himself shall be saved, yet as through fire.* Again, dear God of Work and Rest, may I follow Your lead and do nothing more or nothing less than exactly what You have called me to do. For in the end, nothing else will matter.

Exodus 34:21; Matthew 25:14-30; 1 Corinthians 3:10-15

One Who Will Return

And as for me, I know that my Redeemer lives, and at the last He will take His stand on the earth. Even after my skin is destroyed, yet from my flesh I shall see God.

JOB 19:25-26

O God, You are the One Who Will Return. Long ago, the prophet Daniel spoke these words, *I kept looking in the night visions. And behold, with the clouds of heaven one like a Son of Man was coming, and He came up to the Ancient of Days and was presented before Him. And to Him was given dominion, glory and a kingdom, that all the peoples, nations, and men of every language might serve Him. His dominion is an everlasting dominion which will not pass away; and His kingdom is one which will not be destroyed.* And Jesus, while on earth You also spoke similar words concerning Your eventual return: *But in those days, after the tribulation, the sun will be darkened, and the moon will not give its light, and the stars will be falling from heaven, and the powers that are in the heavens will be shaken. And then they will see the Son of Man coming in clouds with great power and glory.* And after Your resurrection from the dead, the disciples stood and watched You ascend into heaven in a cloud: *And as they were gazing intently into the sky while He was departing, behold, two men in white clothing stood beside them; and they also said, Men of Galilee, why do you stand looking into the sky? This Jesus, who has been taken up from you into heaven, will come in just the same way as you have watched Him go into heaven.* O Savior and King, how I look forward to Your triumphant return! So much of this event remains a mystery to my mind, but I do know that my heart beats hopefully, and my soul waits expectantly. Yes, I will faithfully walk through each day, with my eyes focused on eternity with You. And while doing so, I will cling to Your promise: *But we shall all be changed, in a moment, in the twinkling of an eye, at the last trumpet; for the trumpet will sound, and the dead will be raised imperishable, and we shall be changed. For this perishable must put on the imperishable, and this mortal must put on immortality.* Yes, King of kings, when I look to the clouds, I will rejoice, eagerly waiting for Your glorious Return.

Daniel 7:13-14; Mark 13:24-26; Acts 1:10-11; 1 Corinthians 15:51-53

One that I Seek

But as for me, I will watch expectantly for the LORD; I will wait for the God of my salvation. My God will hear me.

MICAH 7:7

O God, You are the One that I Seek. Your word says: *Set your heart and your soul to seek the Lord your God.* Thank You for the men and women of old who walked before me as an example: *As enemies approached the land of Judah, King Jehoshaphat was afraid and turned his attention to seek the Lord; and proclaimed a fast throughout all Judah. So Judah gathered together to seek help from the Lord ... And he prayed, "O our God, will You judge them? For we are powerless before this great multitude who are coming against us; nor do we know what to do, but our eyes are on You."* I am also reminded of Queen Esther. She spoke to Mordecai concerning the possible extinction of the Jewish nation saying, *Go, assemble all the Jews who are found in Susa, and fast for me; do not eat or drink for three days, night or day. I and my maidens also will fast in the same way. And thus I will go in to the king, which is not according to the law; and if I perish, I perish.* Also, I think of the priest Ezra who was a great leader, concerning the return of the people to Jerusalem from Babylonian captivity: *He set his heart to study the law of the Lord, and to practice it, and to teach Your statutes and ordinances in Israel.* Again, thank You for these and so many others who have gone before me, showing me how to keep my eyes fixed on You. Now, it is my turn to walk by faith, being a living example in my own generation. Help me not to wander, O God; redirect my gaze towards You. Indeed, please become the bull's-eye of my life, targeting You and only You as my Leader. Make this my heart's cry, *O God, You are my God, I will seek You earnestly. My soul thirsts for You, my flesh yearns for You.* Most certainly, Savior God, with a new and determined resolve, *when You said, "Seek My face," my heart said to You, "Your face, dear Lord, I will seek."*

**1 Chronicles 22:19; 2 Chronicles 20:3-4,12; Esther 4:16;
Ezra 7:10; Psalms 63:1; 27:8**

True Life

For what does it profit a man to gain the whole world, and forfeit his soul? For what will a man give in exchange for his soul?

MARK 8:36–37

O God, You are True Life. Sometimes I feel I am on a constant merry-go-round with no start or finish. I'm dizzy with the spinning routine, overwhelmed with the constancy, and yet unsatisfied with the familiarity. And this is life? Then I hear Your words, *If anyone wishes to come after Me, let him deny himself, and take up his cross daily, and follow Me. For whoever wishes to save his life shall lose it, but whoever loses his life for My sake, he is the one who will save it.* O God, show me what this means for me personally. Show me how to get off my own self-absorbed carnival ride so I may truly live. I confess I'm fearful of the unknown and hesitant to deny myself of my daily ritualistic comforts. But my heart is drawn to Your paradoxical words such as these: *Is this not the fast which I choose, to loosen the bonds of wickedness, to undo the bands of the yoke, and to let the oppressed go free, and break every yoke? Is it not to divide your bread with the hungry, and bring the homeless poor into the house; when you see the naked, to cover him; and not to hide yourself from your own flesh? Then your light will break out like the dawn, and your recovery will speedily spring forth; and your righteousness will go before you; the glory of the Lord will be your rear guard. Then you will call, and the Lord will answer; you will cry, and He will say, 'Here I am.' … If you give yourself to the hungry, and satisfy the desire of the afflicted, then your light will rise in darkness, and your gloom will become like midday. And the Lord will continually guide you, and satisfy your desire in scorched places, and give strength to your bones; and you will be like a watered garden, and like a spring of water whose waters do not fail.* O God, I see that True Life comes through giving life to another, especially to those in need. You did this very thing for me, dear Jesus! Help me stop the habitual spin, merciful Savior, so I can willfully obey Your bold but bountiful challenge, *Come, follow Me.*

Luke 9:23-24; Isaiah 58:6-11; Matthew 4:19

True Love

So when they had finished breakfast, Jesus said to Simon Peter, "Simon, son of John, do you love Me?"

JOHN 21:15

O God, You are the God of True Love. And now, You ask each of one of us to be an outpouring of this same love. You explain with clear conviction in Your word: *If you speak with the tongues of men and of angels, but do not have love, you have become a noisy gong or a clanging cymbal. And if you have the gift of prophecy, and know all mysteries and all knowledge, and if you have all faith, so as to remove mountains, but do not have love, you are nothing. And if you give all your possessions to feed the poor, and if you deliver your body to be burned, but do not have love, it profits you nothing.* Dear God, these words are strong words, words that make me think about the motive of my heart and actions. Please Lord, help me to understand what true love is so that I don't fall into "vigorous nothingness." Your Word defines love by saying, *In this is love, not that we loved God, but that He loved us and sent His Son to be the propitiation for our sins.* Ah, so I see and understand that love begins with You. I must receive Your love inside of me before I can give it away; because if I don't have You, I truly have nothing. But with You, I can bear Your fruit. Again, Your word attests to this: *We know love by this, that He laid down His life for us; and we ought to lay down our lives for the brethren.* So Lord, please hear my request for my own heart as well as others far and wide: *I pray that Christ may dwell in our hearts through faith; and that we, being rooted and grounded in love, may be able to comprehend with all the saints what is the breadth and length and height and depth, and to know the love of Christ which surpasses knowledge, that we may be filled up to all the fullness of God.* And then, as a result of this True Love welling up inside of me, cause me to *tend Your lambs and shepherd Your sheep.*

1 Corinthians 13:1-3; 1 John 4:10; 3:16; Ephesians 3:17-19; John 21:15-16

God of the Orphan

For in You the orphan finds mercy.

HOSEA 14:3

O God, You are God of the Orphan. Yes, Lord, You hold the orphan very close to Your heart. *You execute justice for them* and *You are their helper.* And in Your concern and care, You command Your people of old: *You shall not afflict any widow or orphan. If you afflict him at all, and if he does cry out to Me, I will surely hear his cry; and My anger will be kindled.* Dear loving Lord, I ask You then, why are there so many orphans in this world? One reason, I know, is because *the whole world lies in the power of the evil one.* I also realize both abuse and abandonment run rampant due to man's sinful nature. But could another reason for the abundance of orphans be due to the apathy of Your people? For You say to Your own children, *Open your mouth for the mute, for the rights of all the unfortunate. Open your mouth, judge righteously, and defend the rights of the afflicted and needy.* And also, Your word challenges our faith to be real and active: *This is pure and undefiled religion in My sight, to visit orphans and widows in their distress, and to keep oneself unstained by the world.* So dear Lord, wake me up to the needs of the orphans both here and around the globe. Stir my heart to respond to Your heart; show me where to spread Your love, and instruct me how to meet the needs of the ones You hold so dearly. You say to those who walk by active faith, *For I was hungry, and you gave Me something to eat; I was thirsty, and you gave Me something to drink; I was a stranger, and you invited me in; naked, and you clothed Me; I was sick, and you visited Me; I was in prison, and you came to Me ... Truly I say to you, to the extent that you did it to one of these brothers of Mine, even the least of them, you did it to Me.* God of the Orphan, help me to share Your love.

Deuteronomy 10:18; Psalm 10:14; Exodus 22:22-23; 1 John 5:19; Proverbs 31:8-9; James 1:27; Matthew 25:35-36,40

God of the Widow

For the LORD your God is the God of gods and the Lord of lords, the great, the mighty, and the awesome God who does not show partiality nor take a bribe. He executes justice for the orphan and the widow.

DEUTERONOMY 10:17–18

O God, You are the God of the Widow. Yes, Lord, You hold the widow very close to Your heart. In the days of old, You gave this instruction to Your people: *And the Levite, because he has no portion or inheritance among you, and the alien, the orphan and the widow who are in your town, shall come and eat and be satisfied, in order that the Lord your God may bless you in all the work of your hand which you do.* Your word also says that *You are a father to the fatherless and a judge for the widows ... You make a home for the lonely; You lead out the prisoners into prosperity, only the rebellious dwell in a parched land.* And once more Your word proclaims that *You support the fatherless and the widow; but You thwart the way of the wicked.* Dear Lord, because You provide for, care for, and defend the widow, I should do the same. As a matter of fact, You long to work through Your people to meet the needs of all who are afflicted. I have the opportunity to be *an earthen vessel* of Your mighty love. On the other hand, if I am negligent, or even opposed to the widow, then in reality, I am opposed to You—how dangerous. You say to Your children, *For whoever has the world's goods, and beholds his brother (or sister) in need and closes his heart against him, how does the love of God abide in him?* And You implore us, *Learn to do good; seek justice, reprove the ruthless; defend the orphan, plead for the widow.* So dear Lord, keep my heart aware of those who have lost their loved one. Give me words of comfort and hope to speak into their pain and loneliness. Show me how to love them well with Your tender care. And as I enter into the widow's suffering, there, I can expect that my heart will beat more like Yours.

**Deuteronomy 14:29; Psalms 68:5-6; 146:9; 2 Corinthians 4:7;
1 John 3:17; Isaiah 1:17**

Encourager

Now may the God who gives perseverance and encouragement grant you to be of the same mind with one another according to Christ Jesus.

ROMANS 15:5

O God, You are the Encourager. I will cling to this promise: *For the eyes of the Lord move to and fro throughout the earth that He may strongly support those whose heart is completely His.* Thank You for Your undergirding support in every step I take. Jesus, I also thank You for these life-giving words as I daily move forward: *Blessed are the poor in spirit, for theirs is the kingdom of heaven. Blessed are those who mourn, for they shall be comforted. Blessed are the gentle, for they shall inherit the earth. Blessed are those who hunger and thirst for righteousness, for they shall be satisfied. Blessed are the merciful, for they shall receive mercy. Blessed are the pure in heart, for they shall see God. Blessed are the peacemakers, for they shall be called sons of God. Blessed are those who have been persecuted for the sake of righteousness, for theirs is the kingdom of heaven. Blessed are you when men cast insults at you, and persecute you, and say all kinds of evil against you falsely, on account of Me. Rejoice, and be glad, for your reward in heaven is great, for so they persecuted the prophets who were before you.* Dear Lord, I will hold these heavenly blessings tightly as I press through each day, knowing that You are right by my side. Yes, I know You will be with me through joys and trials, in plenty and in need. And as I walk Your direction, I will hear You encouragingly whisper, *Let not your heart be troubled, believe in God, believe also in Me. ... If you abide in Me, and My words abide in you, ask whatever you wish and it will be done for you. ... Be strong and courageous! ... Well done, good and faithful servant; you were faithful with a few things, I will put you in charge of many things; enter into the joy of your master.* Indeed, my Encourager helps carry my load and lightens my steps.

**2 Chronicles 16:9; Matthew 5:3-12; John 14:1; 15:7;
Joshua 1:8; Matthew 25:21**

God of Suffering

Therefore Jesus also, that He might sanctify the people through His own blood, suffered outside the gate. So, let us go out to Him outside the camp, bearing His reproach. For here we do not have a lasting city, but we are seeking the city which is to come.

HEBREWS 13:12–14

O God, You are the God of Suffering. Why suffering, dear Lord? I know the pat answer: because of sin, Satan, and self. But still, my heart and mind wrestle time and again over why a merciful God would allow His children to suffer. I know You provide answers to this hard question in Your word, so that's where my soul will always rest. There, You teach me this truth: if I did not experience suffering, I would not fully understand Your mercy. Indeed, if I only experienced good things, I would certainly walk in prideful independence, having no thought of You at all. Paul writes of this: *And because of the revelations, for this reason, to keep me from exalting myself, there was given me a thorn in the flesh, a messenger of Satan to buffet me—to keep me from exalting myself! Concerning this I entreated the Lord three times that it might depart from me. And He has said to me, "My grace is sufficient for you, for power is perfected in weakness." Most gladly, therefore, I will rather boast about my weaknesses, that the power of Christ may dwell in me. Therefore I am well content with weaknesses, with insults, with distresses, with persecutions, with difficulties, for Christ's sake; for when I am weak, then I am strong.* So I see that adversity is meant to pull me toward You. When I invite You into the midst of my suffering, You will invade me with Your power and Your glory. The alternative is only darkness and despair. Your word points me to the One who suffered most: *For you have been called for this purpose, since Christ also suffered for you, leaving you an example for you to follow in His steps, "Who committed no sin, nor was guile found in His mouth;" and while being reviled, He did not revile in return; while suffering, He uttered no threats, but kept entrusting Himself to Him who judges righteously; and He bore our sins in His body on the cross, that we, might die to sin and live to righteousness; for by His wounds you were healed.* Jesus, Your suffering and death was purposeful and profitable; for it has allowed me to *draw near with confidence to the throne of grace, that I may receive mercy and may find grace to help in time of need.* Thank You Suffering God; by Your merciful hand, please have Your powerful and glorious way in me.

2 Corinthians 12:7-10; 1 Peter 2:21-24; Hebrews 4:16

One Who Seals

In Him, you also, after listening to the message of truth, the gospel of your salvation—having also believed, you were sealed in Him with the Holy Spirit of promise, who is given as a pledge of our inheritance.

EPHESIANS 1:13–14

O God, You are the One Who Seals. I cling to this truth: *But as many as received Him, to them, He gave the right to become children of God, even to those who believe in His name, who were born not of blood, nor of the will of the flesh, nor of the will of man, but of God.* Indeed, I am Your child forever, and *no one can snatch me out of Your hand.* Thank You, dear Lord, for this eternal security. Help me to realize that with this great gift also comes great responsibility; for Your Spirit now resides in me! Please help me to joyfully heed Your words: *But the one who joins himself to the Lord is one spirit with Him. Flee immorality. Every other sin that a man commits is outside the body, but the immoral man sins against his own body. Or do you not know that your body is a temple of the Holy Spirit who is in you, whom you have from God, and that you are not your own? For you have been bought with a price: therefore glorify God in your body.* You also instruct me *not to grieve the Holy Spirit of God, by whom I was sealed for the day of redemption.* O God, I need Your strength in me to overcome my willful ways; I ask for Your help. Thank You for Your patience as I walk out my days as Your maturing child. And thank You for sealing me as Your own through the power of Your Spirit. Yes, only by *grace through faith,* I am Yours today and forever.

John 1:12-13; 10:28; 1 Corinthians 6:17-20; Ephesians 4:30; 2:8

One Who Prophesies

Therefore the Lord Himself will give you a sign: Behold, a virgin will be with child and bear a son, and she will call His name Immanuel.

ISAIAH 7:14

O God, You are the One Who Prophesies. Yes, Lord, You spoke of a promised Messiah all throughout Israel's history: *Then a shoot will spring from the stem of Jesse, and a branch from his roots will bear fruit, and the Spirit of the Lord will rest on Him, the spirit of wisdom and understanding, the spirit of counsel and strength, the spirit of knowledge and the fear of the Lord.* And Your word spoke of His birth: *For a child will be born to us, a son will be given to us; and the government will rest on His shoulder; and His name will be called Wonderful Counselor, Mighty God, Eternal Father, Prince of Peace.* The Messiah's triumphal entry was also foretold: *Rejoice greatly, O daughter of Zion! Shout in triumph, O daughter of Jerusalem! Behold, your king is coming to you; He is just and endowed with salvation, humble, and mounted on a donkey, even on a colt, the foal of a donkey.* His sacrificial death was also prophesied: *He was oppressed and He was afflicted, yet He did not open His mouth; like a lamb that is led to slaughter, and like a sheep that is silent before its shearers, so He did not open His mouth.* Your word spoke also of His resurrection: *For You will not abandon my soul to Sheol; neither will You allow Your Holy One to undergo decay.* And then, Holy God, You also speak of a future kingdom: *And I saw heaven opened; and behold, a white horse, and He who sat upon it is called Faithful and True; and in righteousness He judges and wages war. And His eyes are a flame of fire, and upon His head are many diadems; and He has a name written upon Him which no one knows except Himself. And He is clothed with a robe dipped in blood; and His name is called the Word of God. ... And on His robe and on His thigh He has a name written, "King of kings, and Lord of lords."* O God, nothing catches You off guard. You have always held the past, present, and future in Your divine hands. You proclaimed the good news from the beginning. Therefore, I can rejoice in Your salvation and rest in Your sovereignty. Because the One Who Prophecies is also the One Who Fulfills.

Isaiah 11:2; 9:6; Zechariah 9:9; Isaiah 53:7; Psalm 16:10; Revelation 19:11-13,16

One Who Fulfills

Now all of this took place to fulfill what was spoken by the Lord through the prophet: "Behold, the virgin shall be with child and shall bear a Son, and they shall call His name Immanuel," which translated means "God with us."

MATTHEW 1:22–23

O God, You are the One Who Fulfills. You spoke of the Messiah's lineage and birth place, and it was fulfilled: *Now in the sixth month the angel Gabriel was sent from God to a city in Galilee, called Nazareth, to a virgin engaged to a man whose name was Joseph, of the descendants of David; and the virgin's name was Mary.* And His birth happened just as You said: *And the shepherds came in haste and found their way to Mary and Joseph, and the baby as He lay in the manger.* And His predicted triumphal entry came to pass: *And they brought the colt to Jesus and put their garments on it; and He sat upon it. And many spread their garments in the road, and others spread leafy branches which they had cut from the fields. And those who went before, and those who followed after, were crying out, "Hosanna! Blessed is He who comes in the name of the Lord."* And God, it was no surprise to You that these same voices later yelled, *"Crucify Him!"... And they brought Him to the place of Golgotha ... and it was the third hour when they crucified Him.* But You also fulfilled the good news in His resurrection: *And they found the stone rolled away from the tomb. ... Two men suddenly stood near them in dazzling apparel; and so the women were terrified and bowed their faces to the ground, the men said to them, "Why do you seek the living One among the dead? He is not here, but He has risen. Remember how He spoke to you while He was still in Galilee, saying that the Son of Man must be delivered into the hands of sinful men, and be crucified, and the third day rise again."* God of Time, You fulfilled Your promises down to the hour, minute, even to the second. Redemptive history has happened just as You have planned. And now, my soul waits expectantly for the assigned moment when *the Son of Man will come in a cloud with power and great glory.* Yes, I will wait for this Fulfillment with hopeful longing and eager joy.

Luke 1:26-27; 2:16; Mark 11:7-9; 15:13,22,25; Luke 24:2,4-7; 21:27

God of Those Who Wrestle

Immediately the boy's father cried out and said, "I do believe; help my unbelief."
MARK 9:24

O God, You are the God of Those Who Wrestle. Thank You for Your patience as we search for You; thank You for Your mercy as we question You; thank You for Your loving-kindness as we approach You. I love this story of old: *Then Jacob was left alone, and a man wrestled with him until daybreak. And when he saw that he had not prevailed against him he touched the socket of his thigh; so the socket of Jacob's thigh was dislocated while he wrestled with him. Then he said, "Let me go, for the dawn is breaking." But he said, "I will not let you go unless you bless me." So he said to him, "What is your name?" And he said, "Jacob." And he said, "Your name shall no longer be Jacob, but Israel; for you have striven with God and with men and have prevailed." Then Jacob asked him and said, "Please tell me your name." But he said, "Why is it that you ask my name?" And He blessed him there. So Jacob named the place Peniel for he said, "I have seen God face to face, yet my life has been preserved."* O God, You never cast Your children from Your presence. Your intention is to bless those who seek You. You are a safe place to bring all of my issues, all of my questions, all of my doubts. Give me a settled heart that trusts You, even when I don't understand all that's going on around me. As I wrestle with You, I ask that my faith in You will be strengthened. Yes, Lord, I am determined to have an ongoing undercurrent of trust in the midst of my temporary stream of doubt. You are the Stronger One; You are the Overcomer; You are the Victor of my soul. So hear my mindset and ambition as I wrestle: *Though the fig tree should not blossom, and there be not fruit on the vines, though the yield of the olive should fail, and the fields produce no food, though the flock should be cut off from the fold, and there be no cattle in the stalls, yet I will exult in the Lord, I will rejoice in the God of my salvation. The Lord God is my strength, and He has made my feet like hinds' feet, and makes me walk on my high places.*

Genesis 32:24-30; Habakkuk 3:17-19

Omnipotent

For the LORD your God is the God of gods and the Lord of lords, the great, the mighty, and the awesome God.

DEUTERONOMY 10:17

O God, You are Omnipotent. *You uphold all things by the word of Your power.* Yes, *You made the Pleiades and Orion and change deep darkness into morning, You also darken day into night, You call for the waters of the sea and pour them out on the surface of the earth, the Lord is Your name.* Also, *You established the earth upon its foundations, so that it will not totter forever and ever. You covered it with the deep as with a garment; the waters were standing above the mountains. At Your rebuke they fled; at the sound of Your thunder they hurried away. The mountains rose; the valleys sank down to the place which You established for them. You set a boundary that they may not pass over; that they may not return to cover the earth.* All-powerful One, *nothing is too difficult for You. You show lovingkindness to thousands, but repay the iniquity of fathers into the bosom of their children after them, O great and mighty God. The Lord of hosts is Your name; great in counsel and mighty in deed, whose eyes are open to all the ways of the sons of men, giving to everyone according to his ways and according to the fruit of his deeds. ... Who is able to stand before the Lord, this holy God?* It is only through Your blood, dear Jesus, that I can stand upright. Yes, Your holy power conquered sin and death for me. Therefore, I will humbly bend my knee in reverence to Your name. You are Owner and Operator of all creation, mankind, and history. Indeed, You are Omnipotent.

Hebrews 1:3; Amos 5:8; Psalm 104:5-9; Jeremiah 32:17-19; 1 Samuel 6:20

One Who Confronts

Then the Lord said to Cain, "Where is Abel your brother?"

GENESIS 4:9

O God, You are the One Who Confronts. You confronted Adam and Eve in the garden after they ate the forbidden fruit: *And they heard the sound of the Lord God walking in the garden in the cool of the day, and the man and his wife hid themselves from the presence of the Lord God among the trees of the garden. The Lord God called to the man, and said to him, "Where are you? ... Have you eaten from the tree of which I commanded you not to eat?"* And You confronted King Belshazzar when he misused the articles of Your holy temple: *They drank the wine and praised the gods of gold and silver of bronze, iron, wood, and stone. Suddenly the finger of a man's hand emerged and began writing opposite the lampstand on the plaster of the wall of the king's palace, and the king saw the back of the hand that did the writing. Then the king's face grew pale, and his thoughts alarmed him; and his hip joints went slack, and his knees began knocking together. ... The hand was sent from God.* And You confronted King David through Nathan who said, *Why have you despised the word of the Lord by doing evil in His sight? You have struck down Uriah the Hittite with the sword, have taken his wife to be your wife, and have killed him with the sword of the sons of Ammon.* O God, because You are holy, You must and will confront all evil. Indeed, *it is a terrifying thing to fall into the hands of the living God.* I know it is only by Your grace that I can stand before You. For You mercifully say to me, *If you confess your sins, I am faithful and righteous to forgive you of your sins and to cleanse you from all unrighteousness.* I must remember, Jesus, You bore the brunt of my punishment; You stood in my place; only because of You, I am cleared of my wrongdoing. What an astounding act of love. Therefore, Almighty God, as You Confront, I will humbly confess. Thank You for redeeming me.

**Genesis 3:8-9,11; Daniel 5:4-6,24; 2 Samuel 12:9;
Hebrews 10:31; 1 John 1:9**

One Who Consoles

A bruised reed He will not break and a dimly burning wick He will not extinguish.
ISAIAH 42:3

O God, You are the One Who Consoles. I am *afflicted, storm-tossed, not comforted!* O God, where are You? I am sinking in despair; I am about to hit rock bottom; I am inconsolable. Please God, I need to know You are near; I need to feel Your presence; I long for Your embrace. *Answer me, O Lord, for Your lovingkindness is good; according to the greatness of Your compassion, turn to me, and do not hide Your face from Your servant, for I am in distress; answer me quickly. Oh draw near to my soul and redeem it.* Yes, Lord, You are my only hope. I desperately need You to come. Again, I need to know that You are by my side, struggling with me and for me. *Hasten to my help!* Be still, my soul, so I can hear God's words of comfort. Yes, Lord, calm my heart so I can hear Your words of love: *I will not forget you. I have inscribed you on the palms of My hands. ... You are Mine. ... You are precious in My sight. ... For the mountains may be removed and the hills may shake, but My lovingkindness will not be removed from you, and My covenant of peace will not be shaken. ... Behold, I will do something new, now it will spring forth; will you not be aware of it? I will even make a roadway in the wilderness, rivers in the desert.* God of all comfort, continue to hold me close; I hear You, and I trust You all over again. I will cling to Your words, and I will rest in Your embrace. Yes, *You will revive me again, and bring me up from the depths of the earth.* You indeed, are the One Who Consoles.

**Isaiah 54:11; Psalms 69:16-18; 71:12;
Isaiah 49:15-16; 43:1,4; 54:10; 43:19; Psalm 71:20**

First Love

But I have this against you, that you have left your first love.

REVELATION 2:4

O God, You are my First Love. I pray I will live a life that proclaims You as the One I adore above all else. Indeed, my soul knows *Your love is better than life!* Yes, I want my loyalty to be like Ruth's, who said these words to her mother-in-law: *For where you go, I will go, and where you lodge, I will lodge. Your people shall be my people, and your God, my God.* And I want my faith to be like Job's. When confronted with his most extreme tragedy, he cried out, *The Lord gave and the Lord has taken away. Blessed be the name of the Lord.* And I want my submissiveness to be like Mary's, who, when receiving news of her chosen appointment of bearing the Messiah, said without hesitation, *Behold, the bondslave of the Lord; be it done to me according to your word.* And I want my commitment to be like Paul's who said with absolute affirmation, *But I do not consider my life of any account as dear to myself, in order that I may finish my course, and the ministry which I received from the Lord Jesus, to testify solemnly of the gospel of the grace of God.* Lord, I pray that I keep You as King of my heart, and walk in obedience to Your ways, because this is where I will find real and abundant life. Nothing else rivals You! And I thank You, dear Savior, that my loyalty, my faith, my submissiveness, and my commitment is a mere overflow of what You have already lived out on my behalf. Yes, *I love because You first loved me.* Indeed, You are the One whom I adore above all else.

Psalm 63:3; Ruth 1:16; Job 1:21; Luke 1:38; Acts 20:24; 1 John 4:19

One Who Lavishes

Ho! Every one who thirsts, come to the waters; and you who have no money come, buy and eat. Come, buy wine and milk without money and without cost. Why do you spend money for what is not bread, and your wages for what does not satisfy? Listen carefully to Me, and eat what is good, and delight yourself in abundance.

Isaiah 55:1–2

O God, You are the One Who Lavishes. I love this story from Your word: *Now there were six stone water pots set there for the Jewish custom of purification, containing twenty or thirty gallons each. Jesus said to them, "Fill the water pots with water." And they filled them up to the brim. And He said to them, "Draw some out now, and take it to the headwaiter." And they took it to him. And when the headwaiter tasted, the water had become wine.* Water turned to wine—an amazing transformation! And also, dear Jesus, this story speaks of Your plentiful goodness: *And when it was evening the disciples came to Him, saying, "The place is desolate, and the time is already past. ... We have here only five loaves and two fish." And He said, "Bring them here to Me." And ordering the multitudes to recline on the grass, He took the five loaves and the two fish, and looking up toward heaven, He blessed the food, and breaking the loaves He gave them to the disciples, and the disciples gave to the multitudes, and they all ate, and were satisfied. And they picked up what was left over of the broken pieces, twelve full baskets. And there were about five thousand men who ate, aside from women and children.* From one plate to baskets full—an abundant blessing! Dear Jesus, even to this day, You continue to pour out the new wine of Your Spirit and the broken bread of Your life! Yes, *in You we have redemption through Your blood, the forgiveness of our trespasses, according to the riches of Your grace, which You lavished upon us.* Thank You, O God; because of You, I am no longer an empty vessel nor at a desolate place. Instead, I am amazingly transformed and abundantly blessed.

John 2:6-9; Matthew 14:15,17-21; Ephesians 1:7-8

Lord

And Mary said, "Behold, the bondslave of the Lord; may it be done to me according to your word."

LUKE 1:38

O God, You are Lord. All things belong to You. The sun, moon, and stars all obey You. Dear Lord I, too, want to be under Your authority. I rejoice because *You have brought my soul out of prison.* By Your cords of mercy and lovingkindness, my heart is bound to You. And now, O Lord, my Lord, Your unfailing love has become my life's breath! I want to do Your will; I want to obey Your voice. Help me to remember that *You will never give me more than I can bear* or ask me to do a task that is too difficult, because You are in my midst, helping me through every circumstance. When I begin to weaken with frailty and doubt, please fill me once again, I pray. Help me to respond to Your daily charge over my life: *Be strong, courageous and act; do not fear, do not be dismayed.* Help me to believe *You will not fail me nor forsake me.* Continue to make me strong, O God, and please, awaken my soul to courage! When You ask from Your majestic throne, *Whom shall I send and who will go for Us?* I want to always be ready and willing to respond with awe, *Lord, here I am, send me!*

Psalm 142:7; 1 Corinthians 10:13; 1 Chronicles 28:20; Isaiah 6:8

Lamb of God

For it was the Father's good pleasure for all the fullness to dwell in Him, and through Him to reconcile all things to Himself, having made peace through the blood of His cross.
COLOSSIANS 1:19–20

O God, You are the Lamb of God. Indeed, You declare, *There is no Savior besides Me.* And Your word tells each of us: *You were not redeemed with perishable things like silver or gold from your futile way of life inherited from your forefathers, but with precious blood, as of a lamb unblemished and spotless, the blood of Christ.* Yes, my heart shouts the same words as John the Baptist long ago, *Behold the Lamb of God who takes away the sin of the world!* Dear Lord, through the sacrifice of Your perfect Son, You brought salvation to mankind. Jesus, thank You for laying down Your life to *be the propitiation for the sins of the whole world.* Your blood offers forgiveness; Your blood offers redemption; Your blood offers eternal life. Indeed, You are the One and only Savior. I will worship You today, as well as in my eternal home. John speaks of the days to come: *And I looked, and I heard the voice of many angels around the throne and living creatures and the elders; and the number of them was myriads of myriads, and thousands of thousands, saying with a loud voice, "Worthy is the Lamb that was slain to receive power and riches and wisdom and might and honor and glory and blessing." And every created thing which is in heaven and on the earth and under the earth and on the sea, and all things in them, I hear saying, "To Him who sits on the throne, and to the Lamb, be blessing and honor and glory and dominion forever and ever."* Yes, Lamb of God, I will worship You with my life both now and forever.

Isaiah 43:11; 1 Peter 1:18-19; John 1:29; 1 John 2:2; Revelation 5:12-13

My Champion

If God is for us, who is against us?

O God, You are my Champion. Jesus, You came to *proclaim release to the captives, and recovery of sight to the blind, and to set free those who are downtrodden.* And You also say *You have appeared for this purpose, to destroy the works of the devil.* O God, You are striving for us in all our struggles. Your word triumphantly proclaims; *Who will bring a charge against God's elect? God is the one who justifies; who is the one who condemns? Christ Jesus is He who died, yes, rather who was raised, who is at the right hand of God, who also intercedes for us.* Thank You my Champion, for fighting on my behalf. Thank You for Your valiant sacrifice. In giving Your life, You won the battle over all things, including death. Yes, *the last enemy that will be abolished is death* and You have conquered it! My Champion's tomb is empty, and my soul shouts, *Who is this King of Glory, the Lord strong and mighty. The Lord mighty in battle … the Lord of hosts, He is the king of glory.* So when various trials cycle through, causing fear and dismay once again, please remind me that You have won every battle; and because of You, I hold the victory! Help me to lean heavily on Your promises, claiming each one. Pick me up and set me on my feet once more so I can proclaim this truth with renewed confidence, *Who shall separate us from the love of Christ? Shall tribulation, or distress, or persecution, or famine, or nakedness, or peril, or sword? … But in all these things we overwhelmingly conquer through Him who loved us.* Most assuredly, O God, You are my Champion.

**Luke 4:18; 1 John 3:8; Romans 8:31-34; 1 Corinthians 15:26;
Psalm 24:8,10; Romans 8:35,37**

One Who Warns

And beware not to lift up your eyes to heaven and see the sun and the moon and the stars,
all the host of heaven, and be drawn away and worship them and serve them.

DEUTERONOMY 4:19

O God, You are the One Who Warns. You give us protective instructions for our own well-being. You say to us, *Beware of false prophets, who come to you in sheep's clothing, but inwardly are ravenous wolves. You will know them by their fruits.* God, I ask for Your wisdom so I will not be deceived by the *trickery of men, by craftiness, in deceitful scheming.* And You also warn us about wealth: *But those who want to get rich fall into temptation and a snare and many foolish and harmful desires which plunge men into ruin and destruction.* Please Lord, I ask for Your strength to resist the fleeting temptations of this world. Remind me Your word is *more desirable than gold, yes, than much fine gold.* And You tell us, *Avoid worldly and empty chatter, for it will lead to further ungodliness, and your talk will spread like gangrene.* Dear Lord, I ask for Your discipline concerning the words I speak; please *set a guard over my mouth. Keep watch over the door of my lips* so that I only say words that are edifying to others and honoring to You. And You strongly advise, *Take hold of instruction; do not let go. Guard her, for she is your life. Do not enter the path of the wicked, and do not proceed in the way of evil men. Avoid it, do not pass by it; turn away from it and pass on.* O God, I ask for Your discernment between good and evil; help me to study Your word daily, so that I will know the way in which I should walk. Wise God, I am so grateful You care enough to warn me of all kinds of impending dangers. Again, please help me heed Your instruction, so my soul can enjoy Your paths of peace.

Matthew 7:15-16; Ephesians 4:14; 1 Timothy 6:9; Psalm 19:10;
2 Timothy 2:16-17; Psalm 141:3; Proverbs 4:13-15

God of the Body

For you have been bought with a price: therefore glorify God in your body.
1 CORINTHIANS 6:20

O God, You are God of the Body. You say to each of us, *Do you not know that your body is a temple of the Holy Spirit who is in you, whom you have from God, and that you are not your own?* Convict my heart of this truth, O God. Remind me You love me more than I love myself. I pray that I will take care of my physical body so I can serve You to the best of my ability. I ask for the *fruit of the Spirit—self-control—*when it comes to eating and drinking. For Your word instructs me: *Do not be with heavy drinkers of wine, or with gluttonous eaters of meat; for the heavy drinker and the glutton will come to poverty, and drowsiness will clothe one with rags.* And also, Your word says: *Therefore consider the members of your earthly body as dead to immorality, impurity, passion, evil desire, and greed, which amounts to idolatry.* O God, You know all these fleshly things, although fun for a moment, only lead to a dead end of emptiness, guilt, and shame. And You know me so well because You made me. Therefore, You know what my mind, body, and soul really craves. So cause me to heed Your loving words of warning, and replace my unhealthy physical longings with a spiritual hunger and a thirst for You. Yes, help me adhere to these rich words of rewarding truth: *Lay aside the old self with its evil practices, and put on the new self which is being renewed to a true knowledge according to the image of the One who created him. Put on a heart of compassion, kindness, humility, gentleness and patience; and beyond all these things put on love, which is the perfect bond of unity.* Yes, dear Lord, I want to honor You in every way with the body You have given me. I want to take care of this temple. So *whether I eat or drink or whatever I do, I want to do it all for Your glory.* Please come, and be King of me.

**1 Corinthians 6:19; Galatians 5:22-23; Proverbs 23:20-21;
Colossians 3:5,9-10,12,14; 1 Corinthians 10:31**

God of the Soul

For what will it profit a man if he gains the whole world, and forfeits his soul? Or what will a man give in exchange for his soul?

MATTHEW 16:26

O God, You are God of the Soul. I hear You say to Your children, *Therefore putting aside all filthiness and all that remains of wickedness, in humility receive the word implanted, which is able to save your souls.* And Your people respond, *Indeed, while following the way of Your judgments, O Lord, we have waited for You eagerly; Your name, even Your memory, is the desire of our souls. At night my soul longs for You, indeed, my spirit within me seeks You diligently.* Dear Lord, help me learn from these people of old. For I know there is a void in me that can only be filled by You. And because of Your grace and mercy, Your Spirit has entered in! Indeed, my soul is now richly blessed, abundantly filled. Yes, before knowing You, dear Jesus, *I was dead in my trespasses and sins in which I formerly walked according to the course of this world.* But now, *I am alive together with You (by grace I have been saved), and have been raised up with You and seated with You in the heavenly places, in You.* Indeed, You alone are my only hope, both today, tomorrow, and forever. And *this hope I have is an anchor of my soul, a hope that is both sure and steadfast.* Thank You, my Savior. Your sacrifice is my sustenance. Yes, now my heart truly beats. And because of Your grace, I know I will *obtain the outcome of my faith which is the salvation of my soul.* Therefore, I will sing to You, Savior God; be pleased with my salvation song, *I will bless the Lord at all times; His praise shall continually be in my mouth. My soul shall make its boast in the Lord; the humble shall hear it and rejoice.*

**James 1:21; Isaiah 26:8-9; Ephesians 2:1-2,5-6; Hebrews 6:19;
1 Peter 1:9; Psalm 34:1-2**

God of the Rich

Now the LORD said to Abram, "...I will make you a great nation, and I will bless you, and make your name great; and so you shall be a blessing." Now Abram was very rich in livestock, in silver and in gold.

GENESIS 12:1–2; 13:2

O God, You are God of the Rich. Is being rich a sin? No, but in wisdom, You warn those who have wealth, (and even those who don't have wealth, but long for it): *Those who want to get rich fall into temptation and a snare and many foolish and harmful desires which plunge men into ruin and destruction. For the love of money is the root of all sorts of evil, and some longing for it have wandered from the faith, and pierced themselves with many a pang.* You tell those who are rich, and those who crave it, to *flee from these things and pursue righteousness, godliness, faith, love, perseverance and gentleness.* And Your word also says: *Instruct those who are rich in this present world not to be conceited or to fix their hope on the uncertainty of riches, but on God, who richly supplies us with all things to enjoy. Instruct them to do good, to be rich in good works, to be generous and share.* O Lord, these words are so simple: fix my hope on You, enjoy, do good, be generous, and share. This is the ultimate call of those who are wealthy! It's not to selfishly accumulate more and more, but to bless others from what has been given from above. Help me to embrace this truth with all I have; open the doors to my home, set extra seats at my table, release the pinch of my pocketbook. Yes, decrease the word "mine" from my vocabulary and replace it with "Yours." Please, make me a good steward of all You have placed in my care. Jesus, You gently warn me, *Be on your guard against every form of greed; for not even when one has an abundance does his life consist of his possessions.* Yes, Lord, all I have is Yours. And I hear You say with a promise, *Give, and it will be given to you; good measure, pressed down, shaken together, running over, they will pour into your lap. For by your standard of measure it will be measured to you in return.* O God of Rich Blessings, my heart and my hands are open to richly bless.

1 Timothy 6:9-11,17-18; Luke 12:15; 6:38

God of the Poor

Did not God choose the poor of this world to be rich in faith and heirs of the kingdom which He promised to those who love Him?

JAMES 2:5

O God, You are God of the Poor. You advise: *Better is a dry morsel and quietness with it than a house full of feasting with strife.* O God, I confess, sometimes I am not satisfied with just a "dry morsel." I want more on my plate! Help me cling to You when times are tight; help me trust You as my Provider. For You promise *to supply all my needs according to Your riches in glory in Christ Jesus.* Will You really provide, O God? I'm waiting. Reaffirm my faith. Show me the difference between my needs and my wants. You know best, and You have best; help me believe this, not resent it, when it's not to my liking. Please Lord, cause my heart to pray for a richer faith rather than a more bountiful plate. I must trust You as my Savior; You will come to my aid. Yes, I will believe You, Owner of all things, will provide for my needs, in Your time, in Your way. And while I wait, dear Lord, I pray that I will become more like Paul who said with confidence, *For I have learned to be content in whatever circumstance I am. I know how to get along with humble means, and I also know how to live in prosperity; in any and every circumstances I have learned the secret of being filled and going hungry, both of having abundance and suffering need. I can do all things through Him who strengthens me.* Yes, Lord, keep my eyes from gazing on the culture, looking to it as my standard; this only leads to discontentment. Instead, help me look to You, dear Jesus. And Your word proclaims Your position: *You know the grace of our Lord Jesus Christ, that though He was rich, yet for your sake He became poor, that you through His poverty might become rich.* Ah yes, in every way and for all Your human days, You became poor. Show me how to do this joyfully, faithfully, beautifully. Indeed, I will trust You and thank You for my quiet soul and my dry morsel.

Proverbs 17:1; Philippians 4:19,11-13; 2 Corinthians 8:9

One Who Clothes

Awake, awake, clothe yourself in your strength, O Zion; clothe yourself in your beautiful garments, O Jerusalem, the holy city.

ISAIAH 52:1

O God, You are the One Who Clothes. I love this picture of old: *Now Joshua was clothed with filthy garments and standing before the angel. And he spoke and said to those who were standing before him saying, "Remove the filthy garments from him." Again he said to him, "See, I have taken your iniquity away from you and will clothe you with festal robes."* Thank You, Lord, for Your merciful removal; and then, thank You for Your gracious adornment. Likewise, this ancient parable speaks of You and me: *A certain man had two sons; and the younger of the said to his father, "Father, give me the share of the estate that falls to me."* The younger son gathered everything together and went on a journey into a distant country, and there he squandered his estate. When he had spent everything, a severe famine occurred in that country, and he began to be in need. But when he came to his senses, he said, "I will get up and go to my father." And he got up and came. But while he was still a long way off, his father saw him, and felt compassion for him, and ran and embraced him, and kissed him, saying, "Quickly bring out the best robe and put it on him, and put a ring on his hand and sandals on his feet; for this son of mine was dead, and has come to life again; he was lost, and has been found."* Dear Lord, Your grace is amazing! *You pardon all my iniquities; You heal all my diseases; You redeem my life from the pit; You crown me with lovingkindness and compassion.* O God, thank You. I deserve nothing except death, but You have given me everything, even eternal life. Yes, *I will rejoice greatly in the Lord, my soul will exult in my God; for He has clothed me with garments of salvation, He has wrapped me with a robe of righteousness.*

Zechariah 3:3-4; Luke 15:13-24; Isaiah 61:10

God of the Mountaintop

How lovely on the mountains are the feet of him who brings good news, who announces peace and brings good news of happiness, who announces salvation, and says to Zion, "Your God reigns!"

ISAIAH 52:7

O God, You are God of the Mountaintop. Indeed, on the mountaintop, You spoke profound words of direction and truth. You gave the ten commandments to Moses as protective boundaries on how to live: *You shall have no other gods before Me. You shall not make for yourself an idol. You shall not take the name of the Lord your God in vain.* And Jesus, on the mountaintop, You gave Your disciples encouragement and direction concerning the condition of their heart: *Blessed are the poor in spirit, for theirs is the kingdom of heaven. Blessed are those who mourn, for they shall be comforted. Blessed are the gentle, for they shall inherit the earth. Blessed are the pure in heart, for they shall see God.* And on another occasion, *You took Peter and James and John his brother, and brought them up to a high mountain by themselves. And You were transfigured before them; and Your face shone like the sun, and Your garments became as white as light. A bright cloud overshadowed them; and behold, a voice came from out of the cloud, saying, "This is My beloved Son, with whom I am well-pleased; listen to Him!"* O God, take me to the mountaintop, I pray! Please, *make my feet like hinds' feet, and set me upon my high places.* Yes, Lord, *set my feet upon a rock and make my footsteps firm.* And on these heights, cause me to encounter You in a new and glorious way. For on the mountaintop, away from all the noise, Your words are so very clear, and they ring true to my heart. Yes, dear Lord, I know that what I hear in the heights will be the very truth I need when I walk through the valley. So *lead me to the rock that is higher than I.* I am here, and I am listening.

Exodus 20:3-4, 7; Matthew 5:3-5,8; 17:1-2,5; Psalms 18:33; 40:2; 61:2

God of the Valley

Even though I walk through the valley of the shadow of death, I fear no evil, for You are with me; Your rod and Your staff, they comfort me.

PSALM 23:4

O God, You are the God of the Valley. O dear God, nothing in me wants to be in this difficult place. I'm frightened of the unknown; I'm fearful of the challenges. But at the same time, because You are the faithful Lord over all my days, I wouldn't miss a step. It's better to be in the valley with You than on the mountaintop without You. So right now, even though I don't necessarily feel You are with me, I must believe You are with me: *My presence will go with you and I will give you rest.* And I must hold onto Your promises more than my flesh is currently experiencing them: *I will say to the Lord, "My refuge and my fortress, my God, in whom I trust!" For it is He who delivers me from the snare of the trapper, and from the deadly pestilence. He will cover me with His pinions, and under His wings I will seek refuge.* And I must remember Your clear blessings of the past as I am walking in the misty path of the present: *This I recall to mind, therefore I have hope. The Lord's lovingkindnesses indeed never cease, for His compassions never fail.* And I must cling to Your transparent light rather than be overtaken by the blinding darkness: *The Lord is my light and my salvation; whom shall I fear? The Lord is the defense of my life; whom shall I dread?* And I must choose to hear Your heartbeat instead of being engulfed by a desperate emptiness: *If the Lord had not been my help, my soul would soon have dwelt in the abode of silence. If I should say, "My foot has slipped," Your lovingkindness, O Lord, will hold me up.* God, You are Good, You are Peace, You are Trustworthy, You are my Protector, You are my Companion. Yes, each step of the way I will call out Your name, and by faith, I will willingly walk through the valley.

Exodus 33:14; Psalm 91:2-4; Lamentations 3:21-22; Psalms 27:1; 94:17-18

God of Joy Meeting Sorrow

When a face is sad a heart may be happy.

ECCLESIASTES 7:3

O God, You are the God of Joy Meeting Sorrow. Dear Lord, I am walking in the valley of sorrow, and the road is long and foreboding. My heart is breaking with sadness; my soul weeps for yesterday's mountaintop. Please Lord, I need You. Embrace me now. Sing Your truths to my soul. Yes, let me hear Your promises one by one: *I will lift my eyes to the mountains; from where will my help come? My help comes from the Lord, who made heaven and earth. He will not allow your foot to slip. But he who trusts in the Lord, lovingkindness shall surround him. The Lord will command His lovingkindness in the daytime; and His song will be with me in the night.* Yes, Lord, I am finding out as I walk through this valley of sorrow, I am undergirded by a foundation of joy. Indeed, *the joy of the Lord is my strength.* And no matter the depth of my sadness, I know it will be matched with the height of Your joy. For *when my anxious thoughts multiply within me, Your consolations delight my soul.* O God, thank You. It is an honor to experience the holy conflict of being *sorrowful yet always rejoicing.* Indeed, even as I walk in this valley with a heavy heart, I can and will proclaim with open hands, lifted high, *Hear, O Lord, and be gracious to me; O Lord, be my helper. You have turned for me my mourning into dancing; You have loosed my sackcloth and girded me with gladness; that my soul may sing praise to You, and not be silent. O Lord my God, I will give thanks to You forever.* Dear God, what would I do if You did not meet me in the valley?

**Psalms 121:1-3; 32:10; 42:8; Nehemiah 8:10; Psalm 94:19;
2 Corinthians 6:10; Psalm 30:10-11**

One Who Welcomes the Saints

Precious in the sight of the LORD is the death of His godly ones.
PSALM 116:15

O God, You are the One Who Welcomes the Saints. Yes, Lord, death is a part of life, and rarely is it welcomed on this earth. But You, O God, have Your arms open wide, ready to receive the ones You lead home. In the midst of my sorrow and my loss, my heart will cling to Your promise, *Let not your heart be troubled; believe in God, believe also in Me. In My Father's house are many dwelling places; if it were not so, I would have told you; for I go to prepare a place for you. And if I go and prepare a place for you, I will come again, and receive you to Myself; that where I am, there you may be also.* And in this beautiful place, You promise to *wipe away every tear from our eyes.* Also, in this eternal home *there will no longer be any death; and there will no longer be any mourning, or crying, or pain.* Yes, *the perishable will put on the imperishable, and the mortal will put on immortality.* Therefore, I will hold onto the hope of heaven pertaining to the ones I love and the ones I've lost. And I will also take hope in Your word concerning the story of the apostle Stephen; for when his time had come to leave this earth, *he being full of the Holy Spirit, gazed intently into heaven and saw the glory of God, and Jesus standing at the right hand of God.* Ah yes, You eagerly await the entrance of Your dear children into Your loving home. Most certainly then, I can and will proclaim with heavenly triumph, although mingled with my earthly tears, *O death, where is your victory? O death, where is your sting? The sting of death is sin, and the power of sin is the law, but I am convinced that neither death, nor life, nor angels, nor principalities, nor things present, nor things to come, nor powers, nor height, nor depth, nor any other created thing, shall be able to separate us from the love of God, which is in Christ Jesus our Lord.* Yes, out of depths of my grief I will rejoice, both sobbing and singing, *Thanks be to God, who gives us the victory through our Lord Jesus Christ!*

John 14:1-3; Revelation 21:4; 1 Corinthians 15:53; Acts 7:55;
1 Corinthians 15:55-56; Romans 8:38-39; 1 Corinthians 15:57

God of Atonement

The priest shall make atonement for him in regard to his sin which he has committed, and he shall be forgiven.

LEVITICUS 4:35

O God, You are the God of Atonement. Dear Lord, Your word says: *Without the shedding of blood there is no forgiveness.* I confess, sometimes my heart and mind cannot fully grasp why there must be the shedding of blood. Please give me understanding into this foundational truth, I pray. Again, Your word says: *For the life of flesh is in the blood, and I have given it to you on the altar to make atonement for your souls; for it is the blood by reason of the life that makes atonement.* So I see that because blood represents life, and that my lifeblood is full of sin that leads to death, I need Someone's pure and perfect blood to replace my own. And I also understand the sacrifices of the innocent and unblemished animals in the days of old all pointed to this Someone: the sinless Messiah. Indeed, Your word confirms this truth: *For Christ did not enter a holy place made with hands, a mere copy of the true one, but into heaven itself, now to appear in the presence of God for us; nor was it that He should offer Himself often, as the high priest enters the holy place year by year with blood not his own. Otherwise, He would have needed to suffer often since the foundation of the world; but now once at the consummation of the ages He has been manifested to put away sin by the sacrifice of Himself.* Dear Jesus, You are both the eternal High Priest and the perfect Lamb of God! By faith, I see and understand it was Your lifeblood that wiped away and replaced my lifeblood. This even helps me grasp Your strong figurative statement, *He who eats My flesh and drinks My blood has eternal life, and I will raise him up on the last day. He who eats My flesh and drinks My blood abides in Me, and I in him.* Indeed, by Your grace alone, *I am Yours and You are mine.* I have been atoned for at Your incomprehensible expense; and now, I am forever one with You.

Hebrews 9:22; Leviticus 17:11; Hebrews 9:24-26; John 6:54,56; Song of Solomon 6:3

God of the Generations

One generation shall praise Your works to another, and shall declare Your mighty acts.
PSALM 145:4

O God, You are the God of Generations. *You are the same yesterday, today, and forever.* Therefore, the commands You gave to the Israelites long ago concerning Your holy word also pertain to me today. You say in earnest, *Impress these words of mine on your heart and on your soul; and bind them as a sign on your hand, and as frontals on your forehead. And teach them to your sons, talking of them when you sit in your house and when you walk along the road and when you lie down and when you rise up. And write them on the doorposts of your house and on your gates: love the Lord your God, walk in all His ways, and hold fast to Him.* O Lord, convict my heart to be a lover of Your life-changing word. And then, cause me to be a good steward of these holy truths. Yes, Lord, make Your words be my life-breath and my heartbeat. May I speak of Your wonderful name all the days of my life. If I pass along anything to the next generation, O Jesus, let it be You! Yes, Lord, I will march forward with a divine purpose, resolving to hand down Your words of hope. While doing so, I will cling confidently to this promise as my eternal reward: *"And as for Me, this is My covenant with them,"* says the Lord: *"My Spirit which is upon you, and My words which I have put in your mouth, shall not depart from your mouth, nor from the mouth of your offspring, nor from the mouth of your offspring's offspring,"* says the Lord, *"from now and forever."* O God of the Generations, overtake my heart and permeate my home.

Hebrews 13:8; Deuteronomy 11:18-20,22; Isaiah 59:21

King

My heart overflows with a good theme; I address my verses to the King; my tongue is the pen of a ready writer.

PSALM 45:1

O God, You are my King. *Righteousness and justice are the foundation of Your throne; lovingkindness and truth go before You.* My soul bows down to You; my heart belongs to You. *I will enter Your gates with thanksgiving and Your courts with praise.* There, *I will extol You, my God, O King; every day I will bless You, and I will praise Your name forever and ever. Great is the Lord, and highly to be praised; and His greatness is unsearchable.* Royal One, I humbly thank You for Your greatest unsearchable act—Your life for mine! Loving One, You took off Your *robe of righteousness and wrapped it* around my back while Yours was ripped. Compassionate One, You sweetly held my hand while Yours was pierced. Holy One, You traded in Your crown of glory for one of scorn and shame. All of this for me? O to grasp this *love which surpasses knowledge* ... and to be *able to comprehend the breadth and length and height and depth of it!* King of kings, I am awed by Your act of mercy; I am *drawn by Your lovingkindness;* I am overwhelmed with my inheritance. *Yes, my heart overflows with a good theme:* the King of love has come for me.

**Psalms 89:14; 100:4; 145:1-3; Isaiah 61:10; Ephesians 3:18-19;
Jeremiah 31:3; Psalm 45:1**

Beautiful One

One thing I have asked from the LORD, that I shall seek: that I may dwell in the house of the LORD all the days of my life, to behold the beauty of the LORD, and to meditate in His temple.

PSALM 27:4

O God, You are the Beautiful One. I praise You; I lift my hands high; I love You. *Better is one day in Your courts than a thousand outside.* I see Your beauty in the sanctuary of Your heavens. They are *telling of Your glory, and their expanse is declaring the work of Your hands. Day to day pours forth speech, and night to night reveals knowledge.* How marvelous is Your handiwork, O God. I also feel Your beauty in the sanctuary of my heart. Your goodness and mercy overwhelms me. Yes, You are the Beautiful One to my soul. Your deep love *causes me to be a lily among the thorns.* Thank You, my sweet Redeemer. You lift me up; You make all things new. Continue to beautify me, O Beautiful One. Make me a radiant reflection of who You are, so I, too, will pour out *Your goodness and Your mercy (toward others) all the days of my life.*

Psalms 84:10; 19:1-2; Song of Solomon 2:2; Psalm 23:6

Magnificent

Oh give thanks to the LORD, call upon His name; make known His deeds among the peoples. Sing to Him, sing praises to Him; speak of all His wonders. Glory in His holy name; Let the heart of those who seek the LORD be glad.

PSALM 105:1–3

O God, You are Magnificent. *Heaven is Your throne and earth is Your footstool.* Your heavens are full of Your splendor, and Your earth is full of Your praise. Indeed, *You are the Lord Most High over all the earth; You are exalted far above all gods. Let the heavens be glad, and let the earth rejoice; let the sea roar and all it contains; let the field exult and all that is in it. Then all the trees of the forest will sing for joy before the Lord.* May I, too, join this chorus of thanks and praise. Thank You for Your magnificent wonders; thank You for Your magnificent ways. *With one arm You rule with strength and might, defeating my enemies; and with the other arm, You gently gather me close to You like a shepherd who carefully tends his flock.* Hear me say, Magnificent God, I am glad and I love You with all my heart!

Isaiah 66:1; Psalms 97:9; 96:11-13; Isaiah 40:10-11

My God

My dwelling place also will be with them; and I will be their God, and they will be My people.

EZEKIEL 37:27

O God, You are my God. What an awesome and incomprehensible thought, that I can call You "mine." Yes, You are my God; You are my very breath. You sing to your people, *I will give them a heart to know me, for I am the Lord; and they will be my people, and I will be their God.* Thank You for this love song which plays throughout all of Scripture, and all of time. O God, I love Your song; I sing Your song, each word of its lovely lyrics. Again, You sing, *I have called you by name, you are Mine. … You are precious in My sight and I love you. … Do not fear, I am with you; do not look anxiously about you, for I am your God. I will strengthen you, surely I will help you, and surely I will uphold you with my righteous right hand.* O God, my God, hear me respond to Your love song: *I am His and He is mine!* I want to walk with You, sing back to You, and dance this life with You! What an honor, privilege, and delight. Yes, I will sing, *When I found Him whom my soul loves, I held on to Him and would not let Him go.*

Jeremiah 24:7; Isaiah 43:1,4; 41:10; Song of Solomon 6:3; 3:4

Helper

If the LORD had not been my help, my soul would have dwelt in the abode of silence. If I should say, "My foot has slipped," Your lovingkindness, O LORD, will hold me up. When my anxious thoughts multiply within me, Your consolations delight my soul.

PSALM 94:17–19

O God, You are my Helper. I am a weak and defenseless creature who desperately needs saving! Thank You for not overlooking me when I cry out to You: *I waited patiently for You; and You inclined to me, and heard my cry. You brought me up out of the pit of destruction, out of the miry clay; You set my feet upon a rock making my footsteps firm. You put a new song in my mouth, a song of praise to You.* Dear Savior, because of Your saving love, my soul will no longer be silent! Hear me sing, *Behold, God is my helper; the Lord is the sustainer of my soul. ... For Your Holy Spirit, my Helper,* now dwells in me forever. *I will give thanks to Your name, O Lord, for it is good. For You have delivered me from all my trouble. And my eye has looked with satisfaction upon my enemies.* You make my gloomy thoughts, joy; You make my anxious thoughts, peace; You make my simple thoughts, wise. O God, Your wonderful ways delight my soul.

Psalms 40:1-3; 54:4; John 14:16,26; Psalm 54:6-7

Valiant Warrior

The LORD will go forth like a warrior, He will arouse His zeal like a man of war. He will utter a shout, yes, He will raise a war cry. He will prevail against His enemies.

Isaiah 42:13

O God, You are a Valiant Warrior. You stand *for righteousness, peace, and joy* which You have given freely to all those who believe in You. I thank You, Jesus my Savior, for standing on the frontline of the battle, so I could *have abundant life* now and forever! Protect me, I pray; for the enemy is angry, as You are winning souls with Your love. In heaven and earth, in hearts and minds, the war wages on. *For our struggle is not against flesh and blood, but against the rulers, against the powers, against the world forces of this darkness, against the spiritual forces of wickedness in the heavenly places.* Protect me from the fiery arrows of fear, dismay, confusion, and doubt that the enemy continues to send my direction. Surround me with Your mighty presence; fill me with Your glorious might. *Contend, O Lord, with those who contend with me. Fight against those who fight against me. Take up Your buckler and shield and rise up for my help. Take also Your spear and battle ax and say to my soul, "I am your salvation."*

Romans 14:17; John 10:10; Ephesians 6:12; Psalm 35:1-3

Most High God

It has seemed good to me to declare the signs and wonders which the Most High God has done for me.

DANIEL 4:2

O God, You are the Most High God. *How great are Your signs, and how mighty are Your wonders! Your kingdom is an everlasting kingdom, and Your dominion is from generation to generation.* I praise You; I exalt You; I humbly bow before You. I cherish Your wonders of old: Creator of earth and Sustainer of all mankind, Master of time, and Orchestrator of kings and kingdoms. Nothing escapes You! You have set all things in place, from the first day until the last. *The Lord reigns; let the earth rejoice. … Righteousness and justice are the foundation of Your throne.* Most High God, who am I to stand in Your presence or play a part in Your kingdom? To think, because of Your greatest wonder, Jesus, King of love, *I have been given the right to become Your child.* My face is to the ground; I am baffled; I am awed. Lift me up, and *I will give thanks to You with all my heart; I will tell of all Your wonders. I will be glad and exult in You; I will sing praise to Your name, O Most High.*

Daniel 4:3; Psalm 97:1-2; John 1:12; Psalm 9:1-2

Love

God is love.

I JOHN 4:8

O God, You are Love, and I praise You for all Your attributes. Thank You for daily showing me *patience and kindness*. Thank You for not operating from human *jealousy or arrogance*, but from a pure heart of desire for all of me. Thank You for *not acting unbecomingly or seeking Your own*; instead, You sought the cross for me. There, thank You for *not being provoked and not taking account a wrong suffered*; rather, You chose to be *oppressed and afflicted, yet You did not open Your mouth*. Your steadfast silence brought sweet salvation to my soul. O God, I thank You! Your love does not *rejoice in unrighteousness, but rejoices in truth*. Your love *bears all things, believes all things, hopes all things, endures all things. Your love never fails*. Thank You, Jesus. This is the love You have shown, and faithfully continue to show me, even in my sin. Your love has purchased me; Your love has pardoned me; Your love has redeemed me; O God, Your love sustains me. Daily, cause my heart *to be controlled by Your love* so I may capture others who are longing for Your life-altering touch. Let my heart operate from this compelling truth: *I love because You first loved me.*

**1 Corinthians 13:1-5; Isaiah 53:7; 1 Corinthians 13:7-8;
2 Corinthians 5:14; 1 John 4:19**

Lord of Hosts

Who is this King of glory? The LORD of hosts, He is the King of glory.

PSALM 24:10

O God, You are the Lord of Hosts, Captain of the Angel Armies. Heavenly and Holy God, by faith, I choose to believe You, as well as all the things of You, *things which eye has not seen and ear has not heard, and which have not entered the heart of man; I believe all that You have prepared for those who love You.* Your angels are part of Your divine kingdom, past, present, and future. God of heaven and earth, Your mysteries are marvelous to me! I cannot see the celestial beings nor their *chariots of fire, but I know You command Your angels to encamp around those who revere Your name.* And I cannot feel the brush of angels' wings surrounding me, but I believe *You have given them charge concerning me, to guard me in all my ways.* Nor can I hear their matchless melodies; but I know, Lord of hosts, they worship You all the day long. Hear my heart sing too, *Glory to God in the highest.* You are worthy of all praise. *Praise the Lord! Praise the Lord from the heavens; praise Him in the heights! Praise Him all His angels; praise Him all His hosts!* Yes, as long as I have breath I, too, will praise the Lord.

1 Corinthians 2:9; 2 Kings 6:17; Psalms 34:7; 91:11; Luke 2:14;
Psalm 148:1-2

One True God

Is it not I, the LORD? And there is no other God besides Me, a righteous God and a Savior; there is none except me.

ISAIAH 45:21

O God, You are the One True God. You ask the people You love, *To whom would you liken Me, and make Me equal and compare Me, that we should be alike?* God, there is no one like You! *You declare the end from the beginning and from ancient times things which have not yet been done, saying, "My purpose will be established, and I will accomplish all My good pleasure."* Indeed, You accomplished both Your purpose and Your pleasure at the cross. *You were pleased to crush Him; ... if He render Himself as a guilt offering, He will see His offspring*—me! *He Himself bore the sin of many and interceded for transgressors.* God, there is none like You! No other god sacrifices himself. You are both the Holy King and the Savior. Forgive me when my soul bows to other gods. Why do I sometimes worship worry, fear, and doubt? And why do I sometimes worship earthly comfort, security, and control? Help me, O God, not to fall down before these "blocks of wood." *They cannot answer when I cry to them; they cannot deliver me from my distress.* God, there is no one like You! You are the One True Living God, the One True Loving God. Come live in me, come love through me—for this, too, is *Your purpose and Your pleasure.*

Isaiah 46:5,10; 53:10,12; 46:7; Philippians 2:13

My Shepherd

The LORD is my shepherd.

PSALM 23:1

O God, You are my Shepherd, I shall not want! There is nothing more that my heart desires than to be held by You. Hold me close. *Let Your left hand be under my head and Your right hand embrace me.* There, I will hear Your heartbeat; I will feel Your warmth. Your strong arm is my delight. Whisper words of comfort; whisper words of love. My Guardian, I need You; I love You. What more could I want? Nothing more. Thank You, great Shepherd of the sheep, for tending to my every need. *You know when I am weary; so You make me lie down. How divine are Your green pastures. How sweet are Your quiet waters. Yes, my soul is refreshed; my soul is restored. Continue to guide me along Your paths, which are always right. Keep me close to You, O God, as we walk through the shadows together. I will not fear because You are with me. Your rod and staff will be my comfort.* Yes, I am safe with You. *You will not let even one of Your sheep be lost.* Even when I go astray, You pull me out of the brambly bush. Forgive me when I think I can make it on my own. You overcome my stubbornness with Your faithfulness, and pursue me when I cry. *You know me*, and You run to me once again. O Good Shepherd, thank You! *Thank You for preparing blessings for me in the presence of my enemies. You stand guard as I delight in You. Thank You for lifting my head in Your kind hands, and anointing me with the warm oil of healing. You soothe my mind; You soothe my soul. On and on, on and on. My cup overflows with Your goodness and mercy, now and forever.* What more could I want? Nothing more; my Shepherd is my heart's desire.

Song of Solomon 2:6; Psalm 23:1-6; Luke 15:4; John 10:14

Spirit of Truth

And I will ask the Father, and He will give you another Helper, that He may be with you forever, that is the Spirit of truth, … You know Him because He abides with you and will be in you.

JOHN 14:16–17

O God, You are the Spirit of Truth. You live and abide in me. I thank You, Father, and I thank You, Son, for *breathing Your beautiful Spirit into my being* through grace and faith. I love Your Spirit; I need Your Spirit. You speak to me, You teach me, You remind me, and You help me. I praise You and thank You for Your indwelling. Continue to invade my heart, soul, mind, and strength with Your heart, soul, mind, and strength. Forgive me when I *quench Your Spirit* with fear and doubt. Please, dear Father, cause me to refocus and *set my mind on You; for You bring life and peace.* Remind me, O God, that setting my mind on the Spirit of Truth is a direct result of knowing and believing the *word of truth.* Just as my mind causes my hand to move physically, Your word causes Your Spirit to move in and through me. Word of Truth, Spirit of Truth, fall afresh on me today. You are *freedom to my soul.* I ask You to speak truth to me, so that I may *crush any lies of the enemy under my feet.* I choose truth; I choose freedom; I choose You.

John 20:22; 1 Thessalonians 5:19; Romans 8:6; John 17:17; 8:31-32; Romans 16:20

Perfect One

Therefore you are to be perfect, as your Heavenly Father is perfect.

MATTHEW 5:48

O God, You are the Perfect One, perfect in strength, perfect in beauty, perfect in peace, perfect in righteousness, perfect in love. Heavenly Father, You tell me *to be perfect?* How can I even begin to be like You? Is there any hope for the *heart of man, which is more deceitful than all else and desperately sick?* O God, You know our situation; You see our plight. Yet, You say to each one of our hearts, *Behold, My hand is not so short that it cannot save. Neither is My ear so dull that it cannot hear. But your iniquities have made a separation between you and Me, and your sins have hidden My face from you.* O God, here is my sin. Please God, take away my sin! I praise You, Father, for Your perfect solution to the marred heart of man: *Behold the Lamb of God who takes away the sin of the world!* Thank You, Jesus, for being the *unblemished and spotless One who came to redeem my soul.* Your precious blood covers me. And only because You live in me can I be perfect, mirroring You in strength, in beauty, in peace, in righteousness, and in love.

Matthew 5:48; Jeremiah 17:9; Isaiah 59:1-2; John 1:29; 1 Peter 1:18-19

Creator

In the beginning God created the heavens and the earth.
GENESIS 1:1

O God, You are the Creator. You alone can create something from nothing. You spoke the heavens and the earth into existence, and saw that it was good. *You have measured the waters in the hollow of Your hand, and marked off the heavens by the span, and calculated the dust by the measure, and weighed the mountains in a balance, and the hills in a pair of scales.* Great God, Your enormity and Your grandeur overwhelm me; but, ah, so does Your intimate touch and intricate love. To think, You have made *man to bear Your image*; and this, too, You call *good—even, very good?* Thank You, O Lord. *You are our Father. We are the clay, and You are the potter; and all of us are the work of Your hand.* Forgive me, O God, when *I quarrel with You, my Maker, saying, "What are You doing?"* Help me to trust You, knowing You want only the best for me. And the best for me is You! Make me a vessel that bears Your image for Your glory. Almighty and loving God, hear me praise Your name with the rest of Your creation. *Let the heavens be glad, and the earth rejoice; let the sea roar, and all it contains; let the field exult, and all that is in it. Then all the trees of the forest will sing for joy before the Lord.* Yes, I too, will sing, and I, too, will rejoice in my Creator.

Isaiah 40:12; Genesis 1:26-31; Isaiah 64:8; 45:9; Psalm 96:11-12

Sun and Shield

For the LORD God is a sun and shield; the LORD gives grace and glory; no good thing does He withhold from those who walk uprightly.

PSALM 84:11

O God, You are my Sun and Shield. Your radiant light provides clarity and cleansing, while Your protective hand continually guards and guides. Let me hear You say to my soul each morning, *Awake, sleeper, and arise from the dead, and Christ will shine on you.* O God, just as the sun powerfully rises over the mountaintops, please come, rise, and be beautifully alive in me today. *Make Your face to shine upon Your servant; save me in Your lovingkindness. ... How great is Your goodness which You have stored up for those who fear You.* Continue to turn my face toward You, O God, the living God. Help me to desire the warmth and security found in You alone. Indeed, You are my Sun and Shield. Yes, *Oh Lord, be gracious to me; I have waited for You. Be my strength every morning, my salvation also in the time of distress.*

Ephesians 5:14; Psalm 31:16,19; Isaiah 33:2

Holy One

*Exalt the LORD our God, and worship at His footstool; Holy is He. Moses and Aaron
were among His priests, and Samuel was among those who called on His name; they
called upon the LORD, and He answered them.*

PSALM 99:5–6

O God, You are the Holy One. *Your testimonies are fully confirmed; holiness befits
Your house, O Lord, forevermore.* You are pure and perfect and powerful, righteous and
radiant and rich, majestic and mighty and magnificent. *You reign; You are clothed with
majesty; You have clothed and girded Yourself with strength; indeed the world is firmly
established, it will not be moved. Your throne is established from of old; You are from
everlasting.* O Holy God, I worship You on bended knee. I praise You. For at the center of
Your holiness, I meditate on Your unfailing love, amazing love. To think You sent Your
perfect, holy Son so I may *have the way to come boldly to Your throne of grace! Here, I
receive mercy and find grace to help in time of need.* O King, I come. Purify my lips and
let my voice be heard in unison with the heavenly hosts, singing, *Holy, Holy, Holy, is the
Lord God Almighty. The whole earth is full of His glory.*

Psalms 93:5; 93:1-2; Hebrews 4:16; Isaiah 6:3

Counselor

I will instruct you and teach you in the way you should go; I will counsel you with My eye upon you.

PSALM 32:8

O God, You are the Counselor. Every day, I need You; I cry out to You; I trust You. Help me to *seek You, and search for You with all my heart.* Thank You for Your trustworthy promise that *I will find You.* God of wisdom, *You know the plans You have for me, plans for welfare and not for calamity, to give me a future and a hope.* Thank You for this truth, O God. Give me a heart that seeks You, and only You. *Make me know Your ways, O Lord; teach me Your paths. Lead me in Your truth and teach me. For You are the God of my salvation; for You I wait all the day.* Help me to always remember and comply: *Your word is a lamp to my feet and a light to my path.* Forgive me when I search elsewhere. Direct me to Your light, I pray. In Your word, I cling to the promise: *For who has known the mind of the Lord, that he should instruct Him? But we have the mind of Christ.* Keep me in Your word, O God, that my mind as well as my path may mirror Yours.

Jeremiah 29:13,11; Psalms 25:4-5; 119:105; 1 Corinthians 2:16

Ancient of Days

I kept looking until thrones were set up, and the Ancient of Days took His seat. ... Thousands upon thousands were attending Him, and myriads upon myriads were standing before Him; the court sat, and the books were opened.

DANIEL 7:9–10

O God, You are the Ancient of Days. Through the eyes of Daniel: *Your vesture is white like snow, and the hair of Your head like pure wool. Your throne is ablaze with flames, and its wheels are a burning fire. A river of fire was coming out from before You; thousands upon thousands were attending You, and myriads upon myriads were standing before You. You are the Lord who exercises lovingkindness, justice, and righteousness on the earth; for You delight in these things.* In Your lovingkindness, You sought me, saved me, and You now sing to me. In Your justice, You see all things, You know all things, and You will judge all people. In Your righteousness, You redeem, purify, and perfect. Dear sweet Jesus, I am able to stand upright before the Ancient of Days only because of You. *Yes, You became poor, that through Your poverty, I might become rich.* O God, I thank You; and *I rejoice exceedingly because my name has been written in the book of life.*

Daniel 7:9-10; Jeremiah 9:24; 2 Corinthians 8:9; Luke 10:20

Deliverer

Now the LORD saw, and it was displeasing in His sight that there was no justice. And He saw that there was no man. ... Then His own arm brought salvation to Him, and His righteousness upheld Him.

ISAIAH 59:15–16

O God, You are my Deliverer. In my distress I called upon the Lord, and cried to my God for help; He heard my voice out of His temple, and my cry for help before Him came to His ears. Then the earth shook and quaked. ... because He was angry. Smoke went out of His nostrils, and fire from His mouth devoured; coals were kindled by it. He bowed the heavens also and came down with thick darkness under His feet. And He rode upon a cherub and flew; and He sped upon the wings of the wind. ... He sent out His arrows, and scattered them, and lightning flashes in abundance, and routed them. ... He sent from on high, He took me; He drew me out of many waters. He delivered me from my strong enemy. ... He rescued me, because He delighted in me! Amen! ... I love You, O Lord, my strength; You are my Deliverer! A simple "thank You" is not enough. I will proclaim for the rest of my days, *The Lord lives, and blessed be my rock; and exalted be the God of my salvation!*

Psalm 18:6-19,1,46

Stronghold

But as for me, I shall sing of Your strength; yes, I shall joyfully sing of Your lovingkind-
ness in the morning, for You have been my stronghold, and a refuge in the day of
my distress.

PSALM 59:16

O God, You are my Stronghold. Nothing can touch my soul because of You. You surround me with Your lovingkindness; You shield me with Your strength. *Nothing is too difficult for You. ... Keep me as the apple of Your eye; hide me in the shadow of Your wings.* There, I am perfectly safe; there, I am sweetly secure; there, I will sing for joy! And even when diverse circumstances start swirling about me, I will proclaim, *My soul will wait in silence for God only, for my hope is from Him. He only is my rock and my salvation, my stronghold; I shall not be shaken. On God my salvation and glory rest; the rock of my strength, my refuge is in God.* I trust You, Lord. I need You, Savior. I thank You, Friend. Even *when I am weak, I am strong* because of You. Because of You I will rest; because of You I will sing. *O my strength, I will sing praises to You; for God is my stronghold, the God who shows me lovingkindness.*

Genesis 18:14; Psalms 17:8; 62:5-7; 2 Corinthians 12:10; Psalm 59:17

God of Mercy

So he got up and came to his father. But while he was still a long way off, his father saw him, and felt compassion for him, and ran and embraced him, and kissed him.

LUKE 15:20

O God, You are the God of Mercy. You know the condition of man's heart. We are so lured by *all that is in the world, the lust of the flesh and the lust of the eyes and the boastful pride of life.* You, O God, see us, and You save us from ourselves. I rejoice! *You are rich in mercy, and because of Your great love with which You loved me, even when I was dead in my transgressions, You made me alive together with Christ ... For by grace I have been saved through faith.* To think that *I have obtained favor in Your sight; and that You, my King, have extended Your scepter to me.* What kind of love is this? I want my life to be a life of gratitude because of Your great mercy and kindness. Pull me close, O God, because I am so prone to wander back to the things of this world. The struggle is real and ongoing. So, *search me, and know my heart; try me and know my anxious thoughts; and see if there be any hurtful way in me, and lead me in the everlasting way.* Thank You for Your continual embrace. In Your arms, I will sing of Your tender mercies forever.

1 John 2:16; Ephesians 2:4-5,8; Esther 5:2; Psalm 139:23-24

God of Hope

Now may the God of hope fill you with all joy and peace in believing, so that you will abound in hope by the power of the Holy Spirit.

ROMANS 15:13

O God, You are the God of Hope. Remind my weary heart of all Your joy and peace; cause me to once again put my hope in only You, to again believe in all of You. Today, my spirit fails; I am tired and weak, woeful and wondering. I faithlessly ask, "Where are You, O God?" *Lord, all my desire is before You; and my sighing is not hidden from You. My heart throbs, my strength fails me; and the light of my eyes, even that has gone from me. ... Do not forsake me, O Lord; O God, do not be far from me.* Please, God of Hope, I need You. I am exhausted, and I feel that I am laboring here in vain. *I ask You to create in me a clean heart, and renew a steadfast spirit within me.* Revive me, O Lord. Remind me of who You are! Help me to put my trust in You, even when Your ways are not clear. Strengthen my faith. Make me *steadfast and immovable, always abounding in Your work, believing that it's not in vain.* Redirect my gaze on You; for *You are the only living hope. Just as You raised Christ Jesus from the dead, You can raise me* from this pit. Yes, I will believe in You; yes, I will hope in You. Yes, I will persevere; yes, I will press on. I will not quit. You are here. (So enemy of my heart, and discourager of my thoughts, *Get behind me!*) O God of Hope, I belong to You—fill me with Your power.

Psalms 38:9-10,21; 51:10; 1 Corinthians 15:58; 1 Peter 1:3; Matthew 16:23

Strength

I can do all things through Him who strengthens me.
PHILIPPIANS 4:13

O God, You are my Strength. I cannot live without You; You are the heartbeat of my life—the very breath I breathe. Cause me to breathe deeply, O God, deep into Your wonders, deep into Your love. Continue to *open my eyes to the riches of the glory of your inheritance in the saints and to the surpassing greatness of Your power given to those who believe.* Dear Jesus, I do believe! I humbly thank You that *I am strengthened with power through Your Spirit inside me.* Again, I say thank You with all my heart. *I love You, O Lord, my strength. ... For You are the one who lights my lamp, the Lord my God illumines my darkness. For by Thee I can run upon a troop, and by my God I can leap over a wall.* Yes, I will proclaim, *I love You, O Lord, my strength!* Thank You, Father, for *pouring Your love into my heart through the Holy Spirit.* Now Your love abides in me forever. I thank You, and I praise You. For Your love has become my Strength.

Ephesians 1:18-19; 3:16; Psalm 18:1,28-29; Romans 5:5

Word

In the beginning was the Word, and the Word was with God, and the Word was God.
JOHN 1:1

O God, You are the Word. From the beginning of time, Your words have brought light and life. You speak, and certainly, it will happen; You command, and surely it will come to pass. *The voice of the Lord is upon the waters; the God of glory thunders. ... The voice of the Lord is powerful, the voice of the Lord is majestic.* O powerful and majestic God, to think, *the Word became flesh and dwelt among us.* You have brought light and life to men. And I rejoice because my heart and mind have been captivated by Your Word, Jesus Christ! Thank You for becoming the living and active Word on this earth. Help me to follow in Your footsteps so that I may learn of Your ways. *O, that I may know You!* I humbly thank You that now, today, I can hold Your living Word in my hands; help me to hold You in my heart. Jesus, my Savior and my Friend, I praise You for speaking words to me that are *sharper than any two-edged sword.* Continue to pierce my heart with Your voice of light and life and love. For I know and believe: *the law of the Lord is perfect, restoring the soul; the testimony of the Lord is sure, making wise the simple. The precepts of the Lord are right, rejoicing the heart; the commandment of the Lord is pure, enlightening the eyes.* I crave Your Word; I need Your Word.

Psalm 29:3-4; John 1:14; Philippians 3:10; Hebrews 4:12; Psalm 19:7-8

Provider

Isaac spoke to Abraham his father and said, "My father!" And he said, "Here I am, my son." And he said, "Behold, the fire and the wood, but where is the lamb for the burnt offering?" Abraham said, "God will provide for Himself the lamb for the burnt offering, my son."

GENESIS 22:7–8

O God, You are the Provider. You graciously ordain the *ram in the bush*, in Your time and in Your way. Please forgive me when I question Your timing and doubt Your ways. Remind me *You cause all things to work together for good, to those who love You and are called according to Your purpose.* O God, I do love You. And I do want Your will to be done in my life. So as I patiently wait, I will also eagerly watch. And in this quiet place of trust in You alone, I will remember Your ultimate provision of Your only Son, the sacrificial lamb. O Jesus, You are the ram in the bush! Thank You, sweet Savior, for taking my place on the altar. You have provided salvation to my soul. O God, I praise You. My faith is strengthened. If *You did not spare Your own Son, but delivered Him up for us all, how will You not also with Him freely give us all things?* Yes, You will provide for all my needs, in Your perfect timing and in Your flawless ways. So, *my soul, wait in silence for God only, for my hope is from Him.* Thank You, Father, in advance, for Your beautiful Provision for my every need.

Genesis 22:13; Romans 8:28-32; Psalm 62:5

One Who Defends

The LORD is my light and my salvation; Whom shall I fear? The LORD is the defense of my life; Whom shall I dread?

PSALM 27:1

O God, You are the One Who Defends. *Though a host encamp against me, my heart will not fear; though war arise against me, in spite of this I will be confident.* Yes, when *I am afraid I will put my trust in You. In God, whose word I praise, in God I have put my trust. I shall not be afraid. What can mere man do to me? ... This I know, that God is for me. ...* For You, O God, *are a sun and a shield; You give grace and glory; no good thing do You withhold from those who walk uprightly.* Thank You for Your grace; thank You for Your glory; thank You for fighting and defending Your cherished child. I praise You that *no weapon formed against me will prosper.* Continue to accomplish what concerns me, O great God. And I will continue to *lift my eyes to the hills* and declare with an extraordinary hope, *From where does my help come? My help comes from the Lord, Maker of heaven and earth. ... For You, O Lord, have done great things for me; I am glad.*

Psalms 27:3; 56:3-4, 9; 84:11; Isaiah 54:17; Psalms 121:1-2; 126:3

Great Reconciler

God was in Christ reconciling the world to Himself, not counting their trespasses against them, and He has committed to us the word of reconciliation.

2 CORINTHIANS 5:19

O God, You are the Great Reconciler. Because of Your unfathomable love, *You delivered me from the domain of darkness, and transferred me to the kingdom of Your beloved Son.* Thank You *for drawing me to Yourself with Your lovingkindness.* In this place, You have mercifully chosen not to count my trespasses against me; instead, You faithfully wash them away. Thank You for hearing and answering the plea of Your Son's heart, just before He went to the cross: *I ask … that they may be one, just as We are one; I in them, and You in Me, that they may be perfected in unity.* And because of Your plan, *I, who was formerly far off, have been brought near by the blood of Christ.* And now, I am a *new creature in Christ. Live and reign in me, O God. May Your love compel me to also be a reconciler,* bringing others to Your throne of marvelous grace and peace.

**Colossians 1:13; Jeremiah 31:3; John 17:22-23; Ephesians 2:13;
2 Corinthians 5:14-18**

King of Glory

Lift up your heads, O gates, and be lifted up, O ancient doors, that the King of glory may come in! Who is this King of glory? The LORD strong and mighty, the LORD mighty in battle. … He is the King of glory.

PSALM 24:7–8,10

O God, You are the King of Glory. All power and might belong to You. Heaven is Yours, the earth is Yours, and they are full of Your splendid presence! Continue to open my eyes and *show me Your glory, I pray. May I marvel at all of Your goodness as You unveil it* in my life. Incredibly, Your loving heart's desire is for Your glory to reside and reign in me. *O God, when I consider the heavens … What is man, that You take thought of him? And the son of man that You care for him? Yet You have made him a little lower than God, and You crown him with glory and majesty!* I pray, just as *fire came down from heaven and filled the beautiful temple of old with Your glory*, please come, fill me. King of Glory, come in! Make my purpose in life to be a magnificent display of Your light, causing others to also shout, *Who is this King of Glory?* Please come in, fill me.

Exodus 33:18-19; Psalm 8:3-5; 2 Chronicles 7:2; Psalm 24:10

Peace

Peace I leave with you; My peace I give to you; not as the world gives do I give to you. Do not let your heart be troubled, nor let it be fearful.

JOHN 14:27

O God, You are Peace. I daily need You to live within my soul. Again and again, You calm my wrestling heart. Through the nail-pierced hands of Christ, You give me serenity. Dear Jesus, when my heart once more begins to be troubled or afraid, help me remember and then respond to Your beautiful invitation of, *Come to Me, all you who are weary and heavy-laden and I will give you rest.* Help me to daily take my worries off of my own shoulders and choose to obey Your voice that urges, *Take My yoke upon you, and learn from Me, for I am gentle and humble in heart; and you shall find rest for your souls.* O God, I want to learn from You; I love Your gentle words, and I long for Your humble ways! Here again are my anxious thoughts. Help me now to choose to *pray about everything with thanksgiving, so that I may gain Your peace that passes all comprehension.* I love You, O God of Peace. Always come, and *compose and quiet my soul. Make me become like a weaned child who rests against his mother.* Yes, make my soul like a weaned child within me.

Matthew 11:28-29; Philippians 4:6-7; Psalm 131:2

Portion

Whom have I in heaven but You? And besides You, I desire nothing on earth. My flesh and my heart may fail, but God is the strength of my heart and my portion forever.
PSALM 73:23–26

O God, You are my Portion. You give abundantly; You satisfy completely. Nothing on this earth compares to You. Your words to my heart are *more desirable than gold, yes, than much fine gold; sweeter also than honey and the drippings of the honeycomb.* Dear Lord, keep me close to You. Continue to fill me with Your power and Your promises. Let me not withhold anything from You, calling it "mine." I give You my weakness; I give You my sadness; I give You myself. O God, my Father, how You graciously take these from me as an offering! And *instead of my shame I will have a double portion ... Everlasting joy will be mine!* I praise You; I thank You; I lift my hands high! *How precious is Your lovingkindness, O God! I take refuge in the shadow of Your wings. I drink my fill of the abundance of Your house. And You give me to drink of the river of Your delights. For with You is the fountain of life.* Yes, my heart sings, "You are my Portion forever!"

Psalm 19:10; Isaiah 61:7; Psalm 36:7-9

Alpha and Omega

"I am the Alpha and Omega," says the Lord God, "who is and who was and who is to come, the Almighty."

REVELATION 1:8

O God, You are the Alpha and Omega, the beginning and the end. You are the bookends of life, and You have written every line of every page of every chapter in the story of the past, present, and future. *For wisdom and power belong to You; You change the times and the epochs; You remove kings and establish kings. ... To You, O God of my fathers, I give thanks and praise!* As Your story unfolds, my heart rejoices. I see You, Holy God, pursuing a sinful, stiff-necked people with Your love, which was ultimately *demonstrated at the cross*—Your plan, the climax of Your story! O God of time, You have captured me with this love of Yours. Hold me close to You. I want You to be the Alpha and Omega of my days on this earth. Strengthen my faith when I do not understand your path for me; for *Your ways are higher than my ways, and Your thoughts are not my thoughts.* But I trust You. Make my story match Yours, no matter the circumstances of the day. Live in me—from morning till night, so that I, too, may capture people with Your unending love.

Daniel 2:20-23; Romans 5:8; Isaiah 55:9

Living Water

Every one who thirsts, come to the waters.

ISAIAH 55:1

O God, You are the Living Water. *My soul thirsts for You, my flesh yearns for You, in a dry and weary land where there is no water* to be found. There is nothing on this earth that satisfies the deep longings of my heart; You created me to crave You. Heavenly Father, You promise, *I will open rivers on bare heights, and springs in the midst of valleys, I will make the wilderness a pool of water, and the dry land fountains of water.* O God, my soul is satisfied because of Your Son, Jesus Christ. *He is the way, the truth and the life.* Through Him, *I can delight myself in abundance!* Help me to daily respond to Your invitation of *Come.* Help me to daily *listen carefully to You that I may truly live.* Thank You, Jesus, for the promise in Your words of truth, *Whoever drinks of the water I shall give him ... shall become in him a well of water springing up to eternal life.* Jesus, each day hear my desperate heart's cry, *Give me this water!* Come again, today, this day, fill me completely; fill me abundantly.

Psalm 63:1; Isaiah 41:18; John 14:6; Isaiah 55:1-3; John 4:14-15

Good

Give thanks to the LORD, for He is good, for His lovingkindness is everlasting.
PSALM 136:1

O God, You are Good; You are Good; You are exceedingly Good! All You are and all You do is based upon the goodness of Your love toward Your people. You create and care; You hear and heal; You rescue and redeem. O God, I have been lured by this lovingkindness; and now *my heart overflows with Your good theme.* When I think of You, I must praise You. *Bless the Lord, O my soul, and all that is within me, bless His holy name! Bless the Lord, O my soul, and forget none of His benefits.* Yes, God, You are exceedingly good to me! Thank You that I *can cast all my burdens upon You, because You care for me.* Thank You that no need of mine is too small for You to take notice of, or too big for You to fulfill. *You are intimately acquainted with all my ways. ... Much more than the lilies of the field,* You will give Your goodness to me. Continue, sweet Savior, to feed me with Your words of life, and clothe me with Your adornment of love. Bless You, O God of my heart, for You are exceedingly Good to me!

Psalms 45:1: 103:1-2; 1 Peter 5:7; Psalm 139:3; Matthew 6:28,30

I AM

And God said to Moses, "I AM WHO I AM."

Exodus 3:14

O God, You are the I AM. You have always been and always will be. You are the self-existent One, the self-sustaining One, the source of all power and light; You are the Creator of all creatures and things. You are the Lord of all! Only You, Lord God, can create something from nothing. *You cause breath to enter dry bones that they may come to life.* O God, You are Life! You overwhelm my soul; Your magnitude mystifies my mind. To think, You, this great God of all living things, are also the very One who came to save those destined for death. In love, You say to your people, *"Here I AM."... You have bared Your holy arm in the sight of all nations, that all the ends of the earth may see Your salvation.* O my Lord and my God, I see Your salvation in Your Son Jesus. You, Savior God, have come to earth and proclaimed, *Here I AM!* to my soul. Your voice permeates through me; *I AM the Light. I AM the Word. I AM the Door. I AM the Way. I AM the Shepherd. I AM the Lamb. I AM He, ... the self-existent One who chose to be sacrificed unto death in order to breathe life into souls.* Loving God, only because of You can I say, I am alive; I am Yours; I am awed.

Ezekiel 37:5; Isaiah 52:6,10; John 8:12; 1:14; 10:9; 14:6; 10:14, 1:29; 18:6; Romans 5:5-6

Rock Eternal

*The steadfast of mind You will keep in perfect peace, because he trusts in You. Trust in the
LORD forever, for in GOD the LORD, we have an everlasting Rock.*

ISAIAH 26:3-4

O God, You are the Rock Eternal. You will not be shaken; You will not be moved. *For
who is God, but the Lord? And who is a rock, except our God?* O Holy One, there is none
like You! I choose to trust in You forever. *You are my rock and my fortress and my deliverer, my God, my rock, in whom I take refuge, my shield, the horn of my salvation, my
stronghold.* Thank You, Almighty One, *for hiding me in Your cleft so that I may behold
Your glory passing by.* Loving Lord, You are beautiful to me! Keep my eyes fixed on You,
so that I may praise Your name. And when my faith wavers and *my heart is faint, lead
me back to the rock that is higher than I. For You are a refuge for me, and a tower of
strength against the enemy.* Yes, I am safe and secure with You. Keep me in Your presence so I may *build my house upon this rock.* Because of You, O God of my life, I will not
be shaken, I will not be moved.

Psalms 18:31,1-3; Exodus 33:22; Psalm 61:2-3; Matthew 7:24-25

Almighty One

Now when Abram was ninety-nine years old, the LORD appeared to Abram and said to him, "I am God Almighty; walk before Me, and be blameless. And I will establish My covenant between Me and you, and I will multiply you exceedingly."
GENESIS 17:1–2

O God, You are the Almighty One. *Is there anything too difficult for You? ... And God of our fathers, are You not the God who is in heaven?* You rule over all kingdoms and nations. *Power and might are in Your hand, and no one can withstand You.* Come to our aid, O God, because we bear Your name; we are Your people. *For we have no power to face this vast army that is attacking us. We do not know what to do, but our eyes are on You.* As we fall down and worship You, Almighty God, rise up and fight for us. We believe that *You are able to do exceedingly abundantly beyond all that we ask or think!* Yes, if *You, O God, are for us, who then can be against us?* No, nothing is too difficult for You! God in heaven, glorify Your name through Your people today. Bountifully bless us with Your favor so that *all may see and recognize, and consider and gain insight as well, that the hand of the Lord has done this. And the Holy One of Israel has created it.* Yes, You are the Almighty One, the only One.

**Genesis 18:14; 2 Chronicles 20:6,12; Ephesians 3:20;
Romans 8:31; Isaiah 41:20**

Gentle One

Learn from Me, for I am gentle.

MATTHEW 11:29

O God, You are the Gentle One. With Your few, yet firm words, *Peace, be still,* You calm my troubled heart; *You quiet me with Your love.* Thank You, dear Father, for *bringing good news to the afflicted and for binding up the brokenhearted.* Daily, help me be still enough to receive Your anointing words of healing and hope. The world shouts lies to my mind; but You, Gentle One, whisper love to my heart. Cause me to hear the voice of the Lamb over the *roar of the lion, who is only seeking to devour.* Yet You, O God, *care for me! Here are my anxious thoughts.* Thank You; I love You; I need You. *Your right hand upholds me; and Your gentleness makes me great. You enlarge my steps under me, and my feet have not slipped.* O God, I want to always walk with You. Please fill me each day with the *imperishable quality of Your gentle and quiet spirit,* which is precious in Your sight. Help me be gentle toward others, as You have been so Gentle toward me.

**Mark 4:39; Zephaniah 3:17; Isaiah 61:1; 1 Peter 5:7-8;
Psalm 18:35-36; 1 Peter 3:4**

Humble One

Learn from Me, for I am ... humble in heart.
MATTHEW 11:29

O God, You are the Humble One. You, Maker of heaven and earth, Ruler of all nature, full of power and might, are humble. *Your voice is like thunder ... breaking the cedars;* yet, I hear Your gentle whisper, *"Come to Me." ... You look at the earth and it trembles; You touch the mountains and they smoke;* however, Your gaze of love calms my heart, and Your touch of power heals my soul. You send the tumultuous rain upon the earth; but at the same time, *You gather my tears in a bottle.* You, Mighty One, rule the world in power; yet You serve the people in love. O Humble One, You sit on Your throne high and lifted up; and yet, You chose to *sit among sinners.* Thank You for *emptying Yourself and coming in the form of the bondservant.* King of Glory, You took off Your robe for me! You gave Your life as a *ransom for many.* Your humility in death brought about my salvation in life forever. Hallelujah! O God, teach me to live like You. Pull out by the root any form of pride in my heart. Let it not exist in me, I pray; for pride is a stench to You! Make me humble, Humble One, so that I may bring others before Your almighty throne; and there, directly into Your arms of love.

Psalm 29:3,5; Matthew 11:28; Psalms 104:32; 56:8; Mark 2:15; Philippians 2:7; Matthew 20:28

Strong Tower

The name of the LORD is a strong tower; the righteous runs into it and is safe.

PROVERBS 18:10

O God, You are my Strong Tower. In Your walls You protect me; in Your rooms You provide for me. I will lie down in perfect peace because You are *my keeper who neither slumbers nor sleeps.* With You, I am safe; with You, I am secure. O God, I pray that I will never want to wander beyond Your walls. *Turn my eyes away from worthless things*, the lure of my enemy, whose desire is for me to step outside Your fortress of love. Please guard me from the deceptive temptation of building my own tower of pride, control, or selfish ambition, seeking to *make a name for myself* rather than for You. *Confuse and scatter my plans*, I pray. Cause me to *cease striving and know that You are God.* Remind me the Strong Tower has already been built, and it is not a cold, damp dungeon! Cause me to run to the top of Your Tower, O God, that I might be awed by all that You have created for Your people to enjoy; for You, my King, desire wonderful things for me! I humbly thank You for Your life-giving gifts: mountains of strength, rivers of gladness, fields of freedom. From the height of Your Strong Tower I want to *be the bearer of good news; there, I will lift up my voice, mightily,* and proclaim with abundant joy, *O Lord, how majestic is Your name in all the earth!*

Psalms 121:4; 119:37; Genesis 11:4,7-8; Psalm 46:10; Isaiah 40:9; Psalm 8:1

Great Reward

The word of the Lord came to Abram in a vision, saying, "Do not fear, Abram, I am a shield to you; Your reward shall be very great."

GENESIS 15:1

O God, You are my Great Reward. *I waited patiently for You and You inclined to me and heard my cry. You brought me up out of the pit of destruction out of the miry clay; and You set my feet upon a rock making my footsteps firm. And You put a new song in my mouth, a song of praise to You, my God.* How I love You, O God. You are my treasure; You are the new song in my heart. Yes, once again, You *have rescued me, because You take great delight in me.* Please forgive my wavering emotions that cause me to lose sight of You. Yet, I also thank You for this weakness of the flesh which causes me to cry out to You for help. O, how I need You when the day is dark; and O, how I praise You when the light has come! Continue to shine on me, dear Father, so I might be radiant before others, drawing them ever closer to Your glory. Dear God, *You truly are the rewarder of those who seek You.* Thank You for Your reward of *strength, which causes me to mount up on wings like eagles;* thank You for Your gift of *grace and compassion* that reaches the depths of my soul; and thank You for Your treasure of *abundant lovingkindness that is better than life itself.* Yes, You my God, are my exceedingly Great Reward.

Psalms 40:1-3; 18:19; Hebrews 11:6; Isaiah 40:31; Psalms 103:8; 63:3

Lion of Judah

And one of the elders said to me, "Stop weeping; behold, the Lion that is from the tribe of Judah, the Root of David, has overcome so as to open the book and its seven seals."

REVELATION 5:5

O God, You are the Lion of Judah. Long before the Messiah was born, the patriarch Israel blessed each of his twelve sons, saying to Judah individually, *Judah, your brothers shall praise you; your hand shall be on the neck of your enemies; your father's sons shall bow down to you. Judah is a lion's whelp; from the prey, my son, you have gone up. He couches, he lies down as a lion, and as a lion, who dares rouse him up? The scepter shall not depart from Judah, nor the ruler's staff from between his feet.* O God, from the beginning, You planned from whom the promised Messiah would come. And God, You proclaimed this Lion would possess both incomprehensible peace and undeniable power. For Scripture was fulfilled and it is written: *For it is evident that our Lord was descended from Judah.* Also, You even designated the small city of this majestic King's birth: *But as for you, Bethlehem Ephrathah, too little to be among the clan of Judah, from you One will go forth for Me to be ruler in Israel. His goings forth are from long ago, from the days of eternity. Therefore, He will give them up until the time when she who is in labor has borne a child. Then the remainder of His brethren will return to the sons of Israel. And He will arise and shepherd His flock in the strength of the Lord, in the majesty of the name of the Lord His God. And they will remain, because at that time He will be great to the ends of the earth. And this One will be our peace.* Yes, the Lion of Judah has come, and He will forever reign in both peace and power. And at the sight of Your Majesty, I will bow down in reverential awe.

Genesis 49:8-10; Hebrews 7:14; Micah 5:2-5

Remarkable

Jesus was going throughout all Galilee, teaching in their synagogues, and proclaiming the gospel of the kingdom, and healing every kind of disease and every kind of sickness among the people.

MATTHEW 4:23

O God, You are Remarkable. How extraordinary are the prophetic words that Your angel spoke to Joseph in a dream: *Joseph, son of David, do not be afraid to take Mary as your wife; for that which has been conceived in her is of the Holy Spirit. And she will bear a Son: and you shall call His name Jesus, for it is He who will save His people from their sins.* And this Jesus, Son of God, Son of Man, *walked on the sea,* and *healed the paralytic,* and *drove out demons.* And *there are also many other things which Jesus did, which if they were written in detail, I suppose that even the world itself would not contain the books which were written.* Yes, O God, Your plan of salvation due to Your love for mankind is Remarkable. You knew the *wages of sin is death,* and You knew that Your perfect Son came on our behalf to pay it. So this is the most astounding act of all: *For while we were still helpless, at the right time Christ died for the ungodly. For one will hardly die for a righteous man; though perhaps for the good man someone would dare even to die. But God demonstrates His own love toward us, in that while we were yet sinners, Christ died for us.* Yes, Your salvation story involved the life and death of Immanuel, *"God with us."* Your holy sacrifice is Remarkable to me!

Matthew 1:20-21; 14:25; Mark 2:10-11; 5:12-13; John 21:25;
Romans 6:23; 5:6-8; Matthew 1:23

One Who Proclaims

We proclaim Him, admonishing every man and teaching every man with all wisdom, that we may present every man complete in Christ.

COLOSSIANS 1:28

O God, You are the One Who Proclaims. To think of the awesome night when the angel announced to the shepherds: *Do not be afraid; for behold, I bring you good news of great joy which shall be for all the people; for today in the city of David there has been born for you a Savior who is Christ the Lord.* And then, to accompany this messenger, there appeared with the angel a multitude of the heavenly host praising God, and saying, "Glory to God in the highest, and on earth peace among men with whom He is pleased." I can't imagine the amazing sight and the glorious sound of the greatest news for all mankind. You sent Your Son to save my soul. Thank You! And I hear Your words, dear Jesus, when you announced to these people of old as well as to my heart today, *The time is fulfilled, and the kingdom of God is at hand; repent and believe in the gospel.* To all, You have proclaimed *forgiveness of sins;* to all, You have proclaimed freedom from *a yoke of slavery;* to all, You have proclaimed *redemption from the past.* O God, I pray that all will receive Your good news! Because I hear these proclaiming words of Yours as well: *But take heed; behold, I have told you everything in advance. But in those days, after that tribulation, the sun will be darkened, and the moon will not give its light, and the stars will be falling from heaven, and the powers that are in the heavens will be shaken. And then they will see the Son of Man coming in clouds with great power and glory. And then He will send forth the angels, and will gather together His elect from the four winds, from the farthest end of the earth, to the farthest end of heaven.* O God, by Your grace, I believe and rejoice in every word that You have Proclaimed.

Luke 2:10-14; Mark 1:15; 2:5; Galatians 5:1; Romans 3:24; Mark 13:23-27

Exquisite*

Have you ever in your life <u>commanded the morning</u>, *and caused the dawn to know its place?*   take control

JOB 38:12

O God, You are Exquisite—exquisite in beauty, exquisite in <u>strength</u>. I see Your glory in the <u>faithful rising of the sun</u> *which is as a bridegroom coming out of his chamber, it rejoices as a strong man to run his course.* I see Your splendor in the brilliant colors of the rainbow, a timeless wonder of *Your radiant presence.* I see Your power when You open *the* <u>storehouses of the snow</u>, causing a <u>peaceful purity</u> to blanket the earth.* How exquisite is Your handiwork, O God. I hear the <u>matchless melody</u> of the morning birds; I hear *the trees of the field clapping their hands;* I see the breaking of the mighty ocean waves and I feel the <u>whisper of the calming wind.</u> *All Your creation gives thanks and praise to Your holy name!* And then, I meditate on Your most exquisite work of art—the profound paradox: *Jesus, King of kings,* <u>wrapped in swaddling clothes lying in a manger.</u> Beauty and strength, humility and grace … angels singing, kings bowing, shepherds rejoicing, and my heart proclaiming, "Exquisite!"

earth is alive because of him

Psalm 19:5; Ezekiel 1:28; Job 38:22; Isaiah 55:12;
Psalm 148:1-14; Luke 2:7-14

true meaning
of it all

"Don't be afraid... The Savior has been born
today in Bethleham." Luke 2:10

Extravagant

Your lovingkindness, O LORD, extends to the heavens, Your faithfulness reaches to the skies.

PSALM 36:5

O God, You are Extravagant. Your *love exceeds knowledge*, Your joy springs abundantly, and *Your peace passes all understanding. ... You give Your Spirit without measure ... You forgive my sins without memory*—as far as the east is from the west, so far have You removed my sins from me. ... *My cup overflows* with Your extravagant goodness and mercy! And God of might, You long to *do exceedingly abundantly beyond all that I ask or think according to the power that works within me.* Help me to believe in Your power; strengthen my faith in Your love. Hear me say, *I count all things to be loss in view of the surpassing value of knowing Christ Jesus my Lord.* And this I know, *for to me, to live is Christ and to die is gain*, because heaven, too, will be extravagant. *Eye has not seen and ear has not heard and thoughts have not entered the heart of man, all that God has prepared for those who love Him.* O God, I love You! I love You! I love You! You are Extravagant!

Ephesians 3:19-20; Philippians 4:7; John 3:34, Jeremiah 31:34;
Psalms 103:12; 23:6; Ephesians 3:20; Philippians 3:8; 1:21;
1 Corinthians 2:9

Joy

You will make known to me the path of life; In Your presence is fullness of joy; In Your right hand there are pleasures forever.

PSALM 16:11

O God, You are my Joy. You fill my heart with laughter; You fill my soul with song. Thank You for *coming that I might have life and have it abundantly*. And thank You for speaking to me through Your word so *Your joy may be in me, and my joy may be made full*. God, help me settle for nothing less than all of You. Thank You for Your exceeding abundance. I delight in You; to think, *You delight in me*. I hear You promise, *For the mountains may be removed and the hills may shake, but My lovingkindness will not be removed from you*. Dear God, *though I do not see You, I love You, and believe in You; and I greatly rejoice with inexpressible joy*. Your steadfast love fills me up to overflowing, and a fountain of praise pours from my heart. Sweet Savior, there is no One like You! *For You have been my help. And in the shadow of Your wings I will sing for joy*. Yes, I live and I love because of You.

John 10:10; 15:11; Psalm 18:19; Isaiah 54:10; 1 Peter 1:8; Psalm 63:7

Banner

Moses built an altar and named it The LORD is My Banner.
EXODUS 17:15

O God, you are my Banner. Thank You for Your presence, thank You for Your power. *I can do nothing without You;* However, *I can do all things through You.* Hold your Banner high over me, O Lord; *lift up Your countenance upon me, make Your face shine upon me, give me Your peace.* I long to do Your will; keep me under Your wings. In this place of security, I will rejoice that *Your banner over me is love.* Yes, Your truth was high and lifted up so that I could gain Your love. Thank You, Jesus, for the cross—the Banner which was held up for me to gaze upon. My eyes are fixed on You, my Savior. Through You, I can embrace this life set before me. With You as my confidence, *I will fight the good fight of faith;* and because of Your strength working in me, I will win this battle! *In all things I will overwhelmingly conquer through You, the one who loves me.* God, You are my salvation; You are my victory; You are my Banner.

John 15:5; Philippians 4:13; Numbers 6:25-26; Song of Solomon 2:4;
2 Timothy 4:7; Romans 8:37

Salvation

Behold, God is my salvation, I will trust and not be afraid; for the LORD is my strength and song, and He has become my salvation.

ISAIAH 12:2

O God, You are my Salvation. My heart is desperate for Your words of life; my soul is destitute for works of love. I cry to You, once again, *Save me, O God, for the waters have threatened my life. I have sunk in deep mire, and there is no foothold; I have come into deep waters, and a flood overflows me. I am weary with my crying; my throat is parched; my eyes fail while I wait for my God.* Sweet Savior, help me to remember You—Your strength, Your power, Your might, Your love. Make these be the cords that pull me from the tumultuous waves of my fear, my confusion, my doubt, my dismay. Yes, God, please become *my strength, my song and my salvation* once again. My faith is as *small as a mustard seed*; thank You for asking for no more than that. Because of Your unfailing love, I can already cling to these words of hope: *He sent from on high, He took me; He drew me out of many waters, He delivered me from my strong enemy. ... The Lord was my stay.* Yes, my heart and my soul will soon sing again, *He has become my salvation.*

Psalm 69:1-3; Exodus 15:2; Matthew 17:20; Psalm 18:16-18; Isaiah 12:2

Redeemer

Blessed is the LORD who has not left you without a redeemer today.
RUTH 4:14

O God, You are my Redeemer. Because of You, *I am a new creature; the old things have passed away; behold, new things have come.* Thank You for giving me a *garland instead of ashes, the oil of gladness instead of mourning, the mantle of praise instead of a spirit of fainting.* Dear Father, I praise You, and I humbly thank You; for my redemption cost You Your Son. Yes, *I have been redeemed with the precious blood, as a lamb unblemished and spotless, the blood of Christ.* Sweet Savior, *I want to walk in newness of life with You.* Please continue to *perfect the good work You began in me,* I pray. *Cause me to forget what lies behind and reach forward to what lies ahead.* Help me Father, to *press on toward the goal for the prize of your upward call in Christ Jesus.* Yes, for this *I know, my Redeemer lives;* and as I walk on, I will declare, *My Redeemer is strong; the Lord of hosts is His name; He will vigorously plead my case.* Thank You, Savior; thank You, Friend. I know You are alive in me.

**2 Corinthians 5:17; Isaiah 61:3; 1 Peter 1:18-19; Romans 6:4;
Philippians 1:6; 3:13-14; Job 19:25; Jeremiah 50:34**

Confidence

For the LORD will be your confidence.

PROVERBS 3:26

O God, You are my Confidence. *You only are my rock and my salvation, my stronghold; I shall not be shaken.* Dear Jesus, I do confess to You, however, that I do not always live this way. Forgive me when my faith wavers, and when my eyes wander, and when my steps weaken. Cause me to remember who You are: God Almighty, Strong Creator, Lord of Hosts, King of Glory. Yes, You are my Banner, my Shepherd, my Peace, and my Defense. Remind me, O Lord, You are the great I AM who is a Shield before me and a Foundation beneath me. When I am wearily asking, *From where does my help come?* cause me to say with confidence, *My help comes from the Lord, who made heaven and earth.* You, O God, *will not allow my foot to slip. … You are my Keeper who neither slumbers nor sleeps. You will protect me from all evil; You will keep my soul. Yes, You make my feet like hinds' feet, and set me upon my high places. You train my hands for battle, so that my arms can bend a bow of bronze.* Hear me say with renewed faith, *I can do all things through Christ who strengthens me!* Yes, God, You have become my Confident heartbeat.

Psalms 62:6; 121:1-7; 18:33-34; Philippians 4:13

Website for Chris Baxter

WWW.RESPITEFORTHEWEARY.COM